Wings Around The World

For PETER
My ALPHA and OMEGA

Wings Around the World

Polly Vacher

Grub Street • London

Published by
Grub Street
4 Rainham Close
London
SW11 6SS

First published in hardback in 2006
This edition first published in 2008

British Library Cataloguing in Publication Data
Vacher, Polly
  Wings around the world : the exhilarating story of one
  woman's epic flight from the North Pole to Antarctica
  1.Vacher, Polly 2.Flights around the world 3.Women air
  pilots – Great Britain – Biography
  I.Title
  910.4'1

ISBN 978 1 904943 99 0

Typeset by Roy Platten, Eclipse – roy.eclipse@btopenworld.com

Printed and bound in China by 1010 International Ltd

Contents

Foreword

Few traveller's tales have captured my imagination like this one. Polly Vacher was a mother-of-three when she learned to fly at age fifty. She then flew alone twice round the world in a small single-engined aircraft. Who among us would dream of doing that? Here is the account of her second flight when, at age sixty, she crossed the Arctic Ocean, the Southern Ocean, the Atlantic, the Pacific, the Indian Ocean, and incidentally, landed on all seven continents. Polly writes with sensitivity and humour, not just about flying but about the many people she met along the way.

To fly round the world demanded immense courage, meticulous preparation, generous sponsors, and a sense of mission – in Polly's case raising money for charity. In this frank and unaffected account she invites us to share the challenge and, in spirit at least, to fly with her. Preparations included training to survive a forced landing anywhere, even ditching in mid-ocean. The reader is with her when she skins a squirrel, sleeps in a snow cave, lights a fire without matches, carries a rifle (for polar bears) and learns to grub for food in the wilderness.

This is not a tale of someone jumping into a tiny aeroplane and seeking glory by setting records. Though Polly does not deny the excitement of facing the unknown, she believes passionately in the charity she supports. Moreover, by lecturing to schools in many of the countries where she paused, she has fostered a better understanding between different cultures.

Having myself spent years in the Antarctic on well-found expeditions, I admire the courage of any pilot who can survive heavy icing, raging turbulence, loneliness in the sky and even engine failure – and go on to fly alone for sixteen hours non-stop across the Pacific. This is a rare chance to share the inner feelings and emotions of a very brave woman. Now fly with Polly – for 60,000 miles – and come home safely.

Charles Swithinbank

An Appreciation

by Her Majesty Queen Noor
of the Hashemite Kingdom of Jordan

Αs Patron of Flying Scholarships for the Disabled (FSD), I would like to add my appreciation to this publication by Polly Vacher. All of the author proceeds, as well as a percentage of the publisher's, will go to FSD and will make an enormous difference to the disabled people given the chance to re-build their lives through the challenge of learning to fly.

My late husband King Hussein was involved with the charity from its inception in 1983 when it was established in memory of his wartime hero and friend Sir Douglas Bader. He personally flew with several of the scholars and contributed in many ways to the success of the charity.

Polly Vacher's epic flight was an amazing achievement, not only by the sheer endurance displayed in the pages of this book, but by the funds and awareness raised for FSD worldwide.

I sincerely hope that this book brings the success it so richly deserves.

Acknowledgements

In acknowledging the following contributors to this book, I will never forget the hundreds of people who made *Wings Around the World* possible. Without that support this unique flight would not have taken place. It has been impossible to mention everyone in the book and for this I apologise. Every single person who had anything remotely to do with the flight was important. I wish to say a huge 'thank you' for the many ways everyone has helped to raise the profile of Flying Scholarships for the Disabled.

I am most grateful to Her Majesty Queen Noor of the Hashemite Kingdom of Jordan for kindly writing an appreciation.

Polar expert and glaciologist, Dr Charles Swithinbank read the book with his usual meticulous attention to detail and I am very thankful to him for taking the time and trouble to write the foreword.

My husband Peter has spent hours reading my work and has offered much constructive criticism as well as editing the book for me. Carolle Doyle, the journalist who was commissioned by the *Sunday Telegraph* to follow my first round the world solo flight in 2001, has been through the book with a toothcomb. She has offered much advice on making the narrative flow.

Ambassador Joe Beeman scrutinized the book with his experience as the former United States ambassador to New Zealand. Brian Gorman added his advice both from a diplomat's point of view and from a literary angle. Our son, Brian has read and offered advice too.

Arthur Moore helped me with the description of sun navigation and Mike Cetinich with the techniques of forecasting used by the Jeppesen meteorologists. Dr Jezdimir Knezevich from The Mirce Akademy of System Operational Science in Exeter allowed me to use the detailed research by the two doctoral students, Jurgen Gross and Claude Hertz. Jonathan Selby provided me with a description of Xaxero 'Sky Eye' weather system and Roxanna Diaz Selby researched the Yamana people of Patagonia on my behalf. Neil Gilbert contributed detail on the legal aspect of British permits for Antarctica.

Susie Dunbar spent hours searching for pictures, maps and information and Art Mortvedt, Joe Paulinelli, and Bill Heinecke all suggested essential points that required checking.

My thanks must also go to John Dunbar who was the official photographer for the flight. Many of his photographs appear in the book. Other photos were taken by Aussie Brown (departure formation), Ski Harrison (ditching and dunking), Ant Tuson (Antarctic pictures) and Fin the Doctor (arrival sequence in Antarctica).

Several more people gave advice and I would like to acknowledge Peta Nightingale from Lucas Alexander Whitley, literary agents. Also thanks go to Dan Waddell, Patrick Blackwell, Nissan (Nick) Boury and Alison Lester for their helpful suggestions.

Neither the flight, nor this book would have been possible without the support of numerous sponsors whose names appear at the end. Finally I am grateful to my publisher, John Davies for having the faith to back the story of my voyage to the ice.

Polly Vacher

CHAPTER 1

She's Barking Mad

Jon Fynes, the recently retired Commandant of RAF Cranwell, introduced me. "She's barking mad!" he said with a wry smile, beaming at the students who had packed the hall of Bedstone College, the Shropshire girl's school where Jon was Chairman of the Governors.

I was guest of honour at the annual prize day and after presenting an impressive array of awards I began talking about my polar flight. A rapt silence fell over the hall as I recounted the training and meticulous preparation needed for a round-the-world solo flight in a single-engine aircraft, and there was a gasp as I told them about my engine failure over the frozen Arctic wastes. When I'd finished Jon stood up to thank me. "I told you she was barking mad!" he reiterated with an even bigger grin.

Having now flown over 2,000 hours it is hard to believe that it all began with a sponsored skydive, the idea for which was first planted by a chance remark at another prize day at our own children's school where I learned that you could do a skydive in tandem with an instructor. My next-door neighbour and old friend, Jean Barton, provided the catalyst. She volunteered to commandeer sponsors if I did the skydive for charity. I hated asking people for money, so that seemed easy enough six months before the arranged date. When the time grew closer I began to feel nervous.

As the plane chugged up to 12,000ft I can well remember thinking to myself, "If ever I get out of this alive, I will *never* do it again." Sitting on the metal floor of a Brit-Norman Islander, I was strapped to tall, handsome Andy House who was also contributing to my 'downfall' although for him, it was just another tandem jump. The door opened and a couple of jumpers leapt out.

"Oh my God!" I thought. I could hardly bear to look down. As I sat in the door and Andy checked the straps I felt like running away, but there was nowhere to run. Terror took a grip and my end looked near.

"You will have the time of your life," were Andy's last words indelibly imprinted on my mind. Before I had more time to think we launched into space. After the initial unwelcome feeling of freefalling, I was overcome with the most exhilarating sense of peace and wonder. Once at terminal velocity of 120 mph, the sensation of falling disappeared and I was flying like a bird. The clouds puffed around us and amazingly I could use my arms and legs to move about. I was filled with an unimaginable sense of awe. From that moment there was no looking back.

Nothing is easy for me. I always have to work and work at whatever I do, but I have an inborn determination to 'get there' once I decide to do something. 'Never give up' is my motto. I had to learn to skydive. "If people can't do it, we tell them to take up windsurfing," Dave Emerson, my instructor hinted. "I am NOT taking up windsurfing," I retorted firmly. I decided to go to the United States because I had a greater chance of continuity due to fine weather. "How long will I need to book for?" I asked the school in Florida. "Four days," the voice came confidently over the telephone. "You mean you will get me through in *four* days?" I asked incredulously. "No problem," she replied. I didn't believe her and booked for eight.

They did get me through in four days. I soaked up the magic of skydiving, the atmosphere of fun. I felt freedom and joy. I was flying! I continued to skydive whenever I could and the weather allowed. Little did I know then what an influence this would have on our youngest son, Brian who is now a champion skydiver and full-time instructor.

I made two more visits to the States, but this time to Perris Valley in California where I made many friends and met one of the most wonderfully warm people. Lu Land was known

I really loved skydiving.

as the 'DZ's Mom' (DZ pronounced 'dee zee' stands for Drop Zone). She baked a daily batch of cookies, welcomed students and generally ran the DZ. She took me under her wing and I was entranced at her ability to always find the good in everyone. Her enthusiasm and love was infectious.

Peter, my husband, waited patiently at home. One of the most placid people I know, he is a real antidote to my volatile and somewhat zany character. He is always calm, always patient. He really does live up to his name, 'Peter, the rock'. He is the rock on which my whole life depends. Married in 1966 aged 22 and 23 respectively, I can honestly say that I have never regretted a moment. But how did he cope with a skydiving wife?

"You would never catch me jumping out of a perfectly serviceable aeroplane," he said laughing. He never let on that he was anxious about me doing it, or at least not until many years after I had given it up. In 1994 Peter's job took us to Australia for two years. "I am not going to spend my days standing around watching my wife appearing out of the sky," he announced.

Life is a compromise and it was there that I gave up skydiving and we both learnt to fly. We gained our private pilots' licences in 1994 in Canberra where we lived. Then with just 80 flying hours each we hired an aeroplane and flew ourselves around the circumference of Australia. We flew up the centre to Uluru (Ayres Rock) and Alice Springs and across the Simpson Desert. We landed at Doomadgee, an Aboriginal settlement where we stayed with the local policeman and went on patrol with him, horrified to see what white man's alcohol was doing to the native population.

We were very 'green' and it was a great adventure for us both. Now I realise this is what gave me my love of long distance flying. This was the life! It was as if I had grown wings and become a bird.

On arriving back in the UK we became the proud owners of our own aeroplane. G-FRGN which is known affectionately as Golf November. Golf November is a Piper Cherokee Dakota. It has four seats and one Lycoming 235 horse-power engine. The amazing coincidence was that Golf November was identical to the plane we had hired in Australia and was just two serial numbers away. How could we resist?

'A late convert is a fanatic' and this is certainly true with my flying. I just had to learn more and try to become a better pilot. I went to Bristol to train for my instrument rating so that I could fly in bad weather and cloud because the weather in the UK is so unpredictable and I did not want to be restricted as to when I could fly. Just forty seconds in cloud without instrument training and an aircraft could be totally out of control, even if you are an experienced pilot. A sobering thought.

We had had such fun flying in Australia that we decided to do the same thing in North America. Our middle son Clive was at university in Boston and we knew that we could hire an aeroplane to fly around the States and Canada. I would really need my instrument rating for this so I mentioned my plans to my instructor. It is amazing how a sentence unknowingly uttered can change the course of one's life. She looked at me and said, "Why are you hiring an aeroplane? You've got a perfectly good one yourself."

"Wow," I thought, "perhaps I could fly Golf November to the States." It had not occurred to me that my little aeroplane could fly across the North Atlantic. I knew that professional ferry pilots flew small aircraft across from the States, but I also knew that there are only a few of them and many aircraft are taken to pieces and packed in a crate to be shipped across. Nevertheless, after a lot of research and preparation, in 1997 I accepted the challenge of flying solo over one of the world's most inhospitable stretches of water, the North Atlantic. My flight to Boston via Iceland, Greenland and Labrador took thirty-four hours to get there and thirty-two to fly back. Peter followed in a Jumbo!

By now we had had such fun learning to fly that we were looking for an opportunity to put something back into aviation. A key figure was Pete Thorn. Pete is a very experienced pilot who I affectionately named my 'flying guru'. He is one of the kindest and wisest people I have met. Pete was a Javelin pilot in the RAF and was involved with developing in-flight refuelling. Subsequently he flew Hurricanes and Spitfires for the Battle of Britain Memorial Flight before becoming a full-time instructor at CSE Kidlington. When we came back from Australia, Pete was the examiner who converted our Australian licences to English ones. He introduced us to Flying Scholarships for the Disabled and flying for the disabled in general. This charity was established in memory of one of our most famous World War II pilots, Sir Douglas Bader, to perpetuate his indomitable spirit: "OK, I've lost my legs, but I can still pilot an aircraft." Each year ten flying scholarships are given to people with disabilities. The aim is to help them to re-build their lives and come to terms with their disabilities through the challenge of learning to fly.

My appetite for long distance flying had now become insatiable. I mentioned to our oldest son Julian, himself an airline pilot, that I would like to fly around the world via both the Poles. It had never been done before. "Why do you think it hasn't been done?" he asked. "Because it is very difficult," I meekly replied. "I suggest you fly around the world the conventional way first – that will give you some 'street cred'," was his throw-away remark which led directly to my next big challenge.

It soon became clear that the round-the-world flight could be used to promote Flying Scholarships for the Disabled. A small committee was formed from members of the British Women Pilots' Association. Susie Dunbar, Rosemary Taylor, Valerie Cahill and Sue Rance worked tirelessly to raise funds and support the next flight. Pete Goss, the round-the-world sailor whose catamaran aimed to be the fastest sailing boat ever built, had a brilliant fund-raising idea. He invited individuals to sponsor his attempt by having their names on his hulls. I rang Pete and asked him if he minded if I copied his idea. "Go ahead," he said "and put my name on your wing too." As a result we invited supporters to have their names stencilled on Golf November's wings for a minimum donation of £25 to the charity.

In January 2001 I set out on a four-month adventure to conquer the world, flying east with the prevailing winds generally behind me. It was a grand departure from Birmingham International Airport. The Royal Air Force sent a Harrier jump jet to escort me. What an honour that was. I flew down to

My team which supported the whole project from conception to completion: Sue Rance, Susie Dunbar, Rosemary Taylor and Valerie Cahill.

Australia, crossing the Saudi desert, coping with Indian bureaucracy and flying across the crocodile-infested Timor Sea.

The night before I started my crossing of the Pacific, the largest ocean in the world, sleep eluded me. I was concerned about what lay ahead, and worried that Golf November would be too heavy to take off from the short runway at Coffs Harbour. However, all went well and eight hours later, I landed at Tontouta in New Caledonia just as Cyclone Sose was approaching. Golf November was hurriedly pushed into a hangar and I waited eight days for the storm to abate. The longest leg across the Pacific was from Hilo in Hawaii to Santa Barbara in California, a distance of 2,068 nautical miles. That flight alone took me sixteen hours, nine of which were in darkness.

The North Atlantic again threw up its challenges. Flying up the fiord to Narsassuaq on the south west corner of Greenland, I had to descend to 500 feet to stay beneath the cloud. It was like flying up a tunnel. Steep mountains rose either side with the cloud forming a roof. It was scary, but there was nowhere else to go.

"Yes," I cheered to myself, "now I really *can* start to prepare for the 'big one'." I whipped myself up into an enthusiastic fireball "Yep! I know it is possible to fly around the world via both the Poles – go for it!" In that instant I acquired a new focus as the goal of daunting proportions began to unfold in front of my eyes. There was little time and much to be achieved.

The RAF sent a Harrier to escort my departure for my first solo round-the-world flight in 2001.

CHAPTER 2

Walking with Giants

I n the summer of 2001, one day on the floor of our living room I sat browsing through an atlas, a blank sheet of paper by my side. I had had a hairbrained idea – to fly solo around the world via both the Poles. As Julian had predicted, the flight around the circumference of the world earlier that year had given me some credibility, but I quickly realised that it was just an apprenticeship compared to what I was contemplating. How could I begin to plan for this next flight?

The most challenging areas were undoubtedly the Poles themselves. It would be particularly hard to fly in Antarctica. It is the highest, driest, coldest and windiest continent in the world. Its enormous size, larger than the United States of America and average height of approximately 9,000 ft (2,250 metres) above sea level, meant that I was unsure how my little Piper Dakota, Golf November would perform in such extreme conditions. The Antarctic is subject to twenty-four hours of darkness in winter. The temperatures plummet to -50°C. At Vostok, the remote Russian base, temperatures as low as -89.6°C have been recorded, making this the coldest place on earth. In summer there are twenty-four hours of daylight and the highest temperature recorded at the South Pole itself is -13.6°C. The Pole is 9,355 ft (2,835 metres) above sea level but the air pressure is the equivalent to 10,659 ft (3,230 metres). This would mean that Golf November would be flying at a higher altitude than for her optimum performance. How would she handle in such hostile conditions? No-one could answer this as no Piper Dakota had flown in Antarctica before.

The Antarctic has another seemingly insurmountable problem. The Antarctic Treaty was established in 1959 and involved twelve member countries. There are now forty-five. The treaty states that Antarctica is only to be used for peaceful purposes and protects any mineral wealth from being exploited. Anyone is free to go there but only with the approval of their national government. In reality there is an unwritten understanding between many member states not to support any non-government organisation (NGO) or adventurer in the Antarctic. Governments just do not want to be involved in any search-and-rescue operations which divert their employees stationed there. Understandably, countries with long-term responsibilities in Antarctica are not keen on uncontrolled activities that may damage the ecology.

My other goal, the Arctic, is a vast frozen ocean surrounded by land. A few people live on the surrounding land, mainly Inuit (Eskimos), which belongs to countries such as Russia, Canada and Alaska adjoining the relevant sections. The potential problem over the Arctic should there be a mishap of any sort would be the heaving moving sea ice, which would be difficult although not impossible to land on. In the summer with twenty-four hours of daylight the temperatures can rise to zero at which point the sea ice on the periphery melts and the ice cracks and opens up throughout the area. Should one survive a forced landing on the sea ice then it is the domain of the polar bear, potentially one of the most vicious and hungry animals on earth.

With this knowledge how could I begin to plan for this next flight?

It would be particularly hard to fly in Antarctica, so it seemed sensible to start there. I contacted the British Antarctic Survey and made an appointment to see Adrian Mildwater, affectionately known as 'Chum', the chief pilot. Armed with nothing more than a notepad, I walked into Adrian's office in Cambridge. I was sure he would tell me I was an idiot and a fool even to think of doing such a thing. To my amazement, he spent a couple of hours with me and became quite animated with my ideas.

"Of course it would be possible to do," he said. It was music to my ears. "I suggest you do it in a Cessna Caravan." This is an enormous single-engine aircraft capable of landing in a small area and with enough weight capacity to carry skis for landing on snow. "I wish," I replied. "I have a Piper Dakota, a low-winged four-seater Cherokee. I can't afford another aircraft." He looked surprised but still didn't seem to think it was impossible. "And I won't be able to carry skis," I told him. "That doesn't matter," he said . "There are some gravel runways in Antarctica and it is possible to land with wheels on ice." I was learning by the minute.

Chum was a mine of information. I made copious notes. He showed me maps and charts and told me where to acquire them. He gave me several people's names to contact. He was quite taken with the plan and told me that it was something he would like to do himself one day. I met some of the other Antarctic pilots and sensed the camaraderie amongst these brave people who live and work in the most extreme conditions.

This was a more positive start than I could ever have hoped for and I walked out of the British Antarctic Survey feeling six feet tall (I am only 5 ft 3 in!), on a cloud. I contacted the people Chum

Max Wenden was an experienced Antarctic pilot and one of my 'giants'.

had suggested, and they put me in touch with others. The Antarctic community is small and close knit. They all know and respect each other. Thus I found three out of the four people who were to become what I affectionately called 'my giants'.

Max Wenden, a tall, thin energetic New Zealander was the first person who would earn the accolade of 'giant'. Known to his friends as Maxo, I met him and Lisa, his wife, on one of their visits to her family not far from where I live. Peter and I joined them for a pub lunch and Maxo listened to my plans attentively. He deluged me with a mass of information, especially about flying light aircraft in Antarctica. Maxo had flown a Cessna 180 over the Drake Passage. "Never again," he said. "Why," I enquired inquisitively. "Because Drake Passage is the most dangerous stretch of water in the world. If you go into the water there your chances of survival are very small. It is freezing cold and there are many icebergs. The weather can change in an instant."

It all sounded terrible and I began to have doubts about what I was planning. I too would have to fly across Drake Passage. Lisa had worked many seasons in Antarctica as a mountain guide and between them they told me so much in those two hours that I was swamped by my notes. Thus began a long liaison with Maxo, one of the wisest and most experienced Antarctic pilots I was ever to meet.

I was advised to visit Dr Charles Swithinbank. Charles is an experienced Antarctic glaciologist. He has spent no less than thirty seasons in Antarctica. Coincidentally, I had already been given one of his books by my son Clive. His picture looked formidable on the front cover of *An Alien in Antarctica*. "Would he ever deem me worthy of an interview," I couldn't help wondering, glancing at the photograph of a bearded man in a Russian fur hat. Somehow I plucked up the courage, and as I rang tentatively on his door a tall, kindly man appeared. What a moment! All I noticed were his bright eyes and his genuine smile. Here was someone who ate, slept and dreamt Antarctica and I could tell in the first instant that I was with someone special.

Dr Charles Swithinbank, the polar glaciologist and another of my 'giants'.

He ushered me into his sitting room with its massive floor-to-ceiling book case. Most of the books were on Antarctica and I gazed with awe at the rows of tomes. He sat down and heard me explain my plans so far. Some people have the ability to listen as if you were the only person in the world who has something to say. Charles was one of these. I relaxed, and started talking and asking questions.

Before long I was taken up to the attic where there was a huge chest containing maps of Antarctica. He talked in gentle tones but underlying this, his strong personality shone through and I listened intently as he offered advice, warnings and encouragement.

"Antarctica is a wonderful place," he said as he recounted tales of his flights with Giles Kershaw. Giles was an experienced pilot who started the only commercial airline in Antarctica called Adventure Network International (ANI). They took climbers, sledge haulers, anyone who wanted adventure into Antarctica, and they were responsible for their safety and for their transportation to and from an area with a huge blue-ice runway at Patriot Hills. When Giles died in an air crash, his Scottish wife, Anne took over running the company.

"A conventional radar altimeter is unreliable in Antarctica. The beam penetrates the snow and gives erroneous readings. That is how we first discovered a way to measure the depth of the ice," Charles continued. There was no end to the knowledge he imparted.

I spent much time studying Charles Swithinbank's publications on blue ice runways. These are areas in which katabatic winds remove snow, leaving an icy snow-free surface. They sometimes occur

15

downwind of mountains where locally generated vortices accelerate the wind to high velocities. Boundary-layer turbulence accentuates any small indentations in the surface through sublimation. Blue ice is the name given to these areas. Even heavy wheeled aircraft can land if the surface is level, though pilots feel a high-frequency vibration on touchdown. Ice without a snow cover is inherently blue because it absorbs the rest of the spectrum. As a result, blue ice areas can be identified in aerial photographs. However, the surface needs inspection to ensure that it is free of crevasses and sastrugi, linear humps formed by the wind.

"You sometimes get many days in succession with clear blue skies when it is quite safe to fly," Charles went on in his positive way. "You will just love it." We pored over maps and charts. Charles' complete immersion in Antarctica was enthralling and his enthusiasm for this little-known icy land was so infectious that I found myself picturing the vast continent and determined to fly safely across it.

"Beware of whiteout," he advised. "A whiteout is the biggest danger in the Antarctic. It is not what most people think of as whiteout. It occurs in overcast weather with clouds at any height. This blots out the sun and there are no shadows, thus it is impossible to differentiate between the snow and sky, everything is white and flat. Pilots lose all sense of their height above the ground and they can get disorientated and crash. There is only one way to go if you get into whiteout conditions, and that is to climb." It was as a result of many consultations and e-mails with Charles, that I knew that I was now better equipped to fly in Antarctica.

Art Mortvedt, another Polar veteran, lives and works in Alaska as a bush pilot and survival instructor. He spends the Arctic winter in the south working in Antarctica so his experience would turn out to be invaluable to me. I planned to go for polar survival training to Alaska. Art played a significant role in my flight, which I couldn't have anticipated when I first contacted him. He became my third 'giant'.

It was soon apparent that one of the biggest challenges was to obtain permission to fly in Antarctica. As I've said earlier, generally non-government organisations are actively discouraged from venturing there. Apparently the British author and traveller Michael Palin was made to camp outside the American base at the South Pole. He wasn't even invited inside to warm up or for a cup of coffee. Moreover, it is almost unheard of for a private individual to gain permission to land at McMurdo, the American base on the New Zealand side of Antarctica. However, if something seems impossible, to me it becomes a real challenge.

My first approach was to the American Embassy. They suggested contacting the Foreign and Commonwealth Office (FCO). I arranged a meeting with Neil Gilbert who was in charge of the Polar Division of FCO. Neil had worked in Antarctica and was impressed with my presentation and the detailed knowledge I had already acquired, but said that I would need written permission to land at any government base.

This proved to be a 'Catch 22' situation. To obtain permission to land at McMurdo I had to have permission from FCO, and to gain permission from FCO, I had to have written evidence of permission to land at McMurdo! I asked Neil if he would write to the Americans on my behalf, but this was beyond his remit.

He gave me forms to fill in for a permit to take a British expedition (yes, taking my little aeroplane was deemed an 'expedition') into Antarctica. As mine was the first British-registered aircraft ever to apply for a permit to go into Antarctica (the British Antarctic Survey aircraft are registered in the Falklands), they had to devise a set of forms especially for me.

For my part, I needed runways to land on and there are very few in Antarctica. The runways that do exist, apart from the blue ice runway at Patriot Hills, are operated by the various governments. This was one of the earliest mountains that I had to climb. How could permission be gained to land at the government bases when clearly this was contrary to long established inter-government convention and practice?

By repute the Americans are the most rigid in Antarctica. They certainly have a bigger presence there than any other country. It seemed wise to try to obtain permission to land at their base McMurdo before pushing on any further. It had only once before been done, so I could see that this would require the most delicate and diplomatic handling.

It was a coincidence that led me to a meeting with Terry Boston, more formally known as Lord Boston of Faversham. We had entertained Terry and his wife Margaret in our house for a friend's wedding. Over lunch in a very smart restaurant in London, I revealed my plans. The reaction was one of sheer delight and enthusiasm. "I think we can help," Terry volunteered with a hint of real excitement in his eyes. "One of our greatest American friends is a prominent lawyer and spent several years as US ambassador to New Zealand – we'll give him a call."

That call gave me the opening I needed and I was soon in regular e-mail correspondence with my fourth 'giant', Joe Beeman whose reaction was typical of a lawyer up for a challenge. "I'll organise a meeting for you with Erick Chiang – he owes me a favour," he said. Erick was a senior member of the National Science Foundation (NSF), Polar Division, the body responsible for American operations in Antarctica. Joe and I formulated a plan. I knew that whatever happened I must never put Erick Chiang in a position where he could say 'NO'. I had to avoid a 'NO' at all costs.

I prepared carefully and, with what I hoped would be regarded as a well presented brochure in hand, I set off on a flight to Washington. An hour before the meeting Joe and I met and went through all the possible scenarios over a cup of coffee. Joe is a larger-than-life character with a real twinkle in his eye and I could see that he had every argument up his sleeve. I was very nervous. Not only was I meeting one of the top US officials, an opportunity I never imagined possible, but on this meeting hung the future success of the project. It was crucial.

Ambassador Joe Beeman, a lawyer and retired US Ambassador to New Zealand, who helped to obtain my American permission to fly into McMurdo.

At the appointed hour we met Erick Chiang who greeted us amiably. Joe and he chatted as old friends. "I have invited Dwight Fisher, a very experienced Antarctic pilot, and Bob Wharton, an experienced Antarctic researcher, to join the meeting. Their advice will be invaluable," were his introductory words to me.

They all listened intently to my short presentation. Joe sat quietly in the background. They asked me a few questions to which I apparently gave the right answers. My homework was beginning to pay off. Things seemed to be going my way. Erick told me that Antarctica belongs to no-one and that technically they cannot either refuse or give me permission. All they wanted was for me to execute the flight safely.

"We will make sure that you have the latest most up-to-date weather," he volunteered. This was to play a significant role in the story later on. I asked for a letter of consent so that I could present it to the Foreign and Commonwealth Office (FCO) in order to grant my Antarctic permit. Erick agreed with a smile.

Had it been too easy? Joe and I found a pizza restaurant for lunch. We were both so elated that champagne seemed in order. I asked the waiter for two glasses. His eyes nearly departed from his head and he seemed covered in confusion. Eventually he arrived with two glasses filled with a urine coloured liquid. "Are you sure this is champagne?" Joe ventured to ask. "I can't see any bubbles." The waiter assured us that it was, but vinegar would have been a more accurate description. It didn't spoil the mood although a few sips were all that either of us could manage.

On arriving back at my sister-in-law's house where I was staying, I made phone calls to Max Wenden and Anne Kershaw from ANI whose brains I had been picking. Neither of them could believe that I had been granted permission. It was unprecedented, but time would tell what precarious alleys this would lead me down.

In the meantime, filled with joy and a sense of disbelief, I set off with a new found confidence to drive to Williamsport to visit Lycoming. Lycoming are the manufacturers of my aircraft's engine and I was going to try my persuasive powers on them to sponsor my flight. It was pouring with rain. Lorries were splashing my windscreen and I could hardly see, but I didn't care. I was on cloud nine, and I was savouring the moment. Again, I was successful and Lycoming promised to sponsor me by providing all the parts needed to re-build my engine free of charge. Was there any limit to the good fortune that was flowing my way?

Erick Chiang was true to his word and within a week I had the promised document in my hand. In the meantime Joe had put me in touch with Gillian Wratt, director of Antarctica New Zealand (ANZ). Thanks to Joe's personal contact, Gillian too was happy to support my project. She offered to put me up at New Zealand's Scott Base adjacent to McMurdo where I was to land. She also offered to store my fuel for me.

Everything, but everything, has to be shipped into Antarctica. Aircraft regularly flown in Antarctica use Jet A1 fuel. My aircraft, with its small piston engine, uses Avgas, a high octane leaded petrol. No Avgas is held anywhere on the continent except at Patriot Hills. To be ready for my arrival in the spring, my fuel had to be brought in by ship nearly a year earlier during the Antarctic summer. Gillian Wratt very kindly offered to transport my fuel for me along with the supplies shipped in for Scott Base. She told me to deal direct with Julian Tangaere over the logistics as she was retiring from ANZ. This too turned out to be a 'hornets' nest', but more about that as the story unravels. For now, everything was going smoothly and I couldn't believe my luck.

The next hurdle would be the British Antarctic Survey (BAS). Now that I had permission from the Americans and the New Zealanders would this now turn out to be the biggest challenge of all? Nervously, I set up a meeting in Cambridge with John Pye, head of logistics at BAS. It was raining as I drove into their headquarters.

"Is there something significant about the rain?" I wondered as I tried to look smart and keep dry all at the same time. This really was a cliff hanger. With the rest of the permits in hand and literally hours of hard work not only from me but numerous others, it was even more critical that BAS allowed me to land at Rothera, the British base in Antarctica, and one of the few places available to wheeled aircraft. The whole flight depended on it.

I was introduced to John Pye who is known as JP. His opening words were, "You have published without our permission that you are going in to Rothera – that is a black mark." My heart sunk as I glanced at his desk. I couldn't believe my eyes. There was a copy of my presentation pack and also of The Mirce Akademy book on my first flight 'From B2B'. I had not sent him these, so how had he got hold of them, I wondered.

I replied, "I don't know where you got that from, but I haven't published anything. I have deliberately only told the essential people under sworn secrecy." My heart was sinking by the second and I wished that I had got someone like Joe Beeman to smooth the way for me. JP asked many probing questions, it seemed like a 'third degree' interrogation. I wanted to burst into tears and rush from the room. He continued his interrogation, anxious about my flight, not on any personal level it transpired, but on how it would affect BAS.

"What if something happens to you?" he asked, "BAS will be bound to rescue you." He went on, "If BAS helps you, they will be contravening the agreement and if they don't it will make them look bad." I could see the whole project disintegrating.

"What about the Americans – do you have permission from them?" he enquired with a look that transmitted the feeling, 'I bet you won't have that!' I leant down to my bag and pulled out a copy of the American document. His surprise was evident, as he scrutinised the letter, and this may have been the turning point.

"What about publicity?" JP tried another tack. "Well, there will be publicity because my sponsors need the exposure," I replied. "We are also trying to raise awareness of Flying Scholarships for the Disabled. However, I won't be asking you for permission to send loads of photographers down to Rothera. The Antarctic bit can be very low key." "Oh no!" he responded, "if we do this we will want lots of publicity." I kept thinking "I can't win here."

After a grilling and feeling as if my world had come to an end, JP called the meeting to a close. "You have managed to persuade me, I am now on your side," he said. "But I must persuade the others. Sorry to give you such a hard time."

Once more, I could not believe what I was hearing. "Could I, after all be lucky once more?" I said to myself as I smiled sweetly and bade JP farewell. The outcome was hanging on a thread, but there was still a glimmer of hope as I drove away. A while later, I had a phone call from JP. "I've got you the permission and it will follow in writing." He seemed really pleased.

Inwardly I was shouting 'Yippee'! I asked him how I could help with the publicity and he invited me to Cambridge for a full briefing on the work of BAS so that I could promote the correct facts. This would not be a problem and I knew that I would enjoy learning as much as I could about Antarctica.

I now had all the permissions to hand, American, New Zealand and British. Hopefully there would be no problem with the Antarctic permit from the Foreign and Commonwealth Office. It seemed like a miracle. Max Wenden kept telling me that I was the only person who had managed to get these approvals. I was beginning to feel delighted, but it was far from over.

The next thing was to make sure that I was fully insured for every eventuality including my time in Antarctica. According to the Antarctic Treaty anything taken into Antarctica must be taken out. This had far reaching implications. Should I crash in Antarctica my aircraft would have to be removed and this could be very costly. Global Aerospace had insured my trans-Atlantic flights and my first round-the-world flight. Would they support anything as risky as the polar flight especially in a single-engine aircraft? David Boyce from Aon Insurance had introduced me to Peter Butler and Philip Gregory from Global Aerospace. Over a congenial lunch I presented my proposals. They were captivated by the whole project. Philip had just acquired his private pilot's licence and was full of enthusiasm. They agreed to cover the whole flight including complete coverage of the Antarctic flight as sponsorship. This was music to my ears. I had the final piece for the jigsaw and the green light was finally shining through. Little did I know that the red light would continue to flicker in the background, but at this stage I was elated.

The FCO still required an advertisement about the project to be placed in the *London Gazette*. I wrote a paragraph explaining what was being proposed and had it checked by Neil Gilbert. The following week it was published and I waited anxiously for any opposition. Nothing was forthcoming and as all the obstacles had then been dealt with FCO granted that elusive permit. On that front at least I was ready to go. But it was not going to be as easy as that. Very soon there would be rumblings as the full impact of what I so far had managed to achieve dawned on the tight-knit Antarctic community.

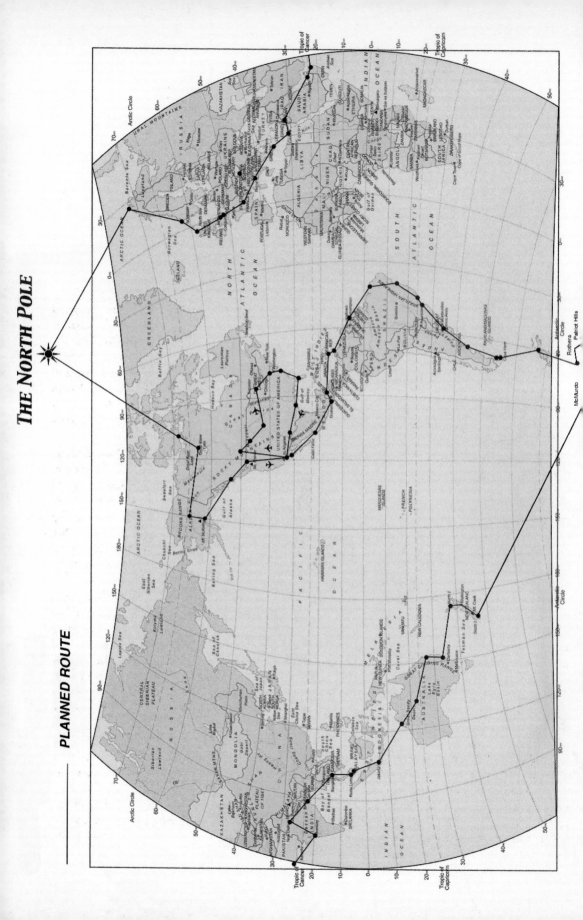

THE NORTH POLE

PLANNED ROUTE

CHAPTER 3

A Logistical Maze

With almost two years to go I started work in earnest. I needed detailed knowledge of conditions in the Antarctic and I shamelessly pestered my 'giants', Charles Swithinbank, Art Mortvedt, Max Wenden (Maxo) and anyone else I could collar for advice. At this stage I had not decided which way round to go. My instincts were to go eastwards to New Zealand, down to Antarctica via the American base at McMurdo and then back up to South America from the British base at Rothera. This would mean crossing the South Pole before the North Pole and would dictate a departure in the northern hemisphere's autumn to catch Antarctica's summer. It would also mean that overall I would have a tailwind pushing me along over the earth's surface, as the majority of the prevailing winds blow from the west to the east.

There was one major consideration and that was the long over-water leg between New Zealand and Antarctica, a distance of 1,917 nm. If I were to fly to New Zealand first and then fly from there to Antarctica I would be flying with the winds behind me most of the way which would be a great advantage. However, a sixteen-hour flight to Antarctica could mean the unpredictable weather there could change dramatically during the actual flight. Should I arrive in the Antarctic and there was fog or a whiteout, there were few alternative options of places to land. If I did the long flight in the other direction from Antarctica to New Zealand, at least I would be flying towards a warmer climate and to a country with lots of alternate airports and help should something go wrong. The whole flight depended on the direction I would choose to fly this leg.

Maxo had grave reservations about going from New Zealand to Antarctica, citing the long flight over water and the potential weather problem. I pondered long and hard over this. Charles had advised me of an area of blue ice where I could land in an emergency, and, as always with conflicting advice, one mulls it over and then takes a decision. In the end I heeded Maxo's warning and decided to route north west over the North Pole first through the Americas to New Zealand. Planning for the Antarctic occupied much of my time, but I tried not to lose focus on the Arctic hazards as well.

It was sometimes difficult to remember that I had to fly safely around the rest of the world, not just the polar regions. With an atlas and ruler I began to plan the entire route. I needed an overall picture and the distance and time required for each leg. Our dining room was commandeered and it was covered with aviation maps and charts. There was only room for one set at a time.

Very soon questions began to pop up. How would I be able to obtain permission to overfly the countries on my route? Saudi Arabia, Suriname, Myanmar and India were particularly tricky. Will Golf November be able to climb over high mountains? She has a normally aspirated engine and above a certain altitude where the air is much thinner it becomes increasingly difficult for her to climb. 16,000 ft is her normal ceiling, but where the air is hot and less dense she struggles to reach 15,000 ft. The Andes had to be crossed, with a minimum safe altitude of 14,000 ft and I was venturing into the Himalayas to Bhutan with mountains up to 17,000 ft. In the Saudi desert I would need a tailwind to push me along as the distances were so long. There would be a huge extra ferry tank in place of the back seats, but even that had its limitations. Eighteen hours would be the absolute maximum I could manage in the air with a safe margin which is called the reserve. Would Avgas (the fuel used in light aircraft) be available where I had to land? If there was no Avgas, could I arrange for some to be transported in barrels?

Each leg of the flight needed to be measured and the questions of permissions, endurance and fuel answered. Then and only then was the flight log placed in a folder, appropriately labelled and added to the pile on the floor. By the time I was ready to leave, I had worked on each section no less than five times. On each occasion the details were checked with painstaking care. The final log was placed, along with the appropriate chart, in a plastic sleeve in a loose leaf binder ready to take with me or for one of my team to bring to me at an appointed place. Weight and space were critical, so I could not take them all.

The charts had been given to me by Jeppesen, an American company and the largest aviation map and chart producer in the world. They also provide a trip planning service mainly for business jets where they obtain overflight clearances and organise fuel and handling. They had been unstinting in their support on my first round-the-world flight so I had naturally approached them again.

"We can provide you with maps, charts and approach plates," Alan Lathan from the Jeppesen European headquarters in Frankfurt had generously offered. "We can organise your handling, fuel and overflight clearances," Steve Card, managing director of Jeppesen UK had said.

So Jeppesen was doing it again. They became my first ever sponsor and gave me support without which I would not have managed the flight. I sent photocopies of the flight logs to Louise Lister at Jeppesen in Gatwick, as she had played a key role in my first round-the-world flight. We had struck up a close friendship, so I was delighted when I heard she would manage the next flight too. The duplicate flight logs allowed Jeppesen to provide 'flight-following', a system whereby I would notify my time of departure and expected arrival time on a particular leg. Jeppesen would await my call to confirm I had landed safely. If no call was made, they would alert the emergency services.

I was very lucky with my sponsors. Shell had provided the fuel for the first round-the-world flight. On my return Steve Dudley had enthusiastically offered to support me again should I be planning another flight. It was Steve from Shell Aviation in Manchester who had initiated the sponsorship. He and Rob Midgley, Shell's technical 'guru', threw themselves into helping with the preparations. Steve had also enlisted Brian Humphries, managing director of Shell Aircraft, who was well aware that Flying Scholarships for the Disabled had been established in memory of Sir Douglas Bader and that Bader was his predecessor at Shell Aircraft. Disappointingly, Steve left Shell before my departure so Lynne Barnes and Julie Wright took over the management of my flight. They had the bright idea to involve Rob Farr from Shell Education. Here was an opportunity to introduce the Shell name to young people but also to broadcast the message of flying for the disabled to schools around the world.

There was also the preparation of my aircraft to consider. My Piper Dakota, a four-seater, single-engined, low-wing aircraft, had already taken me safely across the North Atlantic in both directions and around the world once. By law the engine had to be replaced or completely re-built after 2,000 flying hours. Golf November (as its registration G-FRGN was abbreviated) had very nearly reached that point. I could apply for a 400-hour extension, after all the Lycoming O540 235 hp engine was working well so why change it? However, should the flight take significantly longer than planned I would run out of engine hours. I decided that, costly though it would be, the engine ought to be re-built.

Lycoming came to the rescue. They were excited by the project and had offered to provide the necessary parts for the re-build as sponsorship. This was more than I could have hoped for but the good fortune continued for Steve Jones, managing director of CSE Engineering at Oxford Airport offered to re-build the engine free of charge and promptly took me out to lunch!

Golf November was to have a complete re-spray during the engine re-build. Many aircraft flying in the Arctic and Antarctica are painted black and red. The black absorbs heat from the sun and the red stands out against the snow should there be an accident. It was another safety precaution. Shell Aircraft, the division which operates their business jet fleet, joined forces with Shell Aviation to cover the cost of the re-paint. Instead of the red it was decided to paint it orange to match my orange flying suit that had become something of a trademark as I had worn it on my first round-the-world flight.

Some of the distances to be covered could take over sixteen hours non-stop. Consequently, my little aeroplane had to be converted into a flying fuel tanker. Three out of the four seats had to be removed and a huge aluminium fuel tank placed in the cabin. This was a relatively simple operation. The big question was just how to fit in all the rest of the survival gear and my own personal belongings. These had to be packed so that the aircraft was properly balanced. As Golf November would be loaded beyond its nominal maximum take-off weight, maintaining a perfectly balanced centre of gravity would make its handling easier, and also safer in turbulent weather. In the end my clothes allowance for a year was just 10 kg.

Magnetic compasses tend to be unreliable in the polar regions as they go haywire and give erroneous readings. The first time I experienced this phenomenon it was unnerving watching the dial swivel around at an alarming rate. There are no convenient radio aids to home into in the Arctic. Unlike the early pilots, I had a Global Positioning System (GPS) satellite navigation system, but if the GPS went down for any reason, how would I find my way, particularly over the North Pole? All lines of longitude go south from the North Pole, but which one should I take? Hypothetically I could fly round and round in circles until my fuel and life ran out.

I needed a back-up navigation system and by chance I met the man who could teach me at a meeting of the Royal Institute of Navigation where I was to receive its Certificate of Achievement for my 2001 flight. Arthur Moore, a retired RAF navigator, was to be awarded a Fellowship and after David Broughton, the director of RIN and a keen supporter of my flights had welcomed me, Arthur and I got into conversation. I told him that I would need to learn to navigate by the sun and asked if he could teach me. Arthur gave me his card and a year later I contacted him and lessons in sun navigation began in earnest.

He introduced me to the vagaries of the astro compass. The sun's position is predictable and well tabulated. An accurate reading depends on your latitude, the hemisphere, the date and time. Each year a set of tables is published which enable the declination (latitude) and hour angle (longitude) of the sun to be calculated to establish an exact position. When correctly set the sun compass will give a reading of the true heading. Because the meridians converge at the Poles, true heading can be confusing, with all headings from the North Pole going south. The answer to this is to overlay a rectangular grid and measure the tracks against the new grid.

There was just one problem. Every time Arthur and I met for a lesson there was complete cloud cover. Thus we were never able to take a series of sun-sights and I had to rely on the theory to get me through. My surprise and relief at the accuracy of this method of navigation when actually in the polar regions was overwhelming. The early navigators knew a thing or two!

Every week I went flying with Pete Thorn, my flying mentor. This wonderfully wise man sat patiently beside me and exuded confidence. He never mentioned what I couldn't do. In his mind his students always *could* do it. He is foremost a 'seat of the pants' guy. "Feel the aircraft, you are part of it," he would say and he was right. Golf November became an extension of my being. It was as if I had grown wings. We worked together, Golf November and I. Pete looked on and guided our bonding. Each week we practised emergency procedures and forced landings. He simulated engine fire, engine failure, stalls and unusual attitudes. There was not a stone left unturned and I was to realise later that I owed my life to Pete.

The Astro compass and 'pencil' camera were mounted on the dashboard. The camera was installed by Carlton Television for their documentary.

Another instructor, Martin Barnes, from Bristol Flying Centre put me through my paces. "What are you most worried about?" he asked during my annual instrument rating renewal just before my departure. "A whiteout in Antarctica," I said at once.

As has already been mentioned, Charles Swithinbank had instilled into me the danger of whiteouts. "This is the most dangerous thing that can happen to you over snow-covered terrain. Whiteout is caused by complete cloud cover over a white surface. There are no shadows and it is impossible to tell how high you are above the ground." He emphasized again and again the importance of recognising a whiteout. "Should you be obliged to land, however, don't rely on a radar altimeter as they give erroneous readings over ice."

Charles knew that there are many days in an Antarctic summer when clear blue skies make ideal flying conditions. But the weather can deteriorate in a few short moments. He was determined to make me aware of the possible dangers. "OK", Martin said. "When you descend on final, instead of taking the screen down at 200 ft we will keep the screens up and practice landing blind."

When learning to fly on instruments and for one's annual revalidation, screens are fitted over the aircraft windows to simulate flying in cloud. The examiner can see out through slats on his side as a safety precaution. Descending on the ILS (Instrument Landing System, a radio-controlled beam guiding you in height and direction to the runway), I began to grip the control column and my knuckles went white. My face was probably white too, but I couldn't see that.

"How would I manage to round Golf November out in time and without stuffing her nose into the runway?" I was querying. My eyes were fixed on the altimeter. Muscles tense, nerves jangling, I felt on 'red alert'. When the altimeter registered zero, I pulled Golf November's nose into the landing position and waited for the wheels to touch the ground. It was a tense few moments, but it gave me the confidence to know what to do if I found myself in such dire straits for real. It also emphasised that it was a situation to be avoided at all costs.

There is always more to learn about weather. I bought a book on climatology and learnt all about the Inter Tropical Convergence Zone, where the weather systems of the northern and southern hemispheres meet. This creates huge build-ups of clouds resulting in monsoon. Monsoons are a serious potential hazard which I studied avidly for both my world flights. Every flight around the world inevitably encounters the ITCZ which, although it moves, is always there.

Then there is icing, a nightmare of a hazard for light aircraft. If an aircraft goes into cloud and the temperature is zero or below, ice will build on the airframe. It forms on the fuselage, wings and propeller. It adds huge amounts of weight not always evenly distributed and unbalances the propeller, stressing the engine. Ice is a killer and it can build up in a matter of seconds. Large aeroplanes have de-icing equipment such as heated wings or propeller boots to break off the ice. There are no such luxuries on Golf November.

It was imperative that weather systems with potential icing conditions were fully understood by me and avoided. It is commonly thought that ice accumulation can be simply cured by turning back, but this is a myth. I encountered icing conditions inadvertently in California, unbelievably over Death Valley, one of the hottest places in America. Within seconds the aircraft was covered with heavy ice. I could not see a thing so I called the controller.

"Standby," he said. I thought to myself I don't want to standby. I need to go somewhere else to get out of this icing. I called him again. "Standby," he went again. He must have been having a cup of tea. I did not want to declare an emergency as that creates a whole lot of paperwork and hassle.

I called him again and rather unprofessionally said, "I need your help." He must have put his cup of tea down after that as he was more than helpful. He gave me permission to descend to the minimum safe altitude where it was warmer. Although the temperature was just above zero, the ice was so thick and heavy that it did not melt for over half an hour.

Some light aircraft have fuel-injected engines. They are the lucky ones. The remainder use archaic carburettors, harbouring one of the most frequent accidents to small aeroplanes. As the air is sucked into the carburettor it goes through a narrowed tube or venturi. This has the effect of making the temperature drop significantly. If there is any moisture in the air then the possibility of ice forming in that tube is very real. Not recognised quickly it can block the tube, preventing air and fuel getting to the engine with inevitable dire consequences. It can be prevented by diverting some of the heat from the exhaust system onto the venturi at regular intervals. This needs careful management, though, as heat enriches the fuel/air mixture causing high fuel consumption and possible rough running.

I learnt a lot about carburettor icing from Ross Kelly, the owner of the Piper Dakota we had flown around Australia and a very experienced pilot. Although Ross lives in Australia where you would imagine icing was out of the question, it happens surprisingly frequently in temperatures of up to plus 30°C. He was liberal with his advice on the management of carburettor heat and I was forever grateful to him.

Obtaining visas to enter all the countries en route was another major challenge. Ross Consular in Slough undertook to organise this as sponsorship. It was not as easy as it sounds. Different countries allow differing lengths of time for issue and duration. Suriname in South America for instance will not issue a visa until three weeks before required. This posed an enormous logistical problem. I rang the passport office and explained the situation.

"No problem," they said. "Just fill in an application form and we will send you a second passport." This was wonderful news and eased the situation enormously. I still did, however, have to organise the different passports and visas to arrive in time for me to enter the relevant countries. Wherever possible the passports were delivered by someone meeting me en route. On one or two occasions I rather worryingly had to rely on the mail. Amazingly it all worked without a hitch, thanks to a very efficient Jim Jacobs at Ross Consular.

The Antarctic dominated the preparation. There is no way that Golf November could carry enough fuel to fly from Argentina across the Antarctic continent and up to New Zealand. I needed at least three fuel stops, and it was imperative for fuel to be shipped in to the various bases a year in advance.

I contacted a German shipping company to enquire if they would consider taking fuel to Antarctica for me. I was met with a flat refusal. "There is no way we could carry fuel at the same time as passengers," was their response. There was only one other chance. A Russian ice breaker, the *Kapitan Khlebnikov* was on its way to New Zealand from Vladivostok. It had been chartered as a tourist ship to go to Antarctica. I found the satellite telephone numbers for the ship and after a number of abortive attempts managed to get through to Captain Golikov.

"I am planning a flight to Antarctica next year. Is there any chance that you could transport some barrels of fuel for me?" I tentatively enquired. "I can see no problem," a deep, sexy Russian voice replied with a perfect command of the English language. "You will need to contact John Apps at Quark Expeditions in High Wycombe," he continued. Unbelievable! Here I was talking to a Russian captain on the high seas on the other side of the world and he was telling me to contact someone in High Wycombe, just thirty miles from where I live. The fuel transportation to Rothera and McMurdo in Antarctica on the *Kapitan Khlebnikov* turned out to be the easiest aspect of my Antarctic preparation thanks to the practical approach of Captain Golikov and John Apps who organised it all free of charge. Everything ran smoothly once the fuel was on board. When the ship reached McMurdo it was unable to dock because of the thickness of the ice in the Ross Sea. Undaunted, the Russian crew used their on-board helicopter to carry the fuel to New Zealand's Scott Base, close to McMurdo. The barrels were underslung over the ice. Volunteers from Scott Base rolled the barrels up to their storage shed.

Patriot Hills was the only landing place that was not run by a government department and the only one that handled Avgas. This was where Adventure Network International (ANI) had their base. At a meeting with Anne Kershaw, we discussed the logistics of the Antarctic section of the flight at length. She was on my side, but there was something she wasn't going to disclose and I felt frustrated. It turned out that she was in the process of selling ANI to another company. Nevertheless, she tried hard to get the fuel provision in place, albeit that the price was $4,000 a barrel, mainly due to the cost of positioning the fuel. Although Anne was still working for ANI, she was then answerable to a board of directors and they weren't so keen to support my flight. They wanted to have caches of fuel positioned along my route ready to supply any of their aircraft which might have to come to my aid. This would be at the vast sum of $350,000 and I simply could not justify the expense. Without that, the new company were not prepared to sell me fuel at Patriot Hills or make any exceptions. I understood where they were coming from. ANI had a clean sheet where safety was concerned in the Antarctic and I was asking them to be flexible on behalf of my charity flight. I emphasized that thanks to sponsorship from Global Aerospace and Aon Insurance, I was covered for half as much again than the estimated worst scenario cost of rescue and removal of my aircraft should I crash. They were immovable. I would have to get my fuel another way.

Fuel in the Arctic was not such a problem. I called the airport at Longyearbyen in plenty of time. They have a certain number of barrels of Avgas delivered every year, but it was essential to reserve the required quantity of fuel. The Norwegians are very efficient and speak perfect English.

I planned to fly from Longyearbyen up to the North Pole and across to Resolute Bay, a small Inuit (Eskimo) settlement on Cornwallis Island in northern Canada. I contacted the airport at Resolute Bay. "We don't keep Avgas here," they said. "Oh dear – what do you suggest I do?" I replied. "There is a man called Aziz who runs the local hotel, he may be able to help you."

Thinking this a rather unlikely course, I nonetheless rang Aziz. "No problem," he said. "I have plenty of fuel. It is ten years old but in this cold climate it should be perfectly alright." I thanked him and reserved three barrels.

I was worried about using such old fuel so I made a number of phone calls to people who are experienced at flying in those areas. "It shouldn't be problem," was the reassuring response, so I had to accept that. I did ensure that I went armed with a fuel testing kit, in particular to check for water when refuelling from barrels anywhere on my trip.

CHAPTER 4

Worm and Bulrush Stew

Two thirds of the earth's surface is water. I was faced with the prospect of spending many hours flying over the ocean, so learning to ditch my aircraft safely and to survive was high on my list of priorities. I turned to Bob Wringe at the Fleetwood Nautical College in Blackpool. Bob had spent many years training pilots and rig workers on the North Sea oilfields. "Yes, we can organise a course for you," Bob said. "If you get a small group of about six people together then we can open the facility on a Saturday and devote the whole day to your training."

Bob turned out to be an absolute star. Six pale-faced people turned up for the course, one couldn't even swim. I had done this course twice before, but the thought of the simulated ditching was still terrifying.

The morning was spent in the classroom. Ditching techniques were explained in detail so that I learnt the importance of landing along the direction of the wave. We were also given advice on the type of immersion suit to wear, a suit that, however uncomfortable it may be, must be worn for every flight over water. When the engine dies and all attempts at re-starting have failed then ditching is the only option and, at that moment, there would not even be time to zip the suit up, let alone climb into it. Our instructor talked about life-jackets and then explained the ditching simulation in detail.

There was a lot to cover, so after a quick break for coffee we were hard at it again. A life-raft is the best means of survival but where should it be stored and should it be attached to the aircraft or yourself? There are no hard and fast rules so, after weighing up the pros and cons I decided to attach the life-raft to myself. After all, nothing would be worse than ditching satisfactorily and then watching the life-raft being blown away in the distance. At least if it was attached to me we couldn't be separated.

Lunch was a sombre affair. There was the odd attempt at being jolly, but everyone's minds were focused on one thing. How would we cope with the afternoon's ditching practice? We had to force ourselves to put one leg in front of the other as we walked towards the pool building. The smell of chlorine filled the air in the changing rooms as we pulled on our immersion suits.

We walked into the area. A huge square pool dominated the room which had a high vaulted ceiling and a gallery on one side. Bob introduced us to the two divers. They would be under the water with full breathing apparatus during operations, ready to pull us out if there was a problem. They did not want dead bodies in their pool. This certainly concentrated the mind as there would be no divers in the real world to rescue me. I vowed at that moment to redouble my efforts to be meticulous with my preparation.

Bob showed us the simulator, a two-seater cockpit attached to a huge crane. He gave some final instructions and the first two volunteers gingerly climbed in. Bob stood on the back and shouted the order to begin. The crane wound the cockpit into the air, swivelled it round over the pool and plunged it in.

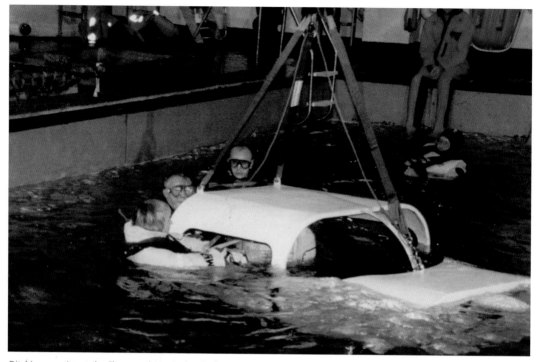

Ditching practice at the Fleetwood Nautical College. Bob Wringe, the instructor and two divers with full breathing equipment are in the water with me.

The orders were simple. Wait until fully submerged to equalise the pressure before attempting to open the door. Get the life-raft out followed by yourself. It was heady stuff and the nerves jangled as we watched. As my turn approached I began to shiver and I wanted to make a bolt for the door. But I climbed in and took a long look at my life-raft to make sure I could get it out. Bob gave the order and the next thing I saw was the water rapidly approaching, it was terrifying.

Splash! The sound no-one ever wants to hear for real. The aircraft began to sink. As the water level rose I tried to judge at what moment to take my last breath. I needed to take in as much air as I could, but judging the exact moment of submersion was not easy because everything was dark and confused under the water. Trying to find the door and the handle to push it open seemed to take forever and the feeling that my breath was running out almost spun me into panic. But panic is the quickest way to disaster and I knew that however difficult it was, I must keep my head.

I chanted orders to myself. "Get the door open – grab the life-raft – you only have one chance, make sure it is right," and then wondered how much longer I could hold my breath and in the next second, would I ever get out? My head was racing as my oxygen level decreased. I couldn't help thinking what it would be like in the open ocean with no-one there to help.

In this situation my thoughts seemed to be rushing in on me like huge birds, crowding and pecking at my very being. At last the door gave way and I wriggled and pushed my way out, grabbing my life-raft. It was stuck! Gasping for air I gave it a mighty tug.

As the life-jacket expanded, I shot to the surface with the life-raft in tow, trod water and fumbled with the toggle to inflate the raft. My arms were like lead. I was exhausted and this was just a heated swimming pool with a simulated wave machine. How would I ever manage in an ocean with cold waves pouring over me? My fingers found the toggle. The life-raft exploded and in a second it was more like a round dinghy. Despite my exhaustion I still had to climb into the life-raft. Bob was swimming around me.

"Don't help me," I panted. "I must do this myself." I clung with determination to the edge of the raft. It seemed so high. I gritted my teeth and hauled on my arms but I couldn't heave my body, weighed down by immersion suit and life-jacket, out of the water. I tried again, but still I could not do it.

"Don't whatever you do help me," I yelled at Bob who was hovering around. "How will I ever manage on my own if I can't even do it here?" I was desperate. "Relax for a minute and calm down," Bob reassured me. I rested, hanging onto the life-raft. Pictures of huge Atlantic waves towering over me filled my imagination. The life-raft had two buoyancy rings making it sit high out of the water. This was necessary as it was imperative that it could withstand oceanic storms. Around the buoyancy rings ropes dangled in loops so that you could climb on them to get into the raft. "I *must* do it," I kept saying to myself, "otherwise I won't have the confidence to do it for real. My arms aren't strong enough – I must do more work in the gym – it wouldn't be funny if this was a real situation."

I had another go and another, but still it was difficult to get enough grip and I was pulling with a distinct disadvantage. The life-raft was too high out of the water, and my arms only just reached the top. I was clutching onto the ropes at the side, trying to get a foothold on one of them and haul myself up on one of the others. Finally, with a superhuman effort I heaved myself up so that I was standing on one of the ropes and collapsed into the life-raft.

"You will have so much adrenalin running in a real situation that you won't have this problem," Bob told me. "Don't forget your own life-raft has a ladder so it will be much easier but we always simulate the worst scenario."

It wasn't over yet. After a brief moment, the raft was bombarded with water. They had turned the hose pipes on and the wave machine was tossing the raft around. The simulated storm was all too real. It was hot and oppressive in the raft with the roof and door tightly closed to keep out the water.

The final test was to be winched out of the raft. A rope was dropped down. I put the strap around my waste and was then hauled up to the balcony above, where I lay feeling exhausted. I was bruised

Trying to haul myself into the life-raft was such a struggle even with my survival gear and life-jacket.

and battered and ached for a week afterwards. It was a salutary lesson, and I realised the gravity of ditching for real.

I could have stayed sitting on the edge of the balcony for hours but Bob was relentless. "When you are dressed come outside and I will show you how to fire flares," he said. It was cold and breezy outside and I still had not got over the immense physical effort and the emotional battering of the afternoon. Firing flares was fun now, but it would be no fun at all if I really had to attract attention in an emergency.

It was an experience which was to have a profound effect on my preparation. It was essential my engine did not fail. But if it did, then I had to have the right equipment in perfect working order. I redoubled my efforts to check and double check every aspect of all I did to ready myself for this challenge. I knew that the outcome would be directly related to the amount of meticulous care I took, not only with the preparation beforehand, but also with the daily care of aircraft, engine, refuelling and all the checks.

Landing in the desert or jungle could be equally forbidding. To increase my chances of survival I spent five days in the Lake District with two ex-marine commandos, Daryl

I was forced to eat worm and bulrush stew whilst on a desert and jungle survival course in the Lake District.

White and Rod Eglin. All went well whilst we were in the classroom, but I was soon to discover that this was the lull before the storm. Together with two other students, Simon Newbery and Howard Lee, I set off across the Lake District in pouring rain. We were weighed down by 35-pound backpacks with only a map and a compass to guide us. Whilst not being able to simulate the heat of the jungle, the Lake District in driving rain was a good, if miserable second best.

We tramped for miles through wet dense undergrowth. Our instructors would appear suddenly from nowhere, and when least expected. We clambered through bogs and waded across swollen streams and rivers only to be told that we had gone in the wrong direction and would have to retrace our steps. Despite ponchos, I was soon soaked to the skin. The niceties of civilised life slipped away and instead of disappearing behind a bush when I needed to attend to a call of nature, I found myself shouting "don't look" as I squatted down. Anything else was too much effort for my tired, sore limbs.

We tramped all day until I thought I could walk no more. In between Daryl and Rod would pop up and give us some instruction in a different aspect of survival. Not only were we learning to survive, but we were also being stretched to our limits and it was interesting to see how much we could stand. All the time, though, a little voice inside me kept saying, "you don't have to do this – you are crazy." It was then that I had to take myself in hand and tell myself that if I gave up before the end, I would never have the confidence to survive should I crash in some remote part of the world.

There was a short break to set up camp and convert our ponchos into tents attaching them to trees and securing them to the ground with sticks before laying out our sleeping mats and bags. We could not dally for long, but we were starving and had to find something to eat before the night exercise. We were hungry and we found some bulrushes which we had been told were nourishing and in desperation we dug up some wriggling worms. Boiling water in a jerry can we added the bulrushes and allowed them to stew. We then dropped the poor worms into the boiling pot. There was no time to feel sorry for them. In fact worm and bulrush stew was quite a delicacy and the worms resembled crunchy chicken! It is amazing what you will eat when you are hungry.

At night the route lay over rough terrain. We climbed up a mountain side through thick trees following a stream. This time we had a radio so our instructors would know should something go seriously wrong. At certain points the stream ran through concrete pipes. There was no other way but for us to climb through the pipes against the rushing water. Doing this with just a head torch on hands and knees in the dark as the water was gushing against us was very testing.

We clambered into the pipe and halfway along Howard shouted, "I've dropped the radio." "What an idiot," I thought although we had all dropped things inadvertently before. Tiredness was getting the better of me but I tried to control it as we all backed down the pipe looking for any sign of the radio.

As we emerged from the pipe, I looked up and saw the instructors standing on the bridge above. "I've lost the radio," Howard said. Daryl was furious and gave him such a dressing down. At this point Howard admitted to having us all on. He had it after all. Daryl was even more furious. You really do not mess with marine commandos.

Finally we flopped into our bivouacs and I dropped fast asleep. I woke in the night to see the stars shining through the trees above. "Where's my tent?" I wondered. "I bet they (the instructors) have been in the night and nicked it," I thought accusingly. Then I looked up the hillside and there was my tent. I had actually rolled out of the side and down the hill without even waking up!

By the end of the week we had learnt how to survive on very little food and water, how to extract water from the desert and how to make fire in the damp of the jungle. We now knew how to build shelters and to survive in atrocious conditions. We were even given live training in being kidnapped and coping with extremely objectionable and aggressive captors.

I would not say it had exactly been fun, but it gave me great satisfaction to finish the course pretty well intact. I was mentally and physically exhausted, filthy and smelly. I then had to face the four-hour drive home. I was so tired, I had to stop at every motorway service station for a caffeine fix. Heaven knows what everyone thought of this ragbag with matted hair and filthy nails and clothes. I was past worrying about things like that. Perhaps everyone gave me a wide berth, I didn't care. When I finally arrived home Peter stripped me off at the door and carried me upstairs and dropped me in the best hot bath I have ever had.

I realised after these courses the importance of being physically fit to fulfil my quest. I started training at the gym, but very quickly found that I cheated on the machines. Aerobics classes were the only hope of obtaining my goal, so a minimum of twice a week and more where possible I worked out intensively for an hour at a time. I gave up coffee. I have an addiction for it, but function better without. It was a big wrench but I resolved not to touch a single cup until I reached Dunedin in New Zealand. Sometimes it was tough especially in South America where every restaurant was filled with the glorious aroma of freshly ground coffee…

CHAPTER 5 Light a Fire

The Antarctic 'network' is such that everyone knows everyone, which led me to Art Mortvedt, a specialist in polar survival techniques, based in Alaska. Before this, though, my flight to Fairbanks, Alaska took me through Calgary where I stopped for a night. I had been put in touch with Steve Penikett. Steve's company, Kenn Borek Air, is the biggest government-contracted commercial aircraft operator in the Arctic and Antarctica. There was so much to learn about the polar regions and I hoped that Steve could help with more advice on flying in those inhospitable environments. On arriving in Calgary I rang him.

"Come on over." he said. "We are expecting you." I was shown into Steve's office to be greeted by a big gruff Canadian. Although he didn't wear high boots and a stetson, I could see them there in my mind's eye. I was amused. "This may be a challenge," I thought to myself. "What do you want to fly over the Poles for? Do you want to have sex at the Poles?" was his opening gambit. "That would be a bit difficult as I shall be on my own," I replied.

Steve pointed to a huge map of the Antarctic on the wall of his office. By now it was familiar to me, but a shiver ran down my spine at the thought of flying over so much ice. We started discussing the logistics of flying in Antarctica. Steve asked me if I had a copy of the Antarctic Flight Information Manual (AFIM). When I said yes it began to dawn on him that I was serious. He picked up his phone and called his chief pilot, Sean Louttit to attend the meeting. I had been in correspondence with Sean previously, picking his brains for information.

The meeting continued. Steve asked me what I planned to do about warming my engine, securing my aircraft on the ice and how I planned to survive should I have to execute a forced landing on the ice. I was able to answer all his questions. He seemed impressed with my preparation.

"Will you need fuel taken in to Patriot Hills?" Steve asked. "Yes," I replied. "That is one of my problems as the only people who can take in my fuel are ANI. But I have talked to Anne Kershaw at ANI and I just cannot afford their price of $350,000. "We can carry some fuel to Patriot Hills for you," Steve offered. Sean Louttit was more cautious. Steve overrode him. "There is plenty of room for three barrels of fuel," he insisted. "We can also cover for your search and rescue (SAR) if you fly at the same time as our aircraft. After all – what can anyone do over the Drake Passage except pass your position so that a boat can rescue you?"

I had been anxious about SAR and fuel transportation to Patriot Hills. This was music to my ears. I hadn't called on Steve expecting anything except advice and here he was offering all this. I asked Steve to put it in writing so that I could pass the information to the Foreign and Commonwealth Office. I must have got on well with Steve because he gave me a lot of his time and his advice was invaluable.

"Our aim," he said "is to see you execute this flight safely. We don't want to see you in a black sack." What a thought. Again I shivered. I realised that this big Canadian had a soft heart underneath all his bravado and I was eternally grateful for his offer of help. He agreed to write a letter in confirmation. Here was the final piece in the jigsaw which had helped to enable me to obtain my Antarctic Permit from the FCO. The hurdles were gradually being overcome.

It was late in the evening when my flight arrived in Fairbanks, so I didn't meet Art Mortvedt until the following morning. Art and I had e-mailed each other back and forth but I had no idea what he would be like and I sat anxiously waiting for him to turn up at the hotel. In walked this big fellow in old denim dungarees, bright red braces and a check shirt. His baseball cap was firmly on his head and his prickly grey beard and moustache gave him the air of a true bushman.

"Hello," he said with a smile and waited patiently for me to pick up my backpack and heave it over my shoulder. I was to learn that patience was Art's trademark and this made a deep impression on me.

We walked out to his car, a beaten-up old VW Beetle which boasted only one seat. I sat on the floor trying very hard to act as thought this was quite normal as we set off on the eighty-mile journey along unmade roads to Art's home at Manley Hot Springs. I clung to whatever I could as we hurtled along.

"Would you like some lunch?" asked Art. I would have done anything to break that journey, so we stopped at a roadside café where I politely ordered a bowl of soup whilst Art had burgers, bacon and eggs all piled up together. He offered me sourdough, an Alaskan speciality and then carried on eating. He is a man of few words and I very quickly learnt to eat in silence until he started a conversation.

Back on the metal floor of the VW Beetle, I saw Fairbanks airport looming up again. I had only seen it in the dusk and now I could really take it in. What an amazing place! It has two parallel runways. One is for the big jets and the other, slightly shorter one is for general aviation. Little planes like mine stood in rows for as far as the eye could see. There were hundreds of them, all different shapes, sizes and colours. Alaska is a huge state and most of it is only accessible by air. In the centre of the two runways is a lake for floatplanes to take off on. It reminded me of the airport in Bangkok where there are two parallel runways with a golf course in the middle.

We drove up and parked near a beaten-up old caravan on the edge of the lake. Here we abandoned the VW and jumped into a Citabria, a light aircraft with just two seats in tandem. We were soon soaring up over Fairbanks and heading north west into the Alaskan wilderness. Forty minutes later, Art said, "There's Manley Hot Springs."

As I looked around I could only see hills and woodland. We descended towards a line of trees, and I could see a river and just one or two houses. As we came closer to the river a tiny airstrip lay hidden amongst the trees. We were soon bumping along the grass and I had my first sight of the real Alaska boondocks. Manley Hot Springs has just sixty inhabitants. I knew that Art and his wife, Dee, lived at 90 Polar Road, but I hadn't realised that theirs was the only house in the road. Art's sense of humour was beginning to dawn on me.

We walked across the only tarmac road in town, through some woods to Art's house and I was taken to my quarters, a little wooden hut hidden amongst the tall pine trees. Art showed me where to get bark to light the wood burning stove and how to light the paraffin lantern. He took me to my own private 'privy' down a path in the woods. I was anxious about bears, but he assured me I would be alright. The smell of pine wafted in the chilly breeze.

I was just settling down in my new home when suddenly I heard a shot and the next moment there was a knock on my door. Art was dangling a dead squirrel. "Here's your dinner," he said with a deadpan face. "Come outside and I will show you how to skin it." He placed the squirrel on the flat roof of the dog kennel and described in detail how to gut and skin it. "Do it later," he said. "Now I have some steak for dinner." His dour sense of humour was trickling through, although I was still wary of this big strong man.

After dinner Art declared that he had some work to do and he had to go out for a while. I agreed to wash up. I kept looking out of the window at the dead squirrel. "Oh my God," I thought. "Have I really got to skin that animal?" My stomach churned as I tried to pluck up courage. I put it off by washing our few dishes as slowly as possible but in the end I ran out of excuses, so I got out my 'multi-tool' and opened the sharpest knife. I resolutely approached the squirrel, holding my breath. First I cut out the genitals and then made a slit up the centre of the animal. I wanted to squeeze my nose to avoid the smell, but there wasn't any smell and my hands were full anyway. I pulled out the gut and threw it away into the wood for other creatures to feed on.

"Keep your mind on the job," I kept telling myself. "You can do anything if you have to." To my amazement, the skin slipped off in one piece. I jointed the animal as instructed. I laid out the skin on top of the dog kennel with the tail nicely displayed beside it. I found an empty margarine pot and put the joints in it and placed the pot strategically in Art's kitchen before going back to my log cabin.

Half an hour later there was a knock on my door. There was Art with the semblance of a smile. "Good job," he said. He was a man of few words, but I knew that I had scored some points. "If you can skin a squirrel, you can skin any animal. The technique is the same for all." I felt a glow of pleasure at my first success. It was certainly not to be my last trial, however.

I soon became acquainted with the metropolis of Manley Hot Springs, and met some of the locals including the mushers who run teams of dogs to pull sledges. This is still an important method of transport in this remote part of the world, and the dogs are loved and respected by their owners. I ate in the Manley Road House, which reminded me of a saloon bar in a John Wayne Western. The welcome was warm and thankfully no-one burst through the door brandishing a gun.

I trekked up the hill to the 'bath house'. Hot springs had been filtered into four concrete baths housed in a huge tent. I lay amongst vines and tropical plants soaking up the goodness of the waters. The therapeutic effect was very welcome after my encounter with the squirrel, even if it did seem a bit incongruous lying amongst grapes and bougainvillea on the edge of the Arctic.

I had two days learning the ways of the Arctic. We looked for bear and found a dead moose. Art was furious. Someone had shot the moose, taken the good pieces of meat and left the rest to rot. He explained that you only kill to eat. "If you kill an animal, like I taught you with the squirrel, you gut it, skin it and joint it properly. You do *not* leave any of the animal to rot." He was emphatic, and I knew then that I was with a true bushman who cared very much for the delicate balance of the environment he lived in. He also explained the importance of using every part of the animal.

"The skin makes beautiful mukluks (Eskimo boots)," he said. "But you must never wrap yourself in the skin of a moose to keep warm. If you do, in the morning it will have frozen solid and you will never be able to move again." What a terrifying thought. "You can wrap yourself in the skin of a caribou as that is softer," he went on, teaching me all the time. I realised how privileged I was to be with such a mentor.

A couple of days later we headed to the river and climbed into another aircraft, this time a Citabria on floats. We were heading up north of the Arctic Circle to the Brooks Range. The weather was not the best and I was glad of the warm clothes I had brought. About an hour into the journey, the weather started to deteriorate. Art found a lake which looked like a small puddle from the air. We had our nose resolutely pointing towards the water and the next moment we were skimming along the surface. In one splashing gliding moment the floats settled on the water. We taxied up but now the plane was more like a boat. Art jumped out in his long wader boots and pulled the rope up onto the shore where he found some bushes to secure it to. There was nothing there except a few reeds and bushes and a small pebbly beach.

Art said simply, "Light a fire." How was I going to do that? Everything was damp and the misty rain enveloped the lake. So now I had the first of many lessons on building and starting fires; and I learnt how to carve an arrow-like point on a suitable stick to which we stuck sausages and roasted them on the fire. All the time I was very aware that we were miles from anywhere.

Art Mortvedt instructed me in polar survival and became one of my 'giants'.

Eventually the rain eased and the mist rose. We were wearing what we would call fisherman's boots. These are waders that will reach up to the top of your thighs, but will fold down neatly to make normal size boots. This was to be our footwear for the rest of the time in the Arctic. Every time we needed to use the floatplane we had to walk in the water to get in, and more importantly to push the floats away from the shore.

We built up speed across the lake and took off towards the north. Another half hour passed. The mountains were getting higher and we were getting lower. Art was feeling his way along under the ever descending cloud. Somehow I didn't feel afraid because by then it was obvious to me that I was with a very experienced Alaskan bush pilot.

The next thing I knew was that we were landing on a fast flowing river. Art had spotted an island in the middle, which he has since named 'Polly's Island'! The rain was sheeting down and we secured the float plane with a rope to overhanging trees. We were already soaked. In no more than four minutes Art had put up the smallest tent I have ever seen. We climbed inside. There was barely room for two of us to sit let alone lie down.

We sat for hours with the rain beating down outside us and Art regaled me with stories of the Eskimos who are called 'Inupiat' in Alaska and 'Inuit' in Canada. Leaving secure teaching jobs further south, he and Dee had come for a year to coach in an Inupiat school. They never left. I asked about bears and Art showed me that he had two guns just in case. "Can they swim?" I anxiously enquired. "Oh sure, they are good swimmers," he said. Until then I had thought I was safe on the island. The rain abated a bit, and we walked outside. We didn't go far as the drizzle soon started again. We sat sheltering under a tree. "How long do you think we will be here?" I tentatively asked Art.

He moved his mouth from side to side, stroking his beard and pondering "Oh could be a day, could be two days," he said. I was beginning to learn one of the most important lessons of survival. There was nothing I could do so I just had to wait patiently and go with the flow. We sat for sometime under the tree, there were long moments of silence. The woods rustled with movements from animals, often unseen and the slow dripping from the trees. We made our way back to the tent, we were still wet through but a calm and warmth was engulfing me. In retrospect, learning to be still was one of the most important survival lessons I had, but it was also a life-changing experience.

Gradually it became dark and it was obvious that we were going to spend the night in this tiny tent in the rain. I spread out my sleeping bag. Art's was beside mine. "Do you snore?" I jokingly asked. "Of course not," was the firm reply.

So here I was, miles from anywhere, with a man I hardly knew in a tiny tent and he had a gun! Nothing for it but to tuck down and sleep as best I could. In fact, he *did* snore and I *did* sleep reasonably well in spite of the damp and fear of strange men and bears.

I was woken with a shout. "Polly, come here quickly." Art's gruff voice penetrated any sweet dreams. I hauled myself out of my sleeping bag. The rain had abated and the river had dropped. I was still wet through. The float plane was beached and I had to help push it into the water again. We loaded our damp things and were soon taking off for what was to be the last leg of the journey.

We rounded a mountain and there lying quietly before us was Selby Lake. This six-mile long stretch of water between two steep snow-capped mountains is hundreds of miles from the nearest road, railway or any other form of communication. At the end of the lake tucked under the mountain and with a tiny beach in front was Selby Lodge. Here we would spend five days in what now seemed utmost luxury.

The days passed quickly as I was instructed in how to hunt, fish, trap and make shelters. Most importantly I had to light fires to melt ice to make water. Without water you cannot survive. In fact I lit several fires a day. "Light a fire," was Art's endless command.

On one occasion we were just about to go out for the day looking for moose and caribou. "Light a fire," he said, and I queried it. "Why do I have to light a fire when we are just going out?" "Light a fire," was the response, so I lit a fire and never dared query again, but I guessed it was just another practice.

We flew over the mountains looking for moose and caribou. "Often you can safely land in trees," Art said. "In the event of an engine failure those trees are better to land in than those." He pointed out the different colours of the leaves which identified the most supple trees to cushion a landing. "Look down there," he went on, "can you see those wolves rounding up the caribou? They are clever with their hunting tactics and the caribou will eventually tire." He was always teaching me and I learnt something every moment.

On arriving back at Selby Lake Art said, "I need to go and check one of the other cabins, I will be away for about two hours, and will return at 9 pm – light a fire and we'll eat when I return." I watched Art's little plane disappear in the distance. I suddenly realised that I was completely alone here north of the Arctic Circle.

"What if he doesn't return?" I wondered to myself. "How will I manage – there are no roads, or railways and he has gone off with my only form of transport?" I was able to control my thoughts and went out to gather wood to make a fire on the shore. As I was collecting sticks I came across a large pile of pooh. "A bear!" I thought, rushing back to the cabin. "What on earth shall I do if he comes after me?" My anxiety grew. I closed and bolted the door, but I knew that a bear could easily break that down. Where could I hide? I looked around. I went upstairs to the sleeping area and found a big chest. "I could get into that," I thought, absolutely terrified. My imagination ran riot.

Time went by, and I plucked up courage. I gingerly opened the door and there was no sign of the bear. I ventured out looking around all the time. Every rustle amongst the trees made me freeze with terror. I picked up some wood and rushed back to the relative safety of the lodge, repeating the whole procedure many times and finally managing to light a fire. Eventually I heard the distant buzz of Art's little aircraft. The relief was overwhelming, although until he had landed I was still looking over my shoulder at every breath.

I rushed up to Art as he taxied in and secured the plane. "Art, Art there's a bear." He didn't look at all worried. "Come and look – I have seen his pooh," I continued. Art lumbered slowly across and came to look with me. He threw his head back and laughed heartily. "That's Hanson, our dog!!"

I just sighed with relief and didn't care that I had made such a fool of myself. Later he showed me real bear pooh and I could see the difference, but the huge paw marks in the sand increased my anxiety too. The bear could hardly be far away and was probably watching us.

There was a hot bath hidden amongst some tall pines. We pumped water from the lake, and filled the large circular tub. We started a fire in the log-burning stove, covered the tub and left it for the day to heat the water. This brought its own worries. I spent the whole day wondering how I would get into the hot tub with a strange man. I needn't have been concerned. Art was much too gentlemanly to embarrass me. After a long hard day canoeing, fishing, building shelters and the inevitable numerous fires, I had the hot tub to myself.

The instructions were clear. You strip off beside the tub. It was -15°C! Shivering as the clothes are shed, you soap yourself and then wash the soap off with a bucket of hot water from the tub. Then you climb in. Bliss! There was something very special about lying in the warm water, gazing up at the top of the pines with the stars twinkling above. My sore limbs were soothed by the heat. It was tempting to stay there for ever. After all, the prospect of climbing out into temperatures well below freezing was not that inviting.

The week's ordeal was drawing to a close. Exhausted, but yet satisfied and more confident that I would be able to survive in the polar regions, we shut the little lodge and nailed wooden protectors to the doors and windows to deter any hungry animals, although even that would not be enough to stop a really determined bear.

Exhilarated after a challenging week, I took a moment to sit outside the hut and soak in a last look at the beautiful lake and mountains. Two mountain peaks rose directly opposite. At that moment the moon came slowly out from behind one of them, passed across the space and disappeared behind the next one. It was as if it was bidding me farewell and good luck for the real adventure which lay ahead. It seemed to wink at me. It was like a reassurance, that in spite of the dangers I would face, I would be safe. It was a moving moment, and a fitting end to an adventure in itself.

CHAPTER 6 Polar Bear Dinner

An engine failure in the polar regions would be the worst scenario imaginable. Although I had spent the ten days in Alaska, there was still more to learn. I had to be able to survive in the extreme cold of the Arctic and Antarctic although I forever prayed that nothing would happen there. The desert, jungles and oceans seemed bad enough but the thought of a disaster in these regions was far the most frightening. So now I flew out to the French Alps where Scotsman Bruce Goodlad was waiting. Bruce had spent many seasons as a mountain guide in Antarctica and he was about to teach me how to survive life in the freezer.

The clitter-clatter of ski boots, the chitter-chatter of happy skiers echoed around as Bruce and I queued for the ski lift in the resort of Chamonix. We had no ski boots and I certainly did not feel like chitter-chatter. I leant against my heavy backpack which I had temporarily put on the floor beside me. My mouth was dry and I was on full alert as the lift arrived and I heaved my pack onto my back. Our mission was deadly serious.

At the top of the lift, the skiers roared off with whoops and shouts of exhilaration as Bruce and I set off cautiously down the other side of the mountain. Wading through deep snow we used ski sticks to test for holes or crevasses that could engulf us. On reaching a small plateau perched on top of a ridge, the lessons began in earnest. I had brought my own state of the art tent designed for Antarctic expeditions and given to me by Mountain Hardware.

I quickly discovered that erecting a tent in the freezing air was very different from putting it up in my garden. I fumbled in the cold and looked anxiously at Bruce who nodded and told me to do it again. I put it up and down with monotonous regularity until I was so familiar with every clip that I became nimble and quick. Should I have to make a forced landing I might very well be injured and this training could make the difference between life or death.

Bruce was concerned that the tent did not have a snow skirt, a six-inch piece of material sewn around the bottom on which snow could be piled to stop the wind whipping underneath the tent and blowing it away. I later solved this on my return when Judi Hussey, a friend and member of the Royal Southern Yacht Club, found a sail maker in Southampton who added the skirt.

With the tent secure we were ready for a hot drink and I turned to my new MSR stove. With big mittens on to keep my hands from the cold, I fumbled with the knob to pressurise the fuel canister. I allowed fuel onto the wick area and broke several matches in my attempts to strike them. After several minutes I got the stove going, scooped some snow into a pan and watched longingly for the snow to melt and finally boil.

Whilst sipping his cup of tea, Bruce never wasted a moment and started teaching me how to clean and change the heater's nozzle. The stove would run on white gas or on Avgas as used in my aircraft, but it required a different size nozzle for each fuel and changing these tiny pieces of

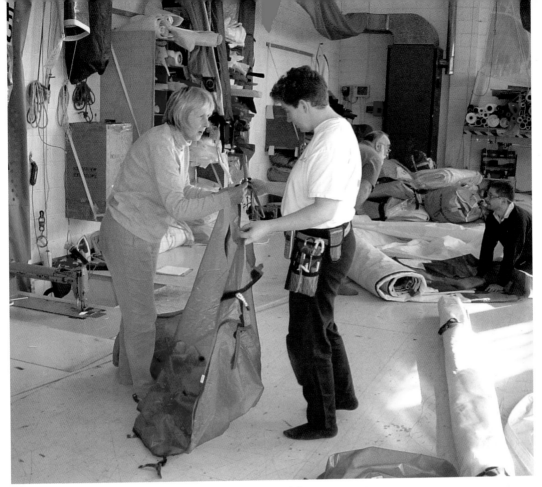

Discussion with the sail maker on the fitting of a snow skirt around the tent.

equipment with frozen hands was far from easy. It was imperative to keep the whole equipment clean, a tricky task with cold hands.

Having erected the tent to Bruce's satisfaction, I had to learn to build a snow wall. It was no good trusting solely to a good tent with strong snow skirts as Antarctic winds blow up to one hundred miles an hour. The added security of a surrounding snow wall was imperative, but unfolding the snow saw with cold hands was frustratingly difficult. Under Bruce's direction I cut blocks of snow and placed them around the tent. Sweat began to pour down my back and my clothes clung to me. It was hot work in spite of the cold mountain air.

The MSR stove had to be lit inside the tent. With temperatures well below freezing and the possibility of high winds I would be forced to stay inside. Tired as I was after a full day's work, I began to dig and hollow out a pit under the front flap of the tent. When we had dug deep enough for both of us to sit on the edge of the tent with our feet touching the bottom we could finally light the stove and boil a saucepan of water to which we added dehydrated fish stew. Never had a meal been so welcome.

We rolled out our sleeping mats. I had one which had duck down in it and would blow up to keep the cold from the ground seeping up. It was an ingenious contraption which would fold up into a tiny roll but yet blow up into a good mattress. We climbed into our sleeping bags for an early night and I was so exhausted that it took no time to drop off to sleep. One never sleeps quite so well on a narrow mattress in cramped conditions, waking with every move and turn. However, the night soon passed and the daily routine began again.

A snow wall is essential protection against the tent being blown away in a blizzard.

Under Bruce's guidance I learnt how to make a snow hole, digging a narrow passage through a high mound of snow and then moulding a sleeping shelf. It took nearly all day to build, but it was snug and the temperature inside remained a permanent zero which was warm considering the conditions. We built a ledge for the candle, a necessary item of survival gear. Not only does the candle give light and a modicum of heat, but it is also an indication of the level of oxygen. It will go out if the oxygen level drops. All this training could be a life saver. If the aircraft crashed and was damaged in such a way that I could not get my tent out, or if the tent should blow away, I would need to build a snow hole or igloo because the aircraft itself would not give me enough protection from the cold.

On the penultimate day of the week a Carlton Television team arrived. They wanted to film my ice survival training. I had become used to being followed by cameras, and indeed welcomed them as it was always an opportunity to promote Flying Scholarships for the Disabled and my sponsors. Having the cameras on me provided an opportunity to re-cap what I had learnt. Under Bruce's patient guidance I ran through all that I had assimilated during the week and then, at the end of the day, Bruce and the television team said goodbye and started their trek to catch the last lift of the day.

I was left on the mountain top all on my own for the night. I was scared but there was no way for me to get down, so I just had to make the best of it. After all, I did have my mobile phone and I had been left a camera to film myself so I was kept busy. I kept telling myself that it was only for a night and if I crashed in the Arctic or the Antarctic heaven knows how long I would be on my own, miles from anyone.

I lit the stove and made myself a brew and then sat looking at the view and wondering what it would be like in Antarctica. Suddenly, as I was drinking my hot tea there was a loud bang and a huge avalanche started tumbling down behind my tent. Then I really was afraid. Once I realised that it would not reach my tent, I rushed to get the camera and managed to film the last bit as it slid mercilessly down the mountainside.

I kept busy as the light began to fade, laying out the mattress and blowing it up. I made sure I had my headtorch to hand and lit the stove once more to make the inevitable stew. It didn't seem to matter what the label said, they all tasted the same. After my meal I tucked into my sleeping bag, desperate to keep warm as the temperature dropped at night. I had some fun propping up the camera and taking film of myself in the dark. I unfolded an old copy of *The Times* which I read by torchlight. It seemed incongruous.

Bruce called me on my mobile phone to check that all was well. "What are you doing?" he asked. "I am down my sleeping bag reading *The Times*," I said with a laugh.

The morning brought its own problems. I decided to walk away from the tent to have a pee. This was a mistake as I fell into the snow up to my waist. I hauled myself out, but if it had been any deeper I would have been in serious trouble. I had just learnt an important lesson, I would never again go far from my base (the aircraft) and I would always test the ground before treading on it. Then I discovered that my matches had become damp and I could not light the stove. Another salutary moment.

I was able to call Bruce and ask him to bring some dry matches, but in the polar climes there would be no-one to bring dry matches, so from then onwards I determined to have little bags of matches in waterproof packets all over the aircraft. During my flight I had at least a dozen packages strategically placed. Without matches there would be no fire. Without fire, snow could not be melted and I could die of thirst.

The most significant features of the training were the pitfalls that I came across. By actually simulating survival in ice conditions I began to identify the weak points I had not previously remotely considered. Yet another reinforcement of the importance of meticulous preparation.

A second trip to France took me to Méribel in the Trois Vallées. This time I was going to learn mountain flying. What a fantastic week flying in the Alps! The scenery was spectacular but I was concentrating in earnest on my technique of landing on ice, snow and glaciers.

A pilot usually expects to land on a tarmac or well marked grass runway. It stretches before you as you come in on final approach. During your initial training you are taught to look down the runway towards the end. From this you learn to judge your height above the ground. Just before landing you flare the aircraft. The nose attitude is changed from pointing down towards the earth to a more flattened angle so that the wheels touch gently and the nose is not plunged into the ground.

Landing on snow is more difficult. Everything around is white. At first it is impossible to judge one's height above the ground. Either you flare too high in which case the aircraft just drops with a huge jolt or you fail to flare in time and risk stuffing in the nose. Like every skill, it improves with practice. It was critical that I was reasonably competent at landing on snow and ice, not only in case of an engine failure and forced landing, but also because I was planning to land on the blue ice runway at Patriot Hills and the sea ice runway at McMurdo, both in Antarctica.

I learnt much more than just landing on snow and ice whilst training in the Alps. For instance it was vital never to fly straight across a mountain ridge as there may be serious downdrafts forcing the aircraft perilously close to the ridge. The safe way to fly is to cross at an angle, then if indeed one is caught in a downdraft the nose can be plunged down the other side of the ridge thus avoiding stalling into the ridge itself.

Mountain waves, rotor waves, updrafts and downdrafts are all features created by mountains. All are potentially lethal. Both times that I have crossed the Rockies in North America, a light aircraft has been lost in the mountains on the same day. On one of the occasions I watched the mountain rescue teams go out and return on two consecutive days without ever finding the aircraft and its unfortunate pilot.

The Arctic is the home of the polar bear. This beautiful creature, who when standing on his hind legs is at least twice my height, is one of the most dangerous animals in the world. Polar bears are usually hungry. Food is scarce and to find seals requires hours of patient waiting by a breathing hole in the ice. As the seal pops up for a breath the bear swipes it with his paw and the seal is dead. The bear hauls the dead seal out of the water and it is not long before there is only a large blood stain in the snow. This is not a pleasant thought and although I had no intention of emulating a seal, I would have been an easy target for a ravenous polar bear.

Shooting was not something I had any desire to do. Nor was I keen to be eaten by a polar bear if I landed on the ice. I procrastinated until I was told that hiding in my aircraft would certainly not protect me as a bear's huge claws would soon rip it apart. So just four months before I was due to leave I made a phone call to the local gun club.

"You will need a firearms licence," I was told. "and it will take at least six months to get that." "How do I get a licence?" I enquired. "Ring the local firearms officer." I rang Keith Jennings at Thames Valley Police and told him that I was due to leave in just four months. He was very obliging and agreed to come and see me the next day. He turned up in a sports jacket and grey flannels. Over a cup of coffee I told him what I was planning to do.

He said, "Normally it does take six months to issue a firearms licence, but in special cases we can issue one in as little as a week." I was impressed by his professionalism, but also his desire to help. Just as he had promised I had my firearms licence within the week.

As a proud possessor of a firearms licence I could now purchase a gun. I contacted the National Rifle Association at Bisley and they agreed to help me. I made an appointment with Stewart Clark, one of their top instructors. When he asked me if I had any experience I confessed that I had had one go at clay pigeon shooting years ago and damaged my shoulder. I also told him that I had had a go at shooting in Alaska and had missed the target every time. He later admitted to thinking, "We've got a right one here!"

Stewart took me to the shop and we looked at a variety of firearms. "I think a .303 rifle will do the job nicely," he said. I looked at several .303s and was filled with horror at the size of them. "How will I ever manage something like that?" I asked with some trepidation. "Wait and see how you get on," Stewart said patiently. "For the time being you can borrow one of the club rifles." We walked to the shooting range. I was chatting away nervously.

When we reached the range Stewart gave me some ear protectors. "Now lie down on this mat," he said, giving me a special rest to lay the gun on. "Now hold the gun like this and look through the sight like this," he demonstrated in his gentle, quiet way. I began to relax. "Breath deeply and when I say fire just pull the trigger." I aimed carefully at the target which was about 200 metres away.

After the shot, the whole target disappeared and came back with a clearly visible mark over the bullet hole. "Wow," I gasped. "That's nearly a bull's eye."

I later went behind the traps and saw how it was done. A couple of people were posted below a bank. After someone has shot a target they lower the whole board with the target on and stick a marker over the hole made by the bullet.

The instruction went on and I began to improve and gain confidence. Stewart was a patient and kind instructor and soon I was able to shoot kneeling on one knee. I found I was quite good at it and Stewart was pleased if a little surprised. Eventually I was able to shoot standing up. After all if I was approached by a polar bear I would not have too much time to position myself comfortably. I would have to be able to 'shoot on the hoof'.

We had a break and walked back to the gun shop. Stewart helped me to choose a rifle. "You must have a good one," he said. "Should you encounter a polar bear you will need one that is man enough for the job." I managed to get a good second hand one. The gunsmith offered to clean and set it up for me. "You can collect it when you come for your next lesson," Stewart assured me.

Stewart Clark taught me to shoot with a .303 rifle at the National Rifle Association at Bisley.

Back at the range I began to shoot with more confidence. I was actually thoroughly enjoying the challenge. "Wow," I gasped, surprised again. "Wow! I've got a bull's eye." I jumped up and down with excitement. Stewart looked nearly as excited as me.

"You've turned out to be a really good shot," he said later. "In fact I have to say that I thought I would have an uphill struggle when you first arrived but you took to it like a duck to water." Fair praise indeed but it was one thing to be a good shot in controlled conditions. How would I manage for real, out there on the ice? Stewart's clear step-by-step instruction had really paid off. On my second visit to Bisley I collected my gun, all polished and well oiled. I felt quite proud.

"You must keep it fully armed all the way across the Arctic region," Stewart advised. "Should you have a forced landing and happen to land near a hungry polar bear you won't have time to load and cock it. And if you have to shoot a bear, don't believe that it is necessarily dead. Keep putting more shot into it. An injured bear can be very dangerous indeed." I was getting more bull's eyes. I thought "If I lived closer to Bisley I would take this up as a hobby." "Make sure that the barrel is always kept clean," Stewart went on, "especially where there is snow. If you get snow in the barrel it can ice up and the whole gun will backfire on you." I was lucky indeed to be in the hands of such a capable instructor.

As I drove away from Bisley I dreaded having to use the gun in anger at a polar bear as it was going to be I who was invading their territory. Nonetheless the idea of becoming a polar bear dinner was not at all inviting. It was hardly my scene to carry a fully loaded gun across the North Pole and into northern Canada but at least it was comforting.

CHAPTER 7
Resolved by Coincidence

I felt as if I was walking a tight rope. True, the permit from the Foreign and Commonwealth Office was in place and I had my written permissions to land at the British base, Rothera and at the American base, McMurdo. However, I was under no illusion that I was home and dry for, at any moment something could change. I was in constant fear that my permit would be rescinded.

I had still hoped that Adventure Network International would allow me to use some of their fuel at Patriot Hills, albeit the charge was $4,000 per barrel. I needed three barrels. It was difficult to justify this price when the flight was for Flying Scholarships for the Disabled. Every penny spent on the actual flight would not be able to go to the charity, which was a constant dilemma. If the flight cost too much, I could just as well have sent a cheque to the charity and stayed at home. However, I did understand how expensive it was for ANI to fly the fuel into Antarctica.

Then Kenn Borek had come to the rescue with an offer to fly fuel in to Patriot Hills.

However, a few weeks before my departure Anne Kershaw left ANI and shortly afterwards ANI terminated all operations in the Antarctic. This would have unforeseen and long-reaching repercussions towards the end of my flight. ANI had given me written permission to go into Patriot Hills where someone would have been available to help with refuelling. With Anne gone it would have been impossible for me to refuel on my own.

Now, though, I got a communication from Steve Penikett at Kenn Borek informing me that as they were no longer going to Patriot Hills, they would fly my fuel to Sky Blu.

Sky Blu is a blue ice runway operated by the British Antarctic Survey. Max Wenden had early been emphatic that it would be safer to land at Sky Blu than Patriot Hills. This was because the blue ice runway at Patriot Hills is in the lee of the Ellsworth Mountains. The katabatic winds sweep down off the mountains and blow the snow off the surface revealing the firm ice. The problem with this is that the winds blow across the runway. Cross wind landings are always more difficult than when the wind is on the nose. The aircraft always cocks into wind so the final approach is at an angle. Just before landing the aircraft has to be straightened and at the same time the aileron placed into wind so that the wind cannot pick up the wing and blow the aircraft over. I was anxious at the prospect of landing on ice for the first time and the likely lack of crosswinds at Sky Blu was a great relief.

I therefore needed to arrange for three barrels of fuel to be at Punta Arenas for the Kenn Borek pilots to pick them up. After a brief panic to find clean fuel drums, Shell Chile organised those and everything seemed to be falling in place.

Things were now hotting up with only a few weeks to departure date. I felt like a juggler trying to keep too many balls in the air. My office was my biggest headache for every day there were numerous letters to be written, a constant stream of e-mails to be answered and telephone calls to be made. I really missed Alice Auckland, a great friend who had acted as voluntary secretary on my first round-the-world flight but who had moved to Scotland.

I was bemoaning this fact to Jill Stuart Clark, who was one of my closest friends and a member of our 'tennis four'. Actually there are five of us, but 'the tennis four' has been going ever since the time we first met when our children were in school together.

"The office is in a terrible mess and I don't have time to sort it out. If you know of someone who would like a voluntary job for a few months, do put them in touch with me," I said. The following day Jill phoned. "Have you thought of having a husband and wife as secretaries?" "Well, no not really," I replied. "I suppose it depends who they are." "How about Chris and myself?" she suggested.

"That would be tremendous. Do you really mean it?" I exclaimed. Jill and Chris came twice a week from then until I departed and order came out of chaos. The filing system was completely revamped. Looking back, I really don't know how I would have managed without them.

We still had the main purpose of the flight to manage, which was to promote and raise funds for Flying Scholarships for the Disabled. My wonderful team of four volunteers, Rosemary Taylor, Sue Rance, Susie Dunbar, and Val Cahill once more helped to organise fund-raising, kept in contact with the sponsors, updated the website and ran the public relations. They worked unstintingly. The names on the wings were selling well. Rosemary was running this campaign to raise funds and she had her hands full with the increased daily mail. Using computer technology, the names were reproduced by Kingfisher Graphics and Alphabet as strips which Peter and I painstakingly adhered to the wings.

Her Majesty Queen Noor of the Hashemite Kingdom of Jordan signing the wing of Golf November.

There were individuals from all over the world, churches, societies, schools, clubs, dogs, cats and even two boa constrictors on the wings. Later, when flying over the more desolate areas, I looked out at the wings and gained enormous strength from reading the list of contributors. If I knew them I used to wonder what they were doing and if I did not I still felt the goodwill 'vibes' that followed me. It was an amazing experience to be buoyed up by so many people from all over the world.

During most of the preparations the project was kept a closely guarded secret. Nevertheless, with so many excellent sponsors supporting the flight it was essential to obtain as much media coverage as possible. To do this the timing was critical. If we announced the flight too early it may be difficult to sustain the media interest. If it was too late then we may not get as much coverage as we needed.

It was decided to hold an official launch in November 2002 just seven months before my departure. CSE Aviation at Kidlington near Oxford provided a hangar. Sponsors, the press and public were invited. Golf November looked splendid in her new colours of orange and black. Major sponsors were invited to the podium to answer questions. Susie organised the press conference with her usual professional approach. It was an exciting moment but also a 'point of no return', now that it was in the public domain.

It was appropriate that Her Majesty Queen Noor of the Hashemite Kingdom of Jordan, who is the patron of Flying Scholarships for the Disabled, was the first to put her signature on the wing. Peter and I flew Golf November into Fairoaks Airport and waited nervously for the royal arrival. We had met Queen Noor on a few occasions before. Her husband, the late King Hussein, had been closely involved with the charity from its inception in 1983. He had even been flying with a few of the scholars. Queen Noor became patron after King Hussein died.

The sky was completely overcast but the rain held off just long enough for the signing. Her Majesty arrived and greeted us like long lost friends, exuding warmth. We had organised an orange pen for her to sign the wing, but we also had a specially prepared signature in vinyl which would not come off during the flight. She laughed and posed elegantly for the cameras. It was a memorable occasion and bode well for the flight.

However, the rumblings of unease concerning my permits continued. It was like a constant drum beat. To date no-one had been given such permission and I was afraid any one could be rescinded at any time. I couldn't help being affected by all the machinations which accompanied the Antarctic section as it dominated everything. Considering it was only 5,000 nautical miles (nms) out of 45,000 nms it took a disproportionate amount of time and energy. The mental exhaustion was building up. It was difficult to sleep. The drum beat grew to a steady crescendo.

The first ill omen appeared in the *Antarctic Non-Government Activities Newsletter (ANAN)*:

> The pilot of a small, home-built, single-engine aircraft was forced to make an emergency landing on sub-Antarctic Marion Island, 2,180 km south-east of Cape Town." (This referred to an aborted attempt in 2002). UK pilot Polly Vacher who is proposing to fly across Antarctica late next year, is to use a slightly larger single-engine Piper Dakota aircraft for her attempt. Details of what arrangements she has to obtain fuel at Ross Island have not yet been made public. *(ANAN – 88/01)*.

Antarctica New Zealand (ANZ) had offered to take my Avgas down to McMurdo on Ross Island in one of their supply ships. It would then be transported the three kilometres on to their nearby facility at Scott Base. On 18th December, 2002 four fuel drums were duly delivered to the dock at Lyttleton in New Zealand ready for embarkation. On 19th December an e-mail arrived from Lou Sanson, the Director of ANZ to say that unfortunately he could not take the fuel. There was just too much pressure for him not to. So where had that pressure come from? None other than the *ANAN* reporter himself.

In such a close-knit community, *ANAN*, an Australian internet journal, was influential and covered all the gossip on events in Antarctica. I had built up excellent relations with the media and had no reason to suspect anything but sympathetic treatment. That was until the autumn of 2002 when an unusually aggressive reporter from *ANAN* rang wanting to have an interview. "Certainly," I replied as I always did because I believed the old adage that any publicity was good publicity.

He came across as belligerent and unpleasant and I began to feel uncomfortable. I quickly realised that I was close to an impossible situation. If I was rude and difficult in return I knew that he would give me a hard time. If I did not answer all his questions he might make it up and get it wrong. This was pressure just when I least needed it. He was curious as to how my fuel was being transported. I refused to tell him. I seriously believed it was none of his business.

Through a process of elimination the reporter found that my fuel was being transported by ANZ. He began his campaign. Lou Sanson said that the reporter rang nearly every day, pressurising him not to carry my fuel. In the end Lou gave in and at the eleventh hour took the decision not to carry the drums. This was a desperate situation. It was late in the season. How was the fuel to be transported for the leg from Antarctica to New Zealand?

Julian Tangaere from ANZ had always been a keen supporter. He suggested ringing John Apps at Quark expeditions in High Wycombe.

"I think we can help," John said. "If you get the fuel to Ushuaia in Argentina by 4th January we'll put it on the ship the *Professor Multanovskiy* which will meet up with the ice breaker *Kapitan Khlebnikov* onto which we'll transfer your fuel." Coincidently the *Kapitan Khlebnikov* was at that moment carrying my fuel to Rothera as a result of my initial phone call to the Captain and him telling me to ring John Apps in High Wycombe! It was also ironic, as the *Kapitan Khlebnikov* would have travelled all the way from New Zealand to South America and would pick up my fuel and take it all the way back. Somewhat unusually it happened to be doing a complete circumnavigation of Antarctica that year.

I contacted Steve Dudley and Julie Wright at Shell in the UK. Steve was about to leave Shell so Lynne Barnes and Julie were taking over. It was panic stations as Christmas was coming and everyone would be away on holiday. Julie said she would organise it. Numerous phone calls went back and forth between Julie and Shell in Argentina. Every time the phone rang I lifted the receiver with trepidation fearing that Shell would say it could not be done. What we did not know was that it is illegal to transport Avgas in drums on the Argentine roads. To get around this, Shell delivered four empty drums to the Aeroclub at Ushuaia and said that they could be filled with fuel on the morning the ship docked. Nothing else could be done and I just had to relax and try to enjoy Christmas.

We had planned a skiing holiday with friends in France. This would make a welcome break and there was no point in cancelling it. On New Year's day in France, I had an e-mail from Art Mortvedt, who had taught me polar survival in Alaska, wishing us a Happy New Year. *"I am here in Punta Arenas, just leaving for Ushuaia,"* it read.

I could *not* believe it. My fuel was due to go from Ushuaia on 4th January and there was Art just about to spend a few days in Ushuaia. I wrote to him and asked him if he would mind checking that my fuel drums were ready for despatch. On 2nd January 2003 I received the following e-mail:

"This morning I inspected your 4 drums sitting together inside the Ushuaia Aeroclub hangar. They appear to be perfect. I opened the bung (lid) of one and felt inside, to be sure that they had been painted inside."

How amazing that someone was prepared to spend so much time and effort on my behalf. Four days later I received the following:

"Today I tried to phone you but there was no answer. Therefore, I felt that it was necessary to make an 'executive decision' on your behalf, since the *Multanovskiy* was sailing this evening for the Antarctic.

"This morning I arrived to the Aeroclub Ushuaia at 9 am, and the Navalia truck arrived at 10 am. As I said in an earlier e-mail your drums 'appeared' to be perfect. When we had them on the truck for re-fuelling, we put 100 litres in one drum and then leak tested it by laying the drum flat in the truck. When the drum leaked profusely, it was obvious that your drums would definitely not do the job.

"What Shell actually sent you is what in Alaska we call a 'snapring barrel', i.e. one end of the barrel comes away in a 'lid' and is secured to the barrel with a tightening ring and a gasket. We use these to store food and gear against bears. When I saw these barrels, I assumed that Shell Buenos Aires had attached a superior gasket and tightening ring to the lids. That definitely was not the case.

"So… my first query was, 'Where in Ushuaia can I buy other drums?' The answer was 'nowhere'. So the second move was to telephone Shell Buenos Aires. No answer to that try, perhaps since it was Saturday. I was given a deadline of 4pm to have the full drums to the ship, and 12 noon was rapidly approaching. The next query went out to Navalia to see how soon they could get us some new drums. That answer was 'two weeks'. One of the other options was to try to 'borrow' some other full Avgas drums that were stored in the Aeroclub hangar. The owner of that fuel was at sea aboard the ship *Orlova*. I had his name, and got the phone and fax numbers of the *Orlova*, but there just didn't seem to be time to get that organised. Plus most of the drums were in pretty poor shape anyway.

"So… with many thanks to the boys at the Aeroclub, one of the team there – Juan Meno – said that there were some drums in the shed behind the office. I went out to have a look at the drums – checking the outside and perusing the inside with a flashlight. I could see no evidence of water or rust. So the boys began rinsing/cleaning the barrels with fresh Avgas. We then transferred the new bungs/'o' rings from the Shell Buenos Aires barrels to the Aeroclub barrels. We filled these barrels with fresh Avgas and they are now tightly sealed.

"I rode with the Navalia truck to the ship, and personally watched the loading of each barrel by the Russian crew, using the crane. The barrels consist of 2 brown, 1 green and 1 yellow/black. Besides transferring the paper labels saying 'for Vacher, store at Scott Base, McMurdo', I also wrote that same information in permanent black marker on the top of each barrel. I checked the barrels just prior to the ship sailing, and they were well secured with cargo straps on a pallet on the starboard side of the ship just aft and under the deck holding the lifeboats. As I suspected, all drum fuel is hauled onboard the ship tied down on the outside decks. Therefore, if your leaky Shell drums would leak fuel out, they likewise would be leaking saltwater in – not a good diet for your engine.

"I watched *Multanovskiy* sail this evening at 2130 UTC. Just prior to sailing I spoke with the Expedition Leader Shane Evoy and his Assistant Ms. Fiona Scott. Fiona will be switching ships at Deception Island to *Kapitan Khlebnikov* and sail with it to McMurdo. I explained to them both how critical it is to get your fuel transferred from the *Multanovskiy* to the *Khlebnikov*. I think Fiona will pay special attention to the transfer of your fuel – especially since I offered her a moose roast someday!

"I don't reckon there is a whole lot more I can do from here. I'm planning to go to Harberton Estancia tomorrow and back to Punta Arenas on Monday. As I see it, however, you will likely want to – through your contacts at Quark:

1. Make sure that the fuel is safely transferred from the *Multanovskiy* to the *Khlebnikov*.
2. Make sure that it is safely offloaded at McMurdo. I emphasise 'safely' because I can see what poor handling has done to some of the drums offloaded here.

3. Make sure – if at all possible – that your drums are stored inside a building at Scott Base. There is always plenty of drifting snow there, and with drifted snow melting on top of the drums there is a chance of water seeping inside the barrel.

"I'm confident that the fuel that went aboard the ship here today is as clean as humanly possible. However – and I'm sure you're already planning this – do conscientiously filter all your fuel along the way.

"I certainly hope that you approve of what's been done. If not, I'm ready to accept the blame. I honestly did what I thought was the best for you under the circumstances.

Sincerely

Art (Mortvedt)

P.S. The total amount of fuel that went into the 4 drums was 800.2 litres"

This story speaks for itself. The fantastic support I received from so many people was truly amazing. I shall never forget it. My flight was all set to go.

CHAPTER 8

A Royal Send Off

I t is doubtful whether I could ever be completely ready as there is always more to learn. It was the eve of my flight and amazingly, I slept well. The 6th May dawned and as we drove out of the drive I glanced back at our home and wondered whether I would ever see it again. I was emotionally mixed up, excited at the prospect of being on my way, but anxious as to what lay ahead.

We arrived early at Birmingham International Airport with plenty of time to spare. Susie Dunbar who was in charge of the PR was already there, always a real stalwart. We did some press interviews and then managed to grab a bacon sandwich for a late breakfast with Susie and Martin Lloyd. Martin had been a Tornado pilot who lost a leg and damaged an arm in a motorbike accident. Without precedent, Flying Scholarships for the Disabled had given him a scholarship so that he could restart his career as a civilian pilot. It was a moving moment when, a couple of years later, Martin presented the charity with a cheque to refund the full cost of his scholarship.

There was a huge amount of equipment to pack into Golf November. With the extra fuel tank and spares to carry there was little space. I had room for just 10 kg (22 lbs) of clothes.

Peter and I went off for a quiet lunch together. My brother, Richard and his wife, Monica came in. They were sensitive to the fact that we wanted to be alone and after a few words melted away. These few last moments together were very precious.

Everyone started to arrive amidst a mêlée of activity, old friends mingling with sponsors and scholars. There were the speeches. Brian Summers, chief executive of Birmingham International Airport, welcomed everyone and Bob Taylor, who had been chief executive before Brian, gave a moving talk. Bob is an inspiration as he is a paraplegic but in true positive fashion he has made a life for himself. He was currently chairman of the trustees of Flying Scholarships for the Disabled and Lord Lieutenant of West Midlands. When I spoke I tried to remember all the right people to thank. I then read the letter which Bunny Currant had written a few days earlier. Bunny had flown Hurricane R4118 in the Battle of Britain, which Peter had rescued from India and over three years lovingly restored it to flying condition. Despite his ninety-two years Bunny was a splendid raconteur. His stories of his experiences flying R4118 alone make your hair curl and are very amusing. What he wrote epitomizes my philosophy on life:

> "Dear Polly,
> Some thoughts about the Poles (*sic*) venture: The Poles themselves and all in between and the aircraft know absolutely nothing whatsoever of this venture which to we humans is or can be, or needn't be of great concern or not. It is up to the pilot totally how she looks upon it and can be of great joy of the unknown anyhow. I see it as an enormous opportunity for both of you (*Peter and Polly*) of 'letting-go' in a very big way indeed to the natural anxieties that we create for ourselves or we don't – It is a great adventure every moment, and we only have ourself (*sic*) to depend on.
> It seems to me that great trust is essential in every aspect of every minute of a very lengthy task.
> Unlike our recent task in 1939 – 1945 you have no real human enemies to cope with thank God. You are in a position of being your own enemy or your own unique spirit on a lovely adventure of great import for one personally.
> I wish you great joy and a happy homecoming. And peace within both of you in a lengthy trial.
>
> God Bless
> Love
> Bunny"

There wasn't a dry eye in the place, but there was no time to dwell on it for I was whisked downstairs for a press conference and then onto the tarmac for a photo-shoot organised by John Dunbar, Susie's husband and photographer, who made it easy for me. Shouts of "Polly look this way" and "Polly wave" and the odd "How are you feeling Polly?" added to the excitement.

We had to be quick. HRH the Prince of Wales was coming to see me off and his programme was timed to the second. Soon the buzz went round that the Prince had landed in a BAe 146. We all got in line, the

HRH The Prince of Wales inspecting his signature on the wing.

Lord Mayor of Birmingham, the lady Mayoress, the Deputy Chief Constable, Bob Taylor, Brian Summers and myself. It was a very emotional moment as the 146 taxied up with the Royal Standard fluttering in the breeze.

For a moment I allowed myself to think, "I can't believe this is happening because of me!" But then the Prince climbed out onto the steps beside the aircraft. He walked down our line up shaking hands and nodding pleasantries. I invited him to inspect Golf November. He

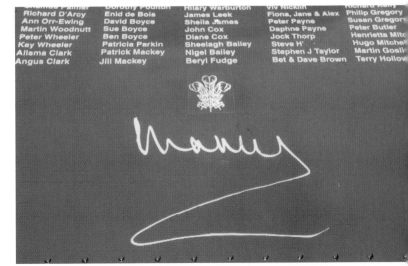

HRH Prince Charles' signature on the wing of Golf November.

asked lots of questions and was fascinated by how everything was squeezed into the tiny cockpit. Golf November's cabin is the size of a normal saloon car. But with the extra survival gear and ferry tank she looked far removed from a motor car. He took a long hard look at his signature on the wing. He was genuinely interested and especially curious to know how I would go to the loo. We posed for the photographers. I was anxious lest he might trip over the wooden post lying on the ground. I need not have worried, the Royal leg was lifted neatly without so much as an apparent glance at the floor below. I couldn't help noticing the remarkable shine on his shoes.

Then we went upstairs to the reception. I found that Prince Charles was talking to Brian Summers as we mounted the stairs and his equerry, Alastair Graham, was looking after me. I was not aware of this being engineered at any moment and I marvelled at the professionalism and attention to detail and protocol. I introduced the Prince to my voluntary committee and helpers – Susie, Valerie, Sue and Ro. When he reached Jill and Chris, I could see him suddenly take stock. Chris had been Prince William and Prince Harry's tutor at Eton and had even been up to Balmoral for the odd week to coach the young princes. "I think we have met somewhere before," the Prince wryly commented. They chatted for a moment and I stood back.

Martin Abbott, principal of Flying Scholarships for the Disabled, introduced the Prince to some of the scholars, and he showed genuine interest. Next came the sponsors, introduced by Sir David Cousins, chairman of

The Prince was introduced to my 'flying guru' Pete Thorn. To the right are Lucy Clements from Jeppesen and Lynne Barnes from Shell Aviation.

The Battle of Britain Memorial Flight sent a Hurricane and Spitfire to escort my departure from Birmingham International Airport.

the RAF Benevolent Fund. It all went so quickly and seemed like a blur. HRH then made an impromptu speech, commentating on what I was about to do and then suddenly he said, "I wonder what the orange suit will be like by the time you get back!" I think this was all a bit of light relief for him. I believe I said a few words, I probably did as I find it hard to keep quiet! I really cannot remember now. His Royal Highness shook my hand and wished me good luck. Clive, our middle son, took over to explain my route to him with a globe which we had brought specially for the occasion.

Julian, our eldest son, had already nipped out and run the engine of Golf November for about ten minutes to warm her up. On reaching the tarmac I kissed all the family except Peter who was missing. I certainly was not going without saying 'good-bye' to him. Someone rushed off to find him. In typical Peter fashion he had taken over looking after Prince Charles so that Clive could come and say his farewells to me. I guess someone sorted it. Soon Peter was running out to give me a big hug. I didn't know whether to laugh or cry. He put his arm round me and we were just reaching the door when he suddenly rushed off again. He had forgotten a bouquet of flowers. One last kiss, and I was on board, trying to find a corner for the much treasured flowers. Too much was happening for me to feel sad, apprehensive or anything else.

I taxied out and the usual routine of checks and radio calls occupied me. I took off and again it seemed unreal. All of Birmingham International Airport came to a halt while I headed south to link up with a Hurricane and Spitfire from the Battle of Britain Memorial Flight which were going to join me for a final flypast. Birmingham Tower air traffic control handed the frequency over to us. I spotted the two World War II aircraft and my heart missed a beat.

"We have you sighted," came over the radio. Feelings of 'déjà vu'. Al Pinner, the very pilot who had escorted my previous departure in a Harrier, was flying the Hurricane. I dropped down to 300 feet as they formated on my wingtips. I just could not believe this was all for my benefit. All too quickly, though, Al and Paul Willis peeled off and I flew away to the north.

On the ground my family and team were still chatting to the Prince as they waited to watch the flypast. When addressing His Royal Highness you are instructed to call him 'Sir'. I later learnt that Julian was chatting in his usual way and kept saying "Charles, what do you think of this," and "Charles – such and such." Nevertheless, I was told that HRH looked as if he was enjoying the informality.

My flight up to Wick in Scotland was uneventful although I was aware that a storm was brewing. The temperature was plummeting. I could hear the pilot of Prince Charles' BAE 146 on the radio as their aircraft climbed above mine. He too was heading to Scotland for his next official engagement. As I crossed over a section of the North Sea to reach Wick I experienced some icing and had to descend to a lower level. It was unnerving flying low across water. I could see the white foam created by the sea as it grew angrier by the minute. With some relief I landed at Wick and taxied into the safety of the hangar, just as the wind was whipping up. The timing was perfect.

Prince Charles chatted with my eighty-nine-year-old mother and family while I prepared to take off for the flypast.

CHAPTER 9

Echo Zero One and Echo Zero Two

I had a little laugh to myself as I entered Norwegian airspace because it was easier to understand the controller on Stavangar radar than it was the one in Scotland. The North Sea looked calm and the sky was scattered with just a few puffy clouds. There was no sign of the storm which had raged for the last three days, delaying my departure from Wick. The odd oil rig sat nonchalantly in the midst of the blue water and the occasional ship floated past. It was as if the tempest of the last few days was but a dream.

The runway at Longyearbyen sits at the foot of the mountain on the edge of the fiord. No trees grow so far north but it is desolate yet beautiful in its own way.

The temperature at 10,000 ft was -9°C. It was lucky that it was a clear day as I would have surely picked up ice if I had had to go into cloud. The sea below, although appearing calm, would have been deadly with its freezing temperatures should ice have forced me down. So it was with a sigh of relief when the airport at Bergen finally came in sight, where a treat was in store. Gunnar (pronounced Goon-ah) Stolton was waiting. He had flown across from Oslo specially to meet me. He runs a charity called A New Day, which uses flight to encourage disruptive children to have a purpose in life. They start by teaching the young ones to build model aircraft. If their behaviour pattern improves they are then able to progress to sailplanes and finally to gain their full licences. We had an hour together discussing this. We compared the work they did with Flying Scholarships for the Disabled which has similar aims of offering a life changing experience but to those with disabilities.

I was overwhelmed by the generosity and friendliness of the Norwegian people. Harold who ran the airport handlers, Norport, looked after me impeccably and absolutely refused to be paid for their services. By now I was exhausted and hungry so I appreciated the lack of hassle. Soon I was making my way up the spectacular coast of Norway. The fiords forced their way between the mountains and I could pick out tiny settlements built on the hillsides. It was so beautiful that I made a promise to myself that I would share all this with Peter one day. I passed over the Norwegian Air Force base at Bodø, destined to play a part in a special treat a few days later. After six hours I landed at Tromsø, pleased to find that my hotel overlooked the fiord and the beautiful Ice Cathedral on the far side. I had just settled down in bed when the phone rang.

"This is Dagfinn from the Aeroclub – would you like to come for a drive into the mountains to see the midnight sun?" Would I ever? How could I refuse? I quickly dressed and went downstairs. A tall handsome man appeared and we were soon driving up into the mountains where we were treated to spectacular views around every corner. I had to keep pinching myself and telling myself that it really was midnight!

Dagfinn and his wife, Sigrid, invited me to stay with them. I was anxious not to be a nuisance to anyone, but they were insistent so I moved into their home – a large wooden red-painted chalet – a day later. All the houses in the street were painted different colours and this added a certain charm to this rather unworldly place. I had a room on the ground floor, but the main sitting room and kitchen were on the first floor. It was typically Scandinavian although there was much evidence of Sigrid's time in Africa with a wonderful array of wooden animals.

I had to wait for five days in Tromsø for clear weather to make the flight to Longyearbyen on Spitsbergen. It was essential to have clear weather now that I was north of the Arctic Circle. Once again any chance of cloud would bring the attendant risk of icing. I went for long walks through wooded and snow-covered hills and was warmly looked after by members of the Aeroclub.

However, I found I still had to slot in the unexpected. While I had been making my way north, Pen Hadow, the intrepid polar explorer, was sledge hauling to the North Pole and Ian Wesley, Pen's PR manager, was suggesting we tried to liaise positions so that I could fly over Pen. This was an added excitement, but I was anxious not to have to deviate from my route which was already long enough over the frozen Arctic Ocean. We kept closely in touch during the next few days. He told me that the temperatures had plummeted to -40°C but had risen again to -10°C.

I also had a call from Jason Roberts, a freelance cameraman, working mainly for the BBC. He had made his home in Longyearbyen, the most northerly town in the world, on the island of Spitsbergen within the Arctic Circle. He had been on his way back from filming in Antarctica and was spending a few days in Germany, when by a fortuitous coincidence he had picked up a copy of *Pilot* magazine at the airport. In it he had found an article about my flight, so he immediately got in touch. He proved to be invaluable with his advice about Longyearbyen and I e-mailed him with many queries leading up to my departure. One of my last queries was, "Are there any hotels in Longyearbyen?" "Yes," he replied. "There are three, but you are staying with me."

It was very difficult for me to refuse and anyway I found it much more congenial to stay in someone's home. Hotels could be very impersonal, although on odd occasions it was a relief to be able to relax on my own.

Anyway, this time Jason rang to say, "The weather is improving. Make sure that you have your cameras ready to film as you fly the approach." I am not that good with cameras but I had to do my best as Carlton Television were making a documentary for which they had also employed Jason to film while I was in Longyearbyen.

At one point during my stay in Tromsø I had had a call from the Norwegian Air Force. "We would like to escort your departure from Tromsø." Wow! "Thank you very much." I replied, wondering how on earth they had heard about my flight. I correctly surmised that it must have been Gunnar who told them.

"Yes, we would like to send two F16s." they went on. F16s are American fast fighter jets! "Thank you very much." My heart missed a beat. "What is your fastest speed?" was the next query. "130 kts." "Oh dear! Our slowest speed is 150 kts and we are not sure yet whether we will be allowed to do this." I was excited at the prospect of having two fighter jets escort me, but I kept my imagination in check as I knew there was every chance it would not happen.

Eventually I had a good weather forecast from Jeppesen in the States. "There is a clear weather window for you to fly up to Svalbard," I was told. It was difficult to control my nerves. This was the first real trial in the polar regions. Several members from the Aeroclub came to wish me 'Good bye and good luck.' I waved cheerily to them as they stood on the edge of the taxiway. I was feeling far from cheerful, but I kept telling myself that this is what I had trained for and I must not pack up now.

I took off and was soon climbing up over the sea. Still feeling anxious I climbed to a cruising altitude of 8,000 ft. I kept asking myself, "Will I get there before it clouds over. Will I find the tiny airstrip? What will it be like?"

I was still pondering to myself when over the radio I suddenly heard, "Golf Foxtrot Romeo Golf November, this is Echo Zero One and Echo Zero Two – we have you on radar." Astonished and excited, I was soon aware that there was an F16 on either wingtip and the pilots were waving and smiling at me.

Then, over the radio came: "G-FRGN this is Bodø Control do you read?"

"Oh go away!" I rather uncharitably said to myself. "Why do they have to call me just at this moment?" Papers went flying as I searched for my camera. "G-FRGN – Bodø Control calling."

I knew that I would have to speak to them as they were after all only trying to look after me, but I spoke to Bodø as briefly as possible. They wanted estimates of time over various en route reporting points so I was able to say "Standby" while I enjoyed the F16s and then did the calculations at leisure.

The F16s very soon overtook me although they were going as slowly as they could. They dropped down 2,000 ft, pulled their noses up and were beside me again. What a thrill! The pilots waved farewell, but before departing they went out in front of me and gave me my own private aerobatic display. A great privilege. I don't know who enjoyed it more, them or me. What I do know is that it helped take my mind off my nerves. By the time they left I was well out over the ocean and the option of turning back was sliding behind me. I now had about four and a half hours to run but was soon straining my eyes for a sight of land. When at first I saw it in the distance it was difficult to discern whether it was cloud or ground. In fact it was both. A thin layer of cloud hung over the island of Spitsbergen and the tall mountain peaks were poking through the top of the clouds.

The outside air temperature had dropped. I looked at the increasing cloud cover over the island and I wondered if I would find a hole through the cloud or whether I would have to fly the published approach with its inherent possibilities of icing. My adrenalin was running on 'high' and my state of alert was increasing by the minute. Flying over cloud-covered icy mountains did not offer the best chance of survival should something happen to my single engine. Through breaks in cloud I could see spectacular mountains, fiords, glaciers and sweeping valleys with virgin snow, not a footprint or mark to show any sign of life. I shivered and tried to enjoy the scenery without dwelling on the negative side of things.

As I closed in on the NDB (non directional beacon) radio aid at Longyearbyen, I spotted a break in the clouds. Below I could see the sea and decided to plunge down below the cloud and fly visually to the runway. I spiralled down and very soon the desolate black strip came into sight. A tall icy mountain flanked one side and the angry looking sea the other. White horses were breaking over the tops of the waves.

I could not help thinking, "God, please don't let me have an engine failure here." Such thoughts were of course completely unfounded. "The engine doesn't know it is over water or mountains," I kept telling myself, but that little demon called 'what if' kept popping up to keep me on full alert. I had an ongoing battle with 'what ifs' throughout my journey and it was not until I was firmly back at home that it completely disappeared. It was a great relief to see the runway and I flew a long downwind leg so that I could take some photos.

As I taxied up I could see not just one cameraman, but two. Little did I know that a camera crew were currently in Longyearbyen filming a series about life in the frozen North. As I opened the door the icy wind hit my face. I clambered out on the wing and Jason came up so I literally tumbled into his arms. The relief to have arrived safely was overwhelming. The other team wanted to do an interview. I asked them to wait while I burrowed in the back of the aircraft to find my Arctic gloves and coat. My body temperature had dropped and I was shivering from the heady combination of the cold and the relief.

With the interviews finished, we pushed Golf November into the hangar. The air may have been cold but the atmosphere and welcome could not have been warmer. Jason drove me along the water's edge to the little town. Longyearbyen has approximately 1,200 inhabitants. The colourful houses had been built into the mountainside on one side of the valley. The wooden church and spire dominate the other side where the museum and a few houses also stand. Jason had converted an old coal shed near the now disused coal conveyor. He had done an amazing job using the best Swedish wood. Little did I know it then, but this was to be my home for ten long days.

During my prolonged stay in Longyearbyen I got to know the little town quite well and thankfully it had a well equipped supermarket and, rather incongruously, a 'Body Shop'. Anxious to move on, however, everyday I contacted the meteorologists at Los Gatos in California and every day it was the same story. "There is a low pressure system sitting over Northern Canada – it is not safe for you to fly." I always double checked with the weather reporter, Lilian, at the airport.

Many of the days were overcast, cold and oppressive. Unfortunately Jason had to go away to film which meant I was in his house alone and I missed the company. Each day I wandered up to the little

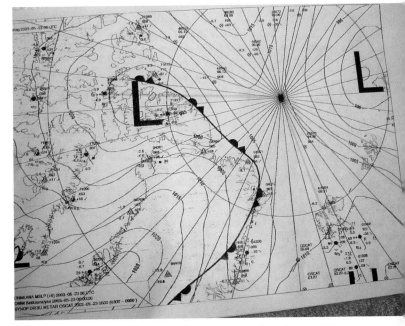

The weather chart I received in Longyearbyen showing the huge low pressure system stubbornly hanging over northern Canada. This held up my flight over the North Pole for ten days.

church and found it was comforting to sit there and meditate. It calmed my nerves and helped me cope with the long wait. I made friends with the local priest who was great fun, and various other people did their best to make my enforced stay a pleasant one.

Tom Stoelsdokken, one of the air traffic controllers, took me out for a meal. Everybody spoke perfect English. I gradually got to know a number of the local inhabitants. Torunn was acting as housekeeper for the priest and I met her on one of my visits to this haven which is the most northerly church in the world. She introduced me to her sister Hilde, a local schoolteacher and her two delightful boys who attended church in national costume. I spent a happy day with them.

Meanwhile Pen Hadow had reached the Pole. He was obliged to camp there as the same weather that was delaying me was preventing the Kenn Borek Twin Otters from flying out to pick him up. The newspapers were making a big thing of it as he was running out of provisions and the battery of his satellite phone, the only means of communicating with the outside world, was going flat.

Would the weather never improve?

CHAPTER 10
All Went Quiet

At last the day came when I received an optimistic weather report. The front had finally moved away and the forecast was good. In the previous ten days I had become accustomed to the little town of Longyearbyen and I had made many friends. Now that the time had finally come I was sorry to leave it behind. Underneath I think I was looking for an excuse to procrastinate and postpone the challenge ahead. As I drove in the taxi to the airport, I felt as if I was going to the gallows.

"Do what you fear and fear will disappear," said the sage. But we all have to cope with the prospect of doing something of which we are afraid. It is not easy to manage. In fact, coping with fear of the unknown was the most difficult aspect of the whole challenge.

I left Longyearbyen wearing silk underwear and a 'tig' suit made of warm down under a Multifabs survival suit fitted with tight neck and arm seals, and a life-jacket.

I got through by changing into an automaton. Automatically I smiled, automatically I checked Golf November thoroughly. Automatically I checked the weather and assimilated the advice from Lilian in the tower. The aircraft was filled with as much fuel as possible, the ferry tank right to the overflow. This was going to be a long flight. I donned my immersion suit and life-jacket and climbed aboard. I checked that my .303 rifle was accessible and loaded. There would be no time to fumble round looking for it if I had a forced landing on the ice and a hungry polar bear was approaching.

I kept busy so as not to dwell on what lay before me. My heart was thumping, and my stomach was churning. I taxied out to the grey runway sitting alongside the icy water with the mountain towering beside. Then suddenly I remembered that I had not informed Canadian customs. I picked up my mobile phone.

"This is just to inform you that I am about to take off from Longyearben and in approximately fourteen hours time I will be landing in Resolute Bay," I told the customs lady on the other end. "You cannot go into Resolute Bay," she replied abruptly. "Why not?" "Because it's not a port of entry," she retorted firmly. "But I am all fuelled up waiting to go," I continued. "You can't," she insisted.

I argued with her, explaining that it was a charity flight in a single-engine aircraft, the weather was good, in fact, anything I could think of to persuade her. She was immovable. I turned off the phone and thought, "Bugger this! I am going anyway."

The wind whistled around the mountains and straight along the runway. A shiver ran down my spine as I revved the engine and took off. Golf November and I climbed up over the icy fiord. I looked at the choppy water beneath and gave a last glance behind me as I left the security of the runway and all my newly made friends. We set course firmly northward. As I climbed away I apologised to the controller, who happened to be Tom, for the delay and explained the argument with Canadian customs.

"What are you going to do?" he asked. "When overhead Resolute Bay, I'm going to declare an emergency," I said. "Can I suggest that if that is your plan, that you file for somewhere else?" "OK, where do you suggest?" I asked. "Yellowknife," he said.

So that is what we did. Yellowknife is over a thousand miles further on from Resolute Bay. There was no chance of ever reaching there on the fuel I could carry! "Who cares?" I thought. "I am going to land at Resolute whatever happens." I had no idea how the Canadians would react. Perhaps they would put me in gaol, but in my bullish mood I could only think that it would make a good story.

Imagine taking off for the North Pole! The mountains of Spitsbergen were fast disappearing under my wing. All that I could see was endless miles of ice interspersed with odd ribbons of open water called 'leads'. It was spectacular, but how would my little craft manage in these low temperatures?

I was frighteningly aware that I was all on my own and that I was flying over vast stretches of ice-covered ocean. My head was full of those 'what ifs' and I tried not to fixate on how Golf November would cope. But if I did come down, if the engine did fail, would I manage? Could I camp on the ice? Would I be found? Would I die?

One cannot be scared for ever. I was busy in the cockpit and my hourly routine kept me occupied. It was important to keep track of the fuel already consumed and the amount left so I did the fuel calculations and checked the instruments. Then I did vigorous leg exercises to prevent deep vein thrombosis, ate a muesli bar and drank some water and so each hour passed. Adrenalin was on permanent fast flow.

In the polar areas the aircraft compass becomes inaccurate and may topple. Satellite navigation by the cockpit Global Positioning System (GPS) then becomes the only means of finding your way. Should the GPS pack up when suspended by a tiny airframe and one engine over the North Pole, which way do you go? All roads lead south, so how do you find the correct line of longitude down which to fly? Without GPS I could use the rest of my fuel and perhaps the rest of my life going round and round in circles. All is flat and there are no landmarks to navigate by.

At this stage, I could still turn round and return to the safety of Longyearbyen and so I might have done had I heeded that little voice that was nagging away. I ignored it and glanced at the names on my wings drawing comfort from those that I knew. I wondered what they were doing 'back home'. Even if the GPS did fail I still had the sun, that one constant which was impervious to magnetic energy and could not fail. At that moment I felt only too grateful to Arthur Moore, the retired RAF navigator who had patiently taken me through the mysteries of the Mk II Astro Compass which I now had mounted on the dashboard of Golf November.

Every half hour I was taking sun-sights and calculating my position. Fortunately the weather was gin-clear aloft so at least I could see the sun. Using the astro compass required a complicated routine. The instrument was awkwardly placed. I could not see the true heading indicator from where I was sitting without the use of a long dentist's mirror. I then had to calculate my position using an almanac, checking the time and date on a set of tables. After all this, the result was perfect. The sun navigation matched exactly with the GPS. It was comforting to know that I had this back up.

The miles ticked slowly behind me. I had a headwind of approximately 30 kts which meant that I only covered the earth's surface at 98-100 nautical miles an hour which was painfully slow. I willed Golf November on and gloried in the sun sparkling off the ice and the blue leads. The reality of it was that I was on my own and there was no-one around should something happen to my engine. Gradually we reached 88°N then 89°N. I became very excited. "Would the GPS read 90°North?"

No-one could tell me the answer to this, not even Bendix-King, the manufacturers and sponsors. In fact it *did* read 90°N for about five seconds. I was so excited that if there had been a table to dance on in my small cockpit, I would have surely done so. Instead, I picked up my satellite phone and called my husband, Peter, back in Oxfordshire.

"I'm on top of the world," I screamed down the phone against the engine noise. "For heaven's sake, head south!" he replied. I did.

The photo of the Global Positioning System reading 89° 54′ north which was the nearest photo I could get to 90°N.

More endless miles of ice, leads and sparkling sunshine were ahead of me as I chugged my way southward. I had a crosswind now, and I had timed the flight so that the sun was directly in front of me as I turned at the Pole. Winds fluctuated and my heart rose and sank accordingly. If I had a bit of a tailwind I was going as fast as 130 kts. My heart rose and then it would sink again as the groundspeed dropped to less than 120 kts.

My spirits moved like the sea rises and sinks beneath that vast expanse of sea ice but I forbade myself to think bad thoughts. Then, silence. That 'sound yet not a sound' which all pilots dread. My engine had stopped. I was over Axel Heiberg Island, one of the most beautiful and hostile places on earth. Mountains rise out of the flat sea ice in sharp peaks like whipped up icing on a cake.

Three minutes earlier the engine had coughed, indicating that my massive cockpit tank was about

YEAR 2003

MONTH	DAY	AIRCRAFT TYPE	REG	PILOT IN COMMAND	OTHER PILOT or CREW	DETAILS	SINGLE-ENGINE DUAL DAY	DUAL NIGHT	COMMAND DAY	COMMAND NIGHT
APRIL	29	PA 28 236	GFRBN	SELF	'	BOURNEMOUTH - OXFORD			0.8	
APRIL	30	PA 28 236	GFRBN	SELF	'	OXFORD TO OXFORD (PHOTO-SHOOT JOHN BURNHAM)			0.8	
APRIL	30	PA 28 236	GFRBN	SELF	'	OXFORD TO OXFORD (PHOTO SHOOT - CARLTON TV)			0.8	
MAY	2	PA 28 236	GFRBN	SELF	1	OXFORD - CONINGSBY (PAR)			1.2	
MAY	2	PA 28 236	GFRBN	SELF	1	CONINGSBY - OXFORD NDB APP			1.4	
MAY	4	PA 28 236	GFRBN	SELF	1	OXFORD - BIRMINGHAM			0.7	
MAY	6	PA 28 236	GFRBN	SELF	1	BIRMINGHAM - WICK DEPREZ ROWJO TYREWELL FLY PAST WITH HURRICAN			3.4	
MAY	11	PA 28 236	GFRBN	SELF	1	WICK - BERGEN ILS			2.4	
MAY	12	PA 28 236	GFRBN	SELF	1	BERGEN - TROMSO ILS			5.5	
MAY	16	PA 28 236	GFRBN	SELF	1	TROMSO - LONGYEARBYEN			5.4	
MAY	26	PA 28 236	GFRBN	SELF	1	LONGYEARBYEN - NORTH POLE - RESOLUTE			14.3	
MAY	28	PA 28 236	GFRBN	SELF	1	RESOLUTE - YELLOWKNIFE			6.7	
MAY	30	PA 28 236	GFRBN	SELF	1	YELLOWKNIFE - FAIRBANKS			9.7	
JUNE	2	PA 28 236	GFRBN	SELF	1	FAIRBANKS - FAIRBANKS			0.8	
JUNE	8	PA 28 236	GFRBN	SELF	1	FAIRBANKS - MANLEY HOT SPRINGS			1.2	
JUNE	9	PA 28 236	GFRBN	SELF	1	MANLEY - FAIRBANKS			1.1	
JUNE	10	PA 28 236	GFRBN	SELF	1	FAIRBANKS - ANCHORAGE			2.4	
JUNE	11	PA 28 236	GFRBN	SELF	1	ANCHORAGE - PRINCE RUPERT			7.8	
JUNE	16	PA 28 236	GFRBN	SELF	1	PRINCE RUPERT - VICTORIA			3.2	
JUNE	26	PA 28 236	GFRBN	SELF	1	VICTORIA - VAN NUYS			8.0	
JUNE	26	PA 28 236	GFRBN	SELF	1	VAN NUYS - EL MONTE			0.7	
						TOTALS THIS PAGE	78.9		75.9	19.4
						TOTALS BROUGHT FWD FROM PREVIOUS PAGE	1491.4	350.5	39.8	1049.2	19.4
						TOTALS TO DATE	1587.3	350.5	39.8	1125.1	19.4

Rt tow 72.6

Entries Certified Correct:

Signed ....

Title ....

A.R.N. ....

Date ....

TOTAL FLYING THIS PAGE .... hrs

GRAND TOTAL FLYING HOURS .... 1567.3 hrs

TOTAL AERONAUTICAL EXPERIENCE .... hrs

SUM OF COLS 1-14 · SUM OF COLS 1-14 · SUM OF COLS 1-12, 13* & 14*

Log book entry of North Pole crossing.

to run dry. This was perfectly normal. I changed onto my first wing tank and the engine purred again. I had plenty of fuel with just two hours left to run and nearly six hours of fuel in the wings. Then the engine stopped.

I went into automatic mode. "Carby heat on, fuel pump on, change tanks," I muttered to myself. My camera went flying. Papers flew to the floor. I rattled through the emergency check list which I had practised over and over with Pete Thorn. Suddenly the engine sprung into life and the relief was enormous.

However, I had no idea whether the engine would stop again, so with sweat pouring down me and adrenalin on overtime, I detoured out over the sea ice. "At least I have a chance of landing Golf November on the sea ice," I thought. There would be no chance of survival over the mountain peaks of Axel Heiburg Island if it happened again.

After that every little sound taunted me as I tried to analyse why it had stopped. Was there ice in the fuel? Ice could certainly block the fuel inlet to the engine and cause fuel starvation. I looked down at the endless miles of ice below and wondered what on earth I was doing. I thought of my family and imagined their lives without me. I queried how I would manage camping on the ice or facing a polar bear...

Unlike Axel Heiburg Island, most of the North Canadian islands are flat. It is almost impossible to differentiate between land and sea ice from the air. All looked flat as I tried to pick out the small islands marked on the map. At last, the runway at Resolute came into sight, which brought intense relief mixed with silent pleadings to my engine to keep going.

I was still shaking when I arrived fourteen hours and five minutes after leaving Longyearbyen. I could not believe that I had landed safely after so long. Had I really crossed the North Pole, the first woman to have done so on her own in a single-engined aeroplane? Totally exhausted and dying to go to the loo, I struggled out of my immersion suit trying not to slip over on the ice. I had not declared an emergency landing after all. The first person I saw was the local policeman who had come out, not to arrest me after all, but simply to make a customs check. He waited while I attended to the necessary call of nature, but he was relaxed and cheerful and he understood. I also had an e-mail from Tom:

"I hope you have safely landed in Resolute. Your HF radio was not too good, so we did not read you too well after departure from Longyearbyen. When I heard of the problem with the customs I personally called the superintendent of that district of the Canadian customs authorities and asked for dispensation from customs clearance for your flight, so you could continue as planned.

"After long discussions and after having explained the purpose of your flight, this was granted, and we tried to convey it to you on the extremely bad HF radio. I really hope you got the message so you did not have to declare emergency to land at Resolute."

People milled around, curious to see this little aircraft that had so valiantly defied nature and crossed one of the most inhospitable stretches of water and ice on earth. They all lent a hand and pushed Golf November into the safe confines of the Kenn Borek hangar. I looked proudly on as she nestled in a corner beneath the fleet of Twin Otters which seemed to look down on her with a smile.

Although I never saw him due to cloud cover, when I actually crossed the Pole, Pen Hadow, that intrepid adventurer, was camping beneath waiting to be picked up after his mammoth solo walk. I had longed to drop him some food supplies as I knew that he was running low. I had no window to open and I knew that if I opened the door in flight I would not be strong enough to close it again. Pen has since written to say he heard me flying overhead. We have met and talked about our experiences of being at the Pole together, which has forged a definite and rare bond between us.

CHAPTER 11

Touched by the Inuit

His name was Aziz and he wore spectacles that balanced perilously on the end of his nose, secured by a long chain around his neck. I never did find out what had brought him so far from India, but I quickly discovered that Aziz *was* Resolute Bay. He ran the airport and a hotel in town, and was mayor of this freezing metropolis of some three hundred souls. He was forty-nine and had come to Resolute aged eighteen. He married an Inuit lady who is a dog musher and takes people to hunt polar bears.

Aziz drove me the three miles into town in his truck. Everywhere there was ice. At first I could not make out the difference between land and sea ice until Aziz pointed out the bay; he chatted all the way into town and showed me to the little wooden church on a hill. "Do you go to church?" he enquired. "They have a service in our little church on a Tuesday evening. You would be most welcome to go." "Do you go?" I asked "No, but please go, you will be most welcome," he insisted.

We drove up to his hotel which was the biggest building in town. Aziz showed me to my room and told me I could have supper whenever I liked as it was laid out on a plate in the dining room. "All you have to do is put it in the microwave. There is a plate for each guest," he explained. "The food is the best in town." I soon got the gist of what to do. I was starving after such a long flight. I bolted my dinner and rushed off to bed where I lay unconscious for eleven hours.

The following day was busy as I was anxious to find out why Golf November's engine had stopped. I had a good look around the aircraft and discovered some white powder near the exhaust stack. I wondered if I had been running the fuel mixture too lean. Bob and Tod, two Kenn Borek engineers who service and maintain the Twin Otters which they run in the Arctic and the Antarctic were at the airport, so I asked their advice.

They were not too sure as they only worked on jet engines so they rang the piston expert back at Kenn Borek headquarters in Calgary. He advised me to get Bob to look at a couple of the spark plugs which he duly did. Everything seemed to be fine. I took Golf November out of the hangar and did a thorough engine run. The test went well, but still there was that niggling query as to why the engine had stopped and whether it would do so again.

Aziz provided me with three barrels of Avgas. I was anxious about that as they were ten years old. Avgas is reputed to deteriorate only very slowly in cold weather but here was just another uncertainty to cope with. I was not out of the woods, or rather ice, yet! We tested the fuel and it was perfect. There was no sign of any contamination. The 'Borek Boys' helped set up my hand pump and we started the long process of re-fuelling Golf November from barrels. This was laborious, flowing the fuel through a hand-held filter as well as the one incorporated in the pump. It was cold but everyone was joking and the time passed quickly in spite of freezing hands. There was nothing but unstinting support from all the Kenn Borek staff.

A few yards across the snow stood the little blue wooden church. The minister, Susan, gave me a really warm welcome and asked me what I was doing in Resolute. Her husband Ali played the keyboard standing up and sang into a microphone at the same time. He was always smiling and encouraging people to sing along with him. My eye was taken to a particular painting on the wall. Looking at the children's drawing of their feet on the wall with the inscription 'I will follow Jesus' I began to ruminate. "Had I really just flown across the North Pole?" I could not believe it. It was like a dream. Yet here I was, so I must have done it.

The Inuit church in Resolute Bay.

Gradually the church filled and in the end there was hardly a seat to spare. There were probably only about twenty people, but it was bulging. The service began. It was all in the Inuit language so I understood not a word. No matter. The text of the hymns were projected onto a screen, but that hardly helped either. I was the only white non-Inuit person there, but I felt comfortable and at home. Everyone smiled. The minister then announced in English, "We get so many visitors to Resolute, but it is rare for us to meet them. We are delighted that Polly has come to meet us." She asked me to come up to the front and tell everyone what I was doing and translated to the congregation as I spoke.

Towards the end of the service Susan invited me to go to the front of the church once more. She asked me if I minded if they all prayed for me. At that point the whole congregation came up to the front and stood in a circle surrounding me. Each person laid a hand on me and I was filled with an overwhelming sense of warmth. Susan and Ali chanted prayers and I felt so deeply happy that I did not want the experience to end. It was one of the most moving moments of my life. I felt a real power being transmitted from these deeply spiritual people as though I were joined to them, yet too humble to be a part of them. I later learnt that this encircling of people is one of the greatest honours the Inuit can give.

At the end of the service I chatted to a young fellow who hunted seals and fish through the ice in the traditional Inuit way. His eyes lit up as he related how he had killed a polar bear recently. I asked him if he ate it and his eyes sparkled as he told me that the flesh of this animal was the best taste of all. It is such a different way of life and a day or two was far too short to begin to assimilate it. But I felt honoured to get just a glimpse.

The following day, much refreshed, I set off for another seven-hour flight across the icy wastes of northern Canada to Yellowknife. Departing the airport at Resolute, I flew a small detour to circle over the little village to say farewell to my newly made friends. I had promised to have their name on my wing. It was the only way I could think to say thank you to them for welcoming me into their community. I often look at their name 'St Barnabas Anglican Church'; and memories of their kindness and generosity of spirit come flooding back.

"Only seven hours to go – please Golf November don't stop again," I thought as my ears listened for every nuance of pitch in her tiny engine.

The frozen tundra of northern Canada looked such a harsh environment, yet I knew that people were living below. It was hard to discern which was sea ice and which was land, yet it was here that McClure, Rae and Franklin explored the North West passage. I dwelt on what I knew of those courageous explorers and thought of the hardships they must have encountered and then of the pioneers who died. It was a salutary thought for there was no room for error. I had to remain alert. Worryingly, the engine failure still remained a mystery. I muttered my checks. "Carby heat on, check oil temperature, check exhaust gas temperature…"The list was long and trotted off the tongue with endless repetition.

Cambridge Bay appeared in the distance, an outpost and relic of the old DEW (Distant Early Warning) Line Stations of the Cold War era. It was a welcome sign of habitation. Flying south, the temperature began to increase and ice gave way to rocks and frozen rock pools. In this desolate area early miners risked life and limb to find gold. I flew over Lupin, a gold mining settlement where there was a beautiful long runway but no sign of life, just a few oil drums. It was hard for me to imagine what life would have been like at the turn of the 20th century where everything would have been brought in by dog sled.

I used carby heat less in direct proportion to the gradual increase in temperature. As mentioned earlier, two students of the Mirce Akademy of Systems Operational Science in Exeter were researching my flight for their doctoral thesis. I had to make a note every hour for them. This kept me busy in the cockpit and took quite a portion of my hourly routine. Here is what I had to record:

At each departure	In flight	At each arrival
Location	Altitude	Location
Co-ordinates	Winds/direction	Co-ordinates
Time	Distance	Time
Fuel load	Fuel consumption	Refuel quantity
Oil refill	Oil temp.	Oil refill
Maintenance	Oil pressure	Maintenance
Battery charge	Cabin temp.	Total distance
Ambient temp.	Ambient temp.	Ambient temp.
Cabin temp.	Engine temp.	Max G-force
Max G-force	Engine RPM	Fuel mix

(reproduced courtesy of Mirce Science)

After six hours some bush-like trees appeared on the ground. I was leaving the Arctic with its strange and, to me, surreal life behind as I flew south. From Yellowknife, I flew over the Yukon into Alaska where the temperature was +30°C in Fairbanks. Peter was waiting, smiling and waving as I taxied in on this now familiar airport. It seemed no time since we had waved farewell at Birmingham, yet so much had happened.

It was to Manley Hot Springs on the edge of the Arctic Circle that I made my first school visit. Shell Education had established an interactive schools' website. Schools around the world were invited to participate and were twinned with schools in the UK. Students followed the flight and participated in solving various problems from the website, comparing the results with their twin school. I visited each school around the world. At the same time Rob Farr from Shell

The most northerly school I visited was in Manley Hot Springs.

Education gave a presentation at the British school twinned with the one I was visiting. It was an exciting way to involve children in geographical, meteorological and mathematical subjects on a practical basis. It also gave me an opportunity to talk to children worldwide about disability.

Art Mortvedt flew Peter and me up to the cabin where I had done my Arctic survival. And it was a joy to be able to show Peter the magnificent scenery where I had undergone some of the most rigorous training. "Light a fire." Art's voice forever resounded in my head.

Flying in formation with Art Mortvedt en route to Manley Hot Springs, Alaska. My husband, Peter was taking pictures from Art's aircraft.

68

CHAPTER 12 Roller Coaster

My cockpit had now become my home and like all homes there were times when it was not as organised as it should have been. Moreover, the tidiness of the cockpit was the least of my concerns as I set out on the long flight from Victoria, Vancouver Island to Van Nuys, California in marginal weather with far too much cloud around for comfort.

Although the minimum safe altitude to clear the mountains was 7,000 ft, dodging in and out of cloud, I had to ask the controller for a descent to 5,000 ft just to keep my wings from icing up. I knew that this would not be high enough to cross the mountains further south so I had to find an alternative route. The easiest way to avoid icing and mountains was to fly along the coast.

I pulled out my charts and tried to fold them to visualise the complete revised route but this turned out to be impossible. Imagine the cockpit with just enough room for me with the control column almost in my chest. On my lap I had an A4 size clip board on which were the current chart, the flight log, the fuel calculation sheet, all the sheets for the research project, and the weather data (amounting to six sheets). The ongoing chart and flight log were in a plastic sleeve.

With things going well, it was not difficult to keep all the papers in order with the relevant chart to hand. On this particular day I had to re-route a long distance out to the coast in thick cloud, with turbulence tossing everything around. I was trying to fly the aircraft, fold the charts, make a new flight log and talk to the controller all at once. This would have been a challenge for a two-person crew. For one it was a nightmare. Charts went flying onto the floor, and as I bent down to pick up one chart, another would drop on the floor the other side.

Thankfully, Pete Thorn had drummed the adage "Aviate, Navigate, Communicate," into my mind so that I would remember to fly the aeroplane above all other tasks. Nevertheless, the cockpit was in a complete muddle and although I tried to tell the controller my new route I was being thrown around the cockpit so much by the turbulence that I kept losing my place. The Seattle Centre controller became understandably impatient.

"You are taking too long – call flight service and call me when you have filed the new plan," he said in an irritated voice. "Oh my God," I thought. "How am I ever going to sort this lot out?" "Aviate first," I kept telling myself as the papers seemed to have a mind of their own. I was ashamed of my incompetence.

"God – if Pete could see me now," I tried to laugh to myself, "he would be horrified." "Fly safely first," I kept repeating to myself whilst trying to restore order in the cockpit. It was a shambles. There was nowhere to put anything. The area beside me, where there is normally a seat, was filled with my life-raft and essential safety equipment. On top of that was a bag with my relevant charts. There was not a corner to spare.

In the end I managed to transfer a garbled message to Flight Service and was able to head to the coast. It was a relief to be away from the mountains which must have been below although I could not see them through the cloud. On reaching the coast the cloud began to lift. The glorious Oregon coastline stretched into the distance. I could now put my house in order and relax once more.

My thoughts went back to when I was in Prince Rupert in northern Canada near the Alaskan border. The most amazing thing happened in this little town which, incidentally, has one of the highest rainfalls in the world. I was met by Joe Paulinelli. He was a keen Rotarian and he and his wife Val hosted me for five days. Joe was holding Kienan, his two-year-old grandchild who has spina bifida and was

Gordon Cooper was an astronaut on the Gemini and Mercury missions.

unable to walk. Joe explained that unfortunately there was a long waiting list at the children's hospital in Vancouver. When the press covered my stay in Prince Rupert it was too good an opportunity not to mention Kienan's story. The resulting newspaper article led to an offer by Hawk Air to fly him and his mother free of charge to Vancouver. A friend put Kienan's name forward for the Shriner's Club, a charity providing expert no-cost orthopaedic care to children in eighteen hospitals in the USA. He has since become a 'Shriner's baby' and will be cared for until he is eighteen. He can now walk with the support of water in a swimming pool, and with the aid of leg braces he is learning to walk on the ground. This extraordinary story enriched the project and made it seem so worthwhile.

Flying Scholarships for the Disabled came sharply into focus over the following six months. I now had to wait for the twenty-four hour daylight of the Antarctic summer but the extra months in America gave me an opportunity to visit schools, Rotary clubs and various societies to talk about the charity.

In Los Angeles I met Bill Murrell who was later to start a Flying Scholarships for the Disabled programme in the USA. Bill organised a lunch with one of the first astronauts, Gordon Cooper. Gordon was one of the seven astronauts on project Mercury. I listened, spellbound as he told me that all the automatic equipment failed on his solo flight in Mercury. He had to fly the spacecraft back to earth by hand. He also broke the space record travelling 3.3 million miles aboard the Gemini spacecraft. He was the first person to execute two space missions.

Ben, Bob, Steve and Brad from Jeppesen looked after me so well with excellent forecasting all the way around the world.

At the start of a circular tour of the States and Canada I now set off northbound from California. The first stop was Los Gatos and I spent a few days meeting the meteorologists from Jeppesen who were responsible for my detailed weather briefings. At last I could put faces to voices.

These guys use state of the art software to ingest, process and display worldwide weather information including satellite imagery, radar, lightning, text reports and numerical model guidance. The system allows the forecasters to predict weather, passing on accurate information and specialised aviation weather maps to pilots wherever they might be on the globe.

From Los Gatos I flew up the west coast of the States and across the Rockies to Calgary. Yes, everyone was wearing cowboy boots and Stetsons. It was the time of the annual stampede and the festive spirit was evident everywhere. The Canadian Business Aircraft Association Exhibition was being held at the same time and several of my sponsors were exhibiting.

Whilst in Calgary I rang Steve Penikett at Kenn Borek. I wanted to keep my name to the fore and ensure that they really would deliver my fuel in Antarctica. "Come on over," said Steve. "Our chief pilot, Sean Louttit is here."

I thanked Steve for the support of his team at Resolute Bay in the Arctic. Then he and Sean reminded me that they were not going to Patriot Hills this year but would be going into another blue ice runway, Sky Blu instead and he repeated his commitment to help me with fuel there.

"Where is your aircraft now?" Steve enquired. "It is here on the airport. Do you want to come and see it?" I asked thinking that as he was so involved he would like to see the Kenn Borek logo on the fuselage. "Well, what's different about it? What do you want me to do – urinate on the wheel?" How could I deal with that? "Well, Prince Charles' signature is on the wing – but maybe you'd want to urinate on that too!" I said trying to give as good as I got.

Sean said, "Shall I show her around the hangar?" "No," said Steve. "He doesn't really mean it as he took me into the hangar last time," I retorted. Steve went on. "You are intimidated by me aren't you?" To which I replied, "No but you *think* I am intimidated by you."

It was a dangerous game. I was relying on Steve's help and it was important that I got it right. He was not the sort of guy who would have appreciated timidity, yet how far could I dare take it? The Kenn Borek hangars were impressive. It was a huge operation. The aircraft were completely rebuilt there between seasons. The professionalism was obvious. "Does Steve speak to everyone like this?" I wondered.

I ordered a taxi to take me back to the exhibition and sat in the reception room to wait for the taxi to arrive. Steve came through and saw me sitting there. "What are you still doing here?" he enquired. "Waiting for a taxi." "Do you want a car?" he asked straight out. "I wouldn't mind one." "How long are you staying here?" "'Til Sunday morning."

He tossed the keys of the car at me and said, "Take the car and drop it back here on Sunday. Drop the keys through the door." "That's very kind of you, thank you so much." "I'm not being kind, I just want you out of here!" He was incorrigible.

In Calgary I also met Tim Mell, a delightful energetic man who marketed headsets for Sennheiser, one of my major sponsors. He took me, dressed up as a cowgirl complete with high boots, waistcoat, and stetson to the Calgary Stampede, where I met Roberta Bondar, the only Canadian woman astronaut. "I feel scared at

All dressed up at the Calgary Stampede with Chris Cooper-Slipper from Field Aviation.

the thought of flying into Antarctica, I can't imagine what it must be like strapped into a spacecraft on the launch pad," I said to Roberta. She was reassuring. "I felt nervous as hell," she said patting me comfortingly. "Every little sound made me jump." Those words gave me that extra bit of courage for the Antarctic.

The wild west really stood out en route to Colorado Springs. I flew over radio aids with such names as 'Crazy Woman', 'Medicine Bow' and 'Muddy Mountain'. I wondered how those names evolved. At Colorado Springs I was taxiing behind a 'Follow Me' car from the far side of the airfield to the terminal when I realised that my right brake had failed. Thank goodness we were going slowly. It would have been undignified to crash into the back of a car guiding me across the airfield.

Soon the brakes were repaired and I was on the treadmill again making a short hop to the Jeppesen headquarters in Denver. This company was started by Captain Jeppesen who bought his first aeroplane, a $500 Jenny in 1927. After an early career barnstorming in the west of the USA,

Diane Earhart is an air traffic controller in St Louis. Despite having multiple sclerosis she is also a flying instructor which is not permitted in the UK.

Golf November had a fifty-hourly maintenance check in St Louis courtesy Ideal Aviation.

aerial survey work led on to operating airmails and it was during that time he began to design instrument approaches for aircraft to fly into airfields in minimum visibility. These sketches grew to become the 'plates' used by the majority of aircraft in the world flying under instrument conditions.

At Piqua in Ohio, Hartzell gave me a new three-blade propeller for Golf November. Although Golf November is an American-built aircraft, fitted from new with a two-bladed Hartzell propeller, and although the Hartzell three-bladed propeller has a UK CAA Airworthiness Approval Note, getting approval from the CAA for Hartzell to fit it to a UK-registered aircraft in the States was a bureaucratic nightmare – worth pursuing though as it would give better ground clearance for landing on the bumpy ice runways. The three elegant scimitar blades were two inches shorter than those of the two-blade propeller. The climb performance was markedly improved and the engine noise was greatly reduced. Hartzell were a substantial sponsor so I was delighted that, as a result of the new propeller being on my aircraft, another one was sold on the first day of the airshow at Oshkosh.

Oshkosh hosts the biggest light aircraft show in the world. Rows and rows of aircraft are parked for as far as the eye can see. 12,000 of them! Many pilots camp underneath their wings for the week of the show. Flying into Oshkosh was a terrifying experience. There were three runways, each marked into three sections. Three aircraft land on one runway at a time. You are told to land on the white dot, orange dot or green dot. It was scary landing with so many

Members of the St Louis branch of 'Women in Aviation' gave Golf November a much needed wash.

Golf November sporting her new three-blade propeller with Mike Disbrow, Nancy Allenbaugh and Larry Zetterlind from Hartzell, the manufacturers, at Piqua, Ohio.

other aircraft landing all around you, but it seemed to work. Golf November was parked in Aeroshell Square, the hub of the show. She had pride of place under the tail of the Orbis DC10, a travelling hospital with a vast network of volunteer medical staff who perform eye operations around the world.

Cornflakes take on a whole different meaning once you have visited Battle Creek better known as Cereal City. It was here that Kelloggs made their name but I had come to experience first hand what the scholars from Flying Scholarships for the Disabled go through to complete their flying course. Battle Creek is an appropriate name, for a battle it is.

A standard Cessna 172 Skyhawk sat in the blazing sun on the tarmac. Sandip Toprani was no standard student, for Sandip has muscular dystrophy, a congenital degenerative disease which saps away at the strength of your muscles, and your confidence too. He may have suffered from lack of strength but he certainly didn't suffer from lack of determination.

"I am having problems with reaching the electric flap lever, and I am not strong enough to push the control column forward," Sandip had analysed to Duncan, his instructor. "Go and work out how you can overcome those problems," Duncan had replied, tossing the aircraft keys to Sandip. It seemed cruel, but it worked miracles.

Sandip sat in the aircraft for two hours, and moved the seat to find a comfortable position. He found that if he locked his elbow against the back of the seat and rested it on the window frame he could lever the control column quite successfully.

"The flaps were more of a problem," he demonstrated to me. "The lever is quite a long way over to the right on the control panel. I found that if I stretched my right leg a little towards the right, I could lean my elbow on my knee, lean my body to the right, grab the sill at the bottom of the panel and flick the flap lever with my thumb. Of course it needed a lot of practice to be quick enough to

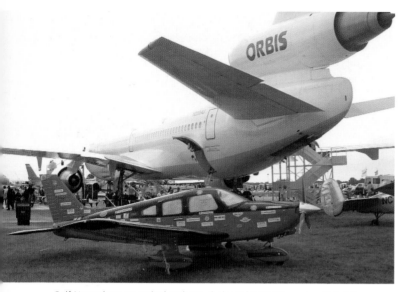

Golf November was parked underneath the Orbis DC10 eye hospital at the Experimental Aircraft Association Airshow at OshKosh.

Sandip Toprani at West Michigan University explains the numerous checks carried out on the aircraft.

manage whilst flying the aircraft." I began to realise how much more was involved for the disabled scholars, than just getting in the aircraft and learning to fly.

"My first solo was exhausting," Sandip continued. "But it was so exhilarating to have achieved it. I shall never forget the wonderful feeling – yep! I've done it!" He later described what the scholarship meant to him. "Before my scholarship I had many problems, mostly psychological," he said. "I just couldn't understand what was happening. I didn't have the confidence to go for an interview for a job for instance. I never thought it would be possible for me to fly. But I gained in confidence, I trained myself to think laterally and develop coping techniques. I also learnt about other people and about team building. I now have a fantastic and very challenging job which I wouldn't have even dared to apply for if I hadn't experienced a flying scholarship."

Martin Abbott, the Principal of Flying Scholarships for the Disabled was also at Battle Creek with his wife Brenda. Leaving the scholars and Peter was heart wrenching once again. As I was walking towards Golf November Brenda reached up to her neck, unfastened a chain with a silver cross on it and gave it to me. This wonderfully generous gesture gave me courage once more and that cross remained around my neck for the duration of my flight.

A couple of days with Lycoming, the manufacturers of Golf November's engine, confirmed that the engine stoppage over the Arctic had been due to an air lock. I must have sucked in air as I drained the ferry tank dry. They gave the engine a thorough check and proclaimed Golf November in excellent condition.

There was, however a moment of embarrassment. On arrival I said to the engineer, "Golf November *makes* oil," which was a rather tongue-in-cheek statement suggesting that she really used

17th December 2003 marked one hundred years since the Wright Brothers' first powered flight from Kitty Hawk. Golf November is at the little airport at the foot of the hill where they took off. The monument to the event is in the background.

very little oil. Two days later the engineer said to me, "We have looked absolutely everywhere and can't understand how she *makes* oil." I thought of that phrase 'divided by a common language' and apologized profusely for the rather strange British sense of humour.

Washington marked the half way point around the States and it was, of course, the source of my American Antarctic permit. Ever since the Australian journalist had successfully stopped ANZ transporting my fuel I had been on edge about maintaining my permits and the final fuel getting to Antarctica. Speaking to Steve Penikett, he told me that Raytheon, the main contractors to the National Science Foundation which runs the United States Antarctic Program, had wind that Kenn Borek, whose aircraft are contracted to Raytheon, were going to transport the fuel. Consequently the following letter was sent to Steve at Kenn Borek on 13th August 2003 just before I arrived in Washington.

From Raytheon Technical Services Company

Mr Stephen Penikett, Kenn Borek Air Ltd
290 McTavish Road NE, Calgary, Alberta T2E 7G5
Canada

Dear Steve,
As you are aware, the US government has a longstanding policy of not supporting private expeditions to the Antarctic except under rare circumstances and by prior agreement. That policy is spelled out in the following NSF statement.

US policy on private expeditions to Antarctica

The objectives and level of the activity of the United States Antarctic Program (USAP) are set forth in President Reagan's directive of February 5th 1982. Achievement of USAP objectives, which center on the conduct of a balanced program of scientific research and include cooperative activities with Antarctic programs of other governments, requires the full commitment of the operational and logistics capabilities available to the USAP. The US government is not able to offer support or any other services to private expeditions, US or foreign, in Antarctica.

In emergency situations, the US is prepared to attempt, in accordance with international law and humanitarian principles, the rescue of private expedition personnel provided that there are no unacceptable risks posed to US personnel and the rescue could be accomplished within the means available to the United States. Such emergency assistance would be limited to the rescue of private expedition personnel and their evacuation would be undertaken in a manner which, in the judgement of the United States, offered the least risk to US personnel, equipment and scientific programs. Once such rescue had been affected, the US would consider its assistance terminated and under no circumstances provide support for the continuation of the expedition.

Private expeditions, therefore, should be self-sufficient and are encouraged to carry adequate insurance coverage against the risk of incurring financial charges or material losses in the Antarctic. The National Science Foundation, as manager of the USAP, reserves the right to seek in accordance with international and domestic law, recovery of all direct and indirect costs of any such emergency search and rescue. The senior US representative in Antarctica may authorize such actions and activities that, in his judgement, best fit this policy guidance on the circumstances and conditions prevailing at the time of application.

As the prime support contractor to NSF on this project, Raytheon Polar Services Company (RPSC) is obligated to follow both the letter and spirit of this policy. We are also obligated to ensure that subcontractors to RPSC follow US government policies while under contract.

Under the terms of our agreement with Kenn Borek Air, we have contracted for the exclusive use of the aircraft in support of the US government's research activities in Antarctica.

It has come to our attention that Kenn Borek Air has offered to provide support for Polly Vacher's Trans-Antarctic flight attempt by moving fuel and by being listed as a Search and Rescue resource. Since it appears the USAP will be providing fuel caches for the deployment of all the KBA Twin Otters used in the Ross Sea region and beyond this season, RPSC is concerned that US government resources are being used to support this private expedition. Furthermore, while the US will attempt to provide assistance in the event of an emergency, the USAP policy is clear. Private expeditions are responsible for coming up with their own contingency plans and are liable for the costs of deploying their own assets to provide for these contingencies. USAP assets are not to be used as part of private contingency plans for the purposes of obtaining insurance or government permissions to mount expeditions.

In response to these concerns, please provide me with a written explanation of how support will be provided to Ms. Vacher and how this will be accomplished without using any USAP resources, either cached fuel or the airframes that are under exclusive contract from mobilization to redeployment. I will need a response by close of business 22nd August, 2003. If you have any questions please contact Kirk Salveson or me at RPSC.

Regards
Steve Dunbar
Director, Science Support Division

Cc: Tom Yelvington, Erick Chiang, Sue Lafratta, Brian Stone
    Dave Breshahan, Al Sutherland, Kirk Salveson

I rang Joe Beeman to ask his advice as I was now concerned that this might lead to my fuel being stopped. He was furious when I told him what I had heard. "Polly," he said. "They would never do something like that over a couple of jerry cans of fuel." Joe tried to reassure me and promised to speak to Erick Chiang from NSF. I had a dreadful nail-biting day worrying about what might happen. As I was staying with friends in Washington they took me out for the day, but my mind was in turmoil.

The children at the school in Acapulco put on a series of traditional Mexican dances in their open auditorium.

"How could people actively try to stop my flight? What would I do if my fuel never got to Antarctica? What if they rescinded my Foreign and Commonwealth Office permit?" I felt distraught, completely washed out with the mental anxiety. I tried relaxing, I tried taking deep breaths, I tried to take an interest in our outing, but I just could not seem to get myself into a positive frame of mind.

I waited and waited for a phone call from Joe. I knew he had managed to arrange a meeting with Erick Chiang at 1530 in the afternoon. The wait was interminable. I was torturing myself with anxiety. What was happening? Surely the meeting must be over by now. Why hadn't Joe rung me?

Finally, the phone rang at 1740. Joe told me that Erick Chiang was "all sweetness and light." He said that Erick realised that he (Joe) knew the law and there was not a leg to stand on. Joe went on, "Erick told me that the FCO was trying desperately to find a way to 'pull' your permit."

"Why would the FCO want to pull my permit?" I asked. "These are my own countrymen." Was I really hearing this? "When the question of Raytheon was raised, Erick was furious," Joe continued. There were so many imponderables to this, it was like a hornet's nest. I rang Steve Penikett who reassured me that he was happy to go on as we had arranged. That at least was a relief. I felt as if I had been in the torture chamber and was given a brief reprieve.

2003 marked the centenary of powered flight when the Wright Brothers achieved their first flight from Kitty Hawk, Kill Devil Hills in South Carolina. I wanted to pay my respects to these two men whose first heavier-than-air flight made such a massive impact on the world, so I made a detour. They flew for just 120ft but that was the start of it all. Landing at Kitty Hawk, the sense of history pervaded the air and I marvelled at the wonders of flight so ingeniously conquered exactly one hundred years before.

Having completed the circular route of the United States and after another hundred-hourly check, Golf November and I flew out of Santa Barbara and down through Mexico where I stayed a night in Guaymas, a delightful seaside town on the edge of the desert. My departure was delayed by a puncture in the taxi taking me to the airport, but the next car to pass stopped and gave me a lift.

Acapulco was awash with noise. Traffic, all night discos and difficult access to the internet were the negative memories, but far outweighed by the warm welcome from the school I visited. The outside theatre surrounded by tiered benches was a hive of activity as the children danced in their traditional brightly coloured costumes and showed me the work they were doing, linked with schools back home through the Shell Education interactive website and my flight.

Away from the sweltering heat of Mexico, Guatemala sat amongst mountainous peaks with a perfect climate. The Mayan people in the streets carrying baskets on their heads took me back a century as I wandered through the cobbled roads of their ancient capital, Antigua. Here John Bell, an American, runs a centre for disabled people called 'Transitions'. The most impressive spot was the workshop where disabled people, themselves in wheelchairs, make wheelchairs for others.

As Golf November and I flew over the border to Belize and across the Caribbean islands to Antigua, I was filled with excitement as I was going to meet Peter again. We settled in to a little rented maisonette for our last five days together before I would face my greatest test – Antarctica.

This Mayan lady in Antigua, Guatemala persuaded me to buy a length of beautiful hand-woven cloth.

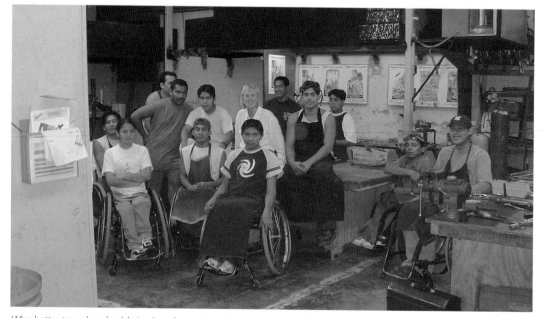

Who better to make wheelchairs than those using them themselves in Guatemala?

CHAPTER 13

Under the Jumbo's Wing

Peter and I spent five beautiful days together in Antigua and although we didn't speak about it, neither of us could shake off the fear of the unknown. Antarctica lay ahead as did the unspoken thought that something might happen to me. Peter did try to book a flight to Tobago to delay the time when we would have to part, but the flight times did not tally with his return flight to the UK. I knew it must be worse for him standing on the sidelines but he was very strong and never let on.

"Well, when you get to New Zealand we won't be worrying about any of these things any more," was the only thing Peter ever said that gave me an indication of what he was going through. I waggled my wings as I took off from Antigua to say good bye to him and our friends there. Four hours later I landed in Tobago.

The magic moment – meeting up with my oldest son, Julian after he landed the Virgin Atlantic 747/400 in Tobago.

Soon after, a Jumbo arrived in Tobago, though it seemed impossible to me that such a large aircraft could land on so short a runway. My heart missed a beat because I knew that our son, Julian, the First Officer on the Virgin Atlantic 747, was at the controls. He was bringing several of my team and the Carlton Television crew to spend five days in Tobago but also on board was Julian's new fiancée, Amanda. I was so excited. They had announced their engagement the day before I left Birmingham but promised that they would wait to get married until I returned. I looked forward to having time to get to know my future daughter-in-law. The jet came to a halt in front of the terminal building. The doors opened and the passengers disembarked. "Golf November - cleared to taxi to the Jumbo," came loud and clear from Tobago tower.

What a moment. I taxied my tiny plane towards the 747 where Julian was standing at the top of the steps and gesticulating for me to taxi under the wing. I wondered if there was enough room as I weaved my way between baggage carts and catering trucks. Susie and John Dunbar were clicking away and the Carlton Television team were running to film my every move. Julian was calmly directing operations and a crowd of people were watching from the perimeter fence. Val Cahill, our treasurer and her husband Dave were waving frantically and there was Amanda looking so calm and beautiful. Golf November resembled an ant

In Tobago I was whisked away to the rhythm of the steel band.

beside an elephant, but she and I felt very proud. It was magic. Julian rushed down the steps and gave me a hug, thrusting a bouquet of flowers into my hands.

Outside the terminal building a steel band was playing and the sound of calypsos filled the air. My feet were itching so I started dancing in the middle of the road as my friends and family laughed and clapped encouragement. Then a huge taxi driver grabbed my hand and we danced. He was wearing a bright blue Caribbean shirt, a marked contrast with my orange flying suit. Hair flying, toes tapping, hot and sweaty, the rhythm of the music engulfed us and we gave ourselves up to calypso. The air was full of festivity and fun as a car purred slowly past, the occupants grinning at our antics. I was whisked into a whirr of waving and photographers. Excited supporters engulfed me with hugs and tears of joy. How I wished Peter had been there to share the moment.

After a few days of relaxing with my family and friends I was once more heading south. The coast of South America loomed into sight on the horizon and huge cloud build-ups like towering mountains hovered menacingly over the coast. As I flew over the rain forests of Suriname the clouds became blacker and thicker. I looked down on a swathe of trees which stretched as far as the eye could see. It resembled a green ocean and I wondered how many different animals and birds lived down there below me. I felt small and insignificant, as I flew across this never-ending forest. The

Patrick, aged 8, at the school in Tobago asked, "If you jump out with a parachute, what happens to the plane?"

clouds were towering above me forming a great, black barrier between me and French Guiana ahead. I entered a tunnel of black cloud, the rain beat down and tossed Golf November and me around. The drumming on the roof was like woodpeckers hammering away and the noise was deafening. All was grey and wet and a quick glance was all that I could allow myself as my eyes scanned the instruments to keep Golf November straight and level. One second of inattention and the altimeter rises or falls 100 ft, the artificial horizon dips and the wings begin to rock. I was working like crazy, hands whisking from the carburettor heat lever to the trim to the mixture lever and back again. My eyes scanned one instrument after the other, checking, checking all the time. There was no let up.

"Keep calm – concentrate, I don't want to die in the rain forest," I thought as I worked to keep Golf November steady. I felt cold although the outside temperature gauge read +20°C. Golf November and I were attacked from above, below and all around as the rain beat its angry rods against us.

After what seemed like an interminable time I landed on the wet tarmac at Cayenne in French Guiana. The rain had abated but there was no fuel available in Cayenne, where I bumped my head on the low cupboard in my tiny hotel room, bugs bit me and I had no Euros to pay for a taxi. As can be imagined, I was thankful to leave Cayenne behind and to cross into Brazil. Because I had been unable to refuel, I could not reach Fortaleza as planned and had to land at Belem. They were not expecting me. It was hot and sticky. It took several hours to get through customs but I finally left the airport and reached the haven of my hotel room.

I made several stops along the lengthy coastline of Brazil where the warmth of the people raised my spirits again. Sergei and Kiara looked after me in Fortaleza where beautiful fishing boats with elegant bending masts called Jangadas floated peacefully. Life was fun. Jose Vieira put Golf November

Jangadas boats at Fortaleza.

in a smart hangar in Recife where she was given a long overdue wash. I was entertained by Ernani from the Rotary Club and Wagner Monteiro escorted my departure in a helicopter. All of which made me forget my concerns about Antarctica – temporarily.

As I broke through the total cloud cover the stunning city of Rio de Janeiro lay below. The runway was surrounded by the waters of the natural harbour. Margi and Gerrard Moss were waiting at the airport. They were about to embark on a year-long project in a flying boat to measure water pollution throughout Brazil, but still they made time to entertain me. Next, I flew on to the teaming city of Sao Paulo where I was met by two sponsors, Dr Knezevic from the Mirce Akademy and Roberta from Shell. We spent a day at the school of St Paul's where the children proudly displayed their work associated with the flight.

Sao Paulo is also the place where Ayrton Senna is buried. Dr Knezevic and I went to pay homage to the man whom many consider to be the world's greatest ever racing driver. His grave, adorned with flowers, is in the middle of a large green field on the side of a hill overlooking the city. I stood nearby and tried to focus on what made him so great. I had seen a video about his life and what shone out so loud and clear was his meticulous attention to detail. I had tried to emulate this with my preparation. But he had died doing what he had to do. Here was both an example and a note of caution for what I would face in Antarctica.

In Porto Allegre, Luis the handler greeted me and glancing at Golf November he said, "There are two seats in the aircraft." I looked at him quizzically as I only had one seat in the cockpit. "Yes, one for you and one for God." I remembered this when the going got tough.

An accidental meeting with Marcos in Porto Allegre resulted in Golf November once more being offered hangarage. The hangar was on the other side of the airport and a group of fellow pilots took us back to the terminal. We all piled into a car and the guy in front serenaded us on a guitar. It was

The view over my wingtip of the harbour at Rio de Janeiro.

crazy! When I left the following morning Marcos unpinned his pilots wings and gave them to me. I was humbled by his gesture.

The River Plate stretched beyond the horizon like a huge snake curling through the brown countryside with the great city of Buenos Aires stretching out on its furthest bank. I had special permission to land at Aeroparque, a small airport in the centre. Cities can look much the same from the air, but this one looked different as it sprawled along the banks of the river. The buildings looked neat and inviting. I couldn't help a quiver of excitement as I came in on final to such a historic place.

Taxiing in at Aeroparque I noticed a Piper Dakota on each wing. The Argentine Air Force, which was to prove so vital later in my trip, use Piper Dakotas, identical to mine, for initial training. I came to a halt on the apron and rousing music filled the air from the air force band. What a welcome! I was presented with champagne and flowers and introduced to Jorge Reta, the head of PR for the Argentine Air Force, who said to me, "My name is Jorge (pronounced Haw Hay) – call me George." Jorge, was the spitting image of James Mason, the film star, and he was no less charming. The Chief of the Air Staff hosted a breakfast and Jorge took me to a reception at the British Embassy.

I was a guest at The Air Force Hotel. Needing to change some money, I wandered into the local shopping area and found a bank. They were not able to change travellers' cheques, but told me of a bank that did. I took a taxi which drove me for about half an hour through the city to another bank which couldn't change my cheques either, but they told my taxi driver where he could take me. We drove into the very centre of the city. A policeman standing across a 'no entry' street, moved the bollards especially for my taxi to park. The driver got out of his cab and escorted me to a little money changer down a dark and dingy street. I kept glancing behind as I had heard that Buenos Aires wasn't always safe. Everything seemed innocuous and the taxi driver looked after me. I finally got my money. Jorge was alarmed when I told him the story. "You could have been kidnapped, Polly," he said. "That would have caused an international incident."

Airports in Argentina are run by the military. At the airfield of Trelew, Jorge (yes, another Jorge) the airport manager took me into his office. On his desk under a sheet of glass he had photos of his family which he proudly showed me. He pulled out a small card with a pre-Raphaelite-type picture of 'Queen of the Skies'.

"I want you to take this," he said "I carried it whenever I went flying." He asked me if I believed in God. I pulled out the cross which Brenda had given me and put the picture in my breast pocket. It was another memorable gesture. Later the poem on the back of the picture was roughly translated:

Queen of the Skies
As beautiful as a star
Pure and radiant
Fountain of the purest love
Our hope lies in you
Dear Mother, dear mother, Queen of the skies

If our wings are broken
At the end of our flight
Before touching the ground
Open your arms to us
Dear Mother, dear mother, Queen of the skies

The Andes rose in the distance. The snow-capped mountains looked benign enough in the brilliant sunshine. Climbing to 14,000 ft, I had to cross these mountains at their most southerly point to reach Ushuaia, my next destination. With the canula in my nose, I switched on the oxygen flow from the cylinder behind my seat. I had a new 'on demand' oxygen system so that I would only use the oxygen I actually needed. As a result I only needed to carry a smaller cylinder. The new device took some getting used to. Its computer only allowed oxygen to flow when I breathed in. Often it missed a breath which was a bit disconcerting. When this happened I looked anxiously at the gauge but I soon realised this was normal. The skies were clear and over the peaks I spoke to Ushuaia Tower. "Golf November descend to 9,000 ft," was the instruction after clearing the highest mountain.

Ushuaia lies tucked in the foothills of the Andes on the edge of the Beagle Channel, looking south to Cape Horn and Antarctica. Further clearance was forthcoming and the rapid descent to the airport was like skiing down the mountainside. Permission was granted to land on the old runway, now the home of the Aeroclub Ushuaia. I taxied through scores of people waving and shouting. What a welcome! Not just for me though, as I discovered that it was the annual festival with a huge barbecue being held at the Aeroclub.

A moving moment when Marcos gave me his wings in Porto Allegre.

Golf November was pushed into a hangar and I was taken for something to eat. There were about 600 people there. I spoke no Spanish, but just then a lady came pushing through the crowd. "Hello," she said in almost perfect English. "My husband is British, he would like to meet you but feels that you have too many people to talk to already and you won't want to speak to him."

"Of course I would like to meet him," I replied. The lady had long dark hair and was very beautiful. "My name is Roxanna," she shouted as we pushed through the crowd clinging to each other. Her husband, Jonathan, was to

The Selby family who looked after me so well during my long stay in Ushuaia.

Pilu, from the Aeroclub Ushuaia who helped Art with my fuel drums and Jonathan Selby who repaired my HF radio. Jonathan was my fifth 'giant'.

become my fifth 'giant' and I was very glad to meet him. "If there is anything I can do to help while you are here, please ask me," he said in a diffident manner. "Well yes, there is something," I said. "I am having a problem with my HF radio. I just don't seem to be able to get a signal." "That is something I am sure I can help you with," he said with more confidence.

A few days later Jonathan spent time sorting out my portable HF radio. After all the 'experts' who had looked at it, Jonathan managed to solve the problem in under two hours. Jonathan and Roxanna, together with their lively daughter, Gabriela, became friends and confidants. They entertained me to meals and Roxanna taught me Spanish. Above all they became my family during what was to prove a long wait in Ushuaia. Metaphorical clouds were thickening as I started down a slippery slope over which I had little control.

chapter 14

Strangled by Politics

There is a legal requirement for all aircraft to have regular maintenance checks, and one of my planning headaches was to find a competent light aircraft mechanic in the remote places. Pilu, an instructor from the Ushuaia Aeroclub, had recommended an engineer in Rio Grande on the east coast of Patagonia, north of Ushuaia. So early in the morning I took off from Ushuaia and flew along the Beagle Channel, that spectacular ribbon of water, stretching through the mountains from the Atlantic to the Pacific. There was a tailwind blowing me at a healthy 165 knots across the ground, but on turning north towards Rio Grande the groundspeed was only 98 knots. There was an 'on the nose' headwind and the flight seemed endless.

Golf November was in excellent order, so there were no specific requirements, just the normal 150-hour inspection. I gave Carlos, the engineer, the check list which unfortunately was in English. He said he would manage. He seemed very confident. Carlos' dog had been prowling around the hangar looking angrily at me. I am not afraid of dogs, in fact I positively love them, but as I walked out of the hangar it took a nip out of the back of my leg. Was he rabid? The thought crossed my mind but I put it firmly behind me.

The Aeroclub of Rio Grande organised a barbecue in my honour. The Argentines cannot live without a barbecue at least once a week but in this part of the world, where the temperature never rises high enough to sit comfortably outside, they build barbecues indoors. At one end of the club house was a huge open fireplace with a barbecue grill. It was an evening of laughing and joking and I felt whipped up by the sense of fun and joviality. My Spanish was improving by the minute and I was able to pick up the gist of much of the banter around the table. When I looked lost someone translated for me and I had the greatest of times.

The next day Alex and Marcello from the tourist board drove me through heavy snow to the missionary school in Rio Grande where eleven to seventeen-year-olds are taught skills, predominantly associated with farming. An elderly man with a strong face came to meet us. Dressed in traditional baggy trousers called bombacha and huge boots or botas, Padre Tico led us into his office and gave us yerba mate, the Patagonian infusion made from local herbs. The drinking vessel is generally shaped like an hour glass without a handle. Padre Tico had a wonderful collection of mate containers, only surpassed by his repertoire of stories. I listened as I sipped the drink through a silver bombilla. I had been introduced to it in Ushuaia where at first I wondered if it was some form of drug. It was harmless but it did have a noticeably stimulating effect.

Soon Golf November's 150-hourly check was complete. Everyone was at the airport to see me off. I had spoken to Alejo Contreras who promised assistance in Punta Arenas, my next stop, and was expecting me. I had become increasingly anxious about the fuel for my ongoing flight to the Antarctic. Would it get to Punta Arenas and would Kenn Borek's aircraft take it on to Antarctica? Just at that moment though, I put my niggling fears behind me as I was engulfed in a whirl of friendliness and warmth. Golf November was gleaming in spite of the overcast skies. The snow that had fallen all the previous day when I visited the missionary school had stopped.

Several members of the Aeroclub accompanied me for the first fifteen miles and I glanced out to see a Cherokee Six on one side and an Archer on the other. Adrenalin flowing and every nerve on alert, we flew in close formation at 800 feet over the undulating snow-clad hills. Flying so close to other aircraft is thrilling as everyone's life depends on the skill of the others and there is no room for error. It was exhilarating as we skimmed over the snow and it was like dancing on air. It felt good to be alive, but soon there would be a more sinister cloud hanging over me.

"Good-bye Polly – good luck for your flight – we love you" came over the radio from the two aircraft and I watched them turn away and head back to Rio Grande. Alone once more I set off into the unknown. The temperature was -5°C and I was vigilant, watching for the first sign of ice building on the wings. The Magellan Strait lay before me and on the other side the airfield came in sight. It is situated about 15 km from the town of Punta Arenas on flat, open windy countryside. No-one seemed to be expecting me.

"Where was Alejo?," I wondered. "He couldn't have received my message." Eventually a man came out from the Ministry of Agriculture. He wanted to know if I had any food on board. He led me across the tarmac to the passport office. "Where are you going next," he enquired. "Antarctica," I replied, perhaps rather too glibly. "Oh no, you are NOT," he said emphatically. "That is not allowed in a single-engine aircraft." I held my council, greatly relieved that I had already planned to leave from Argentina where they were more liberal.

The previous year Q Smith and Steve Brooks had ditched in a Robinson R44 helicopter in the Drake Passage. They were rescued by a Chilean naval vessel. Episodes of this kind do not give the authorities a lot of confidence and do nothing to further the cause of light aviation in the Antarctic regions.

Somehow Alejo heard that I had arrived and sent a message that he would be there in twenty minutes. In the meantime Ramon, a swarthy dark-haired air traffic controller, invited me up to the tower – a rare opportunity to meet the guys at the other end of the 'mike'.

Every aircraft movement was recorded on a strip of stiff paper. They gave me my 'strip' to keep. They spoke in detail about the terrible time when Q and Steve went down. They were nervous about light aircraft flights to Antarctica and they kept telling me to be careful, which did nothing to improve my already stretched nerves.

Alejo (pronounced Al–lay–ho), arrived. What a character! He looked like Puck with his pointed red/grey beard and his twinkling eyes. Over the course of the next days I discovered that he ate raw conger eel and what he called 'vegetarian salad' which turned out to be a mound of uncooked ground beef with a raw egg floating on the top! His brain worked overtime as he continuously scurried around in top gear. He worked for DAP, a Chilean aviation company which runs aircraft down to the Antarctic. They fly mainly to King George Island. Alejo's brief was to help expeditions to Antarctica. A bundle of energy, he speaks faster than most people can think. He ran everywhere. I had never met anyone more positive. 'Everything is possible' is his motto.

It was not long before I would need a huge injection of his positive thinking. Alejo knew Art Morvedt, Max Wenden and Charles Swithinbank really well and had enlisted Art's help in monitoring Q and Steve's flight the day they ditched and I discovered that the memory of this near-fatal flight hung like a cloud over Punta Arenas.

The ghosts of the early explorers haunted the streets of this windy town on the Magellan Strait. Shackleton had been here. The thought of his expedition where his men ended up camping under upturned boats for four and a half months in below freezing temperatures filled me with horror. "How did they survive with very little to eat and nothing to warm them up day after day?" I kept

The MSR stove doubled as an engine heater which I regularly practised using so that I could quickly set it up in Antarctica.

thinking and felt glad that for me there was sponsorship available for the very best Antarctic equipment.

The fuel problem which had been niggling away constantly at the back of my mind, was now beginning to dominate my thoughts. Kenn Borek had changed their routing yet again. They were not now going into Sky Blu. When I had first spoken to them they were due to land on the ice runway at Patriot Hills, but they had changed their plan to go to the British airstrip at Sky Blu instead. Now Kenn Borek had changed back to Patriot Hills which would cause me all sorts of problems. Not only would it be more difficult to land there but I knew that it would be deserted until the end of November which was another six weeks away. This made me anxious. I was not physically strong enough to move full barrels of fuel on my own. Also it would be impossible to hand pump the fuel into my aircraft without help. It is a minimum two-person operation.

"How would I get Golf November started in the extreme cold even if I could manage to refuel her myself?" I thought, in spite of the fact I had a specially adapted engine heater and engine cover. Would it really be wise to go into such an inhospitable place totally unaided? The runway might be covered with uneven snowdrifts and there would be no-one there to indicate where the drifts were. Without skis in a light aircraft this could be fatal. I rang Maxo in New Zealand to ask his advice about Patriot Hills. What he said depressed me further. "It is positively dangerous for you to go there when no-one is around," he said. He was quite adamant that I should not attempt it but then he was always so concerned for my safety.

The Hotel Isla Rey Jorge in Punta Arenas is a mecca for Antarctic expeditions. There was a lot of bustle in the friendly entrance hall which resembled a sitting room with several arm chairs and piles of books. Børge Ousland, a Norwegian and Thomas Ulrich, a Swiss had just arrived back from crossing the Patagonian ice cap on foot. This was the first time this had been done and it was exciting to listen to their stories. I also met Paul Olai Olssen who had cycled from Patagonia to Alaska passing through the notorious Darian Gap. You never knew who you would meet next.

Alejo took me back to the airport where the Kenn Borek pilots had just arrived in their Twin Otters. Sean Louttit was in excellent spirits. "We will load your fuel for you, Polly. We will put two barrels in one aircraft and one in the other." What a star! Sean had not been that supportive at the meeting in Calgary with Steve Penikett. Sean too thought it was too dangerous for me to go into Patriot Hills on my own, which put me in a real quandary. He then said "The British Antarctic Survey is always sending aircraft up from Rothera to Sky Blu. I am sure they will put a barrel or two of fuel on board for you." He then added, "but I suppose it will depend on Cambridge." My heart sank.

"Should I speak to the base commander in Rothera or direct to BAS's headquarters in Cambridge?" I asked myself. "Or should I just ask Sean to deliver the fuel to Rothera regardless of having permission?" It was like playing Russian roulette. The last was not an option. All along I had played it 'by the book' and done everything 'up front'. It did not seem a good idea at this stage to start doing anything differently, although in retrospect it may have been the best way.

The Aeroclub had kindly put Golf November in their hangar. Some drops of oil appeared beneath the engine, running down the exhaust pipe. We took off the cowling but the leak eluded us. Panic! "What *could* be wrong?" Worried about the fuel and now the state of the aircraft I found tempting thoughts invading my mind, "The easiest thing would be to pack up and fly home. After all I can always have Golf November shipped back," that little voice went on. "I am not a quitter," I sternly knocked myself back into shape.

Jorge, the president of the Aeroclub, promised to get his engineer to look at Golf November the next day. As for the fuel situation, I decided to ask Peter's advice and he, in turn, asked his friends for a consensus of opinion. He was spending the evening with the Jordan Eleven, a group of friends who met during a vintage car rally in Jordan. They are all very capable people and Peter put the question to them as to whether I should speak to officialdom about my fuel. It was generally agreed that I should do so, which just reinforced what I was thinking. "After all," said Bernard, a highly experienced and successful business man, "they are human, and all they want is your safety and well being. They will be excited about what you are doing and want to help."

Sleep was becoming increasingly difficult. I woke several times in the night with all the problems churning around in my head. I tried all the methods of relaxation I could think of, but nothing seemed to relieve the tension which had built up. It was a constant tussle. "You can cope with much more than this," I chided myself. The morning finally came and I caught the early bus to the airport. Using my mobile phone, I spoke to the Rothera station commander who, as it turned out, was in the Falkland Islands. When asked about whether BAS could help getting fuel to Sky Blue, his reply was, "My instinct is to say 'no', but I will speak to Cambridge." It was just as Sean had predicted.

"If it had been two years ago it would have been easy, but we have such a lot of fuel to transport ourselves," the station commander went on. I explained about Patriot Hills and about how difficult it would be to go in there without any support. He was immovable. "Why can't people take decisions on their own," I asked myself, "without always having to refer it to someone else – where is the initiative these days?" I was feeling belligerent.

Taking the 'bull by the horns' I rang Cambridge. In retrospect it was a hasty decision. I was harangued with a third degree questioning as if I was a naughty schoolgirl. I tried to defend myself by pointing out that I had done everything 'above board' and that I was ringing for some advice and asking for their help. "We will have to take this to a higher level," was the curt response. "Oh dear!" I thought, tears welling up. "The Jordan Eleven and my instincts weren't right this time."

The iron grip was tightening. It was like being a fish out of water, I didn't know which way to turn for the best. I felt cross. I vented my anger to myself. "Where is the spirit of adventure, pride in our country – why are there always people trying to stop me doing something?"

On the surface I kept control and took a command decision. "I will get Kenn Borek to take the fuel to Rothera and if BAS won't move it on for me, I'll route direct to McMurdo and just miss going over the Pole. It will be a compromise, but at least I will be able to get across." Immediately things felt better. "After all, I have enough fuel in McMurdo to fly back to the Pole and then return to McMurdo." I remembered the eight barrels sitting at Scott Base just three km away from McMurdo.

A number of appointments were lined up for the following day. The engineer was due to look at the oil leak and various television and media interviews were arranged. The wind was howling across the airfield. Sitting in the cold hangar reading my book, I was beginning to freeze to the bone. Again the feeling of self pity was all enveloping like a cold damp fog. I wanted to be alone. It is always the easy way out to sit quietly and muse on problems on one's own. But it wasn't to be. A whole group of people insisted I join them in the smart new airport canteen. A wonderful sound filled the air and I stood up and looked over the balcony. There was a large group of children singing their hearts out. Two adults were playing guitars, all were wearing national costume. How incongruous it seemed compared to the mounting problems. It helped me come to grips with myself and I set to work on trying to create a way through the maze of obstacles. Then journalists, photographers and translators arrived and I realised I was going to have to put on a smile and pretend everything was fine. After all, the entire purpose of the flight was to promote flying for the disabled, and I wasn't going to let them down.

Time means nothing in southern Chile.

Bouncing down the stairs of the hangar, I did the interviews and posed for the photographers, a broad grin fixed permanently on my face. "The engineer will come exactly at six," were Alejo's very words, but the engineer had his own agenda and didn't turn up until 1845. I had been at the airport for ten hours and was frozen to the marrow.

"They haven't tightened the screws enough after the 150-hour check," was the engineer's diagnosis. He set about rectifying the problem in a methodical way, checking, tightening all the way round. He seemed to know what he was doing and had apparently fixed the problem. Not being an engineer I trusted him implicitly.

Back in town at last, I had a quick wash and change and walked across the square to a very smart hotel where I was the guest of honour at a special dinner. Everyone was waiting and sipping their Pisco sours, the lethal Chilean national drink. I decided to splash out and join them. The drink very soon took effect. People were laughing and giggling. Jorge from the Aeroclub and John, the British Consul, own the hotel which used to be a private house where Shackleton was a guest. John is a cellist so we chatted about music. The dinner was delicious and provided a panacea from the tensions of the day.

At 0730 the next morning the phone in my room rang. It was Sean Louttit. "Sorry Polly, but I had an e-mail last night from Steve Penikett to say that we couldn't after all take your fuel, even to Rothera." Why had Steve so suddenly changed his mind? It was he who offered to transport the fuel in the first place and he was reneging at the eleventh hour. I asked Sean why there was this sudden change.

"The British Antarctic Survey has contacted the Americans, the Australians and the Italians," he said. "How can anyone be so actively destructive in such a short time?" I thought. So in desperation I rang Peter.

"Leave it with me." He always exuded such confidence. I rang off and sat numbed on the edge of my bed. It was like awaiting a death sentence. Soon Peter rang back to say that the decision had been rescinded. I rang Sean to tell him but all he said was, "I will need it in writing."

"How much more?" I moaned to myself as I rang Peter once more. As a result of his efforts, the following fax was sent from the British Antarctic Survey at Cambridge:

When my fuel was left behind, I had just enough avgas to make one attempt to get across the continent of Antarctica by a new direct route to McMurdo.

Further to our telephone call today.

Last year BAS agreed to store a small qty of drummed avgas at Rothera for Polly Vacher "Wings Around the World." Two drums of Avgas are already at Rothera. We/you did not specify how this fuel would be delivered to Rothera. On the of this (sic) existing agreement BAS will accommodate a few more drums for your (exclusive) use at Rothera. We note your intention to deliver this using Kenn Borek Twin Otters currently in Punta Arenas.

You should note that the agreement for the ferry routing these Twin Otters through Rothera is between BAS and the chartering National Programmes – USAP AAD & ENEA, not with Kenn Borek.

You can see therefore that it is not for BAS to agree/disagree to these aircraft carrying your fuel. This is a matter for Borek, yourself and the charterers to resolve. So contrary to my message of yesterday BAS will accept this fuel at Rothera, but as discussed BAS are unable to move this fuel onwards from Rothera to a deep field fuel cache.

Alejo came to the rescue. We took a taxi to the airport as fast as we could. The crews were already in the aircraft. On the ground were my three barrels of fuel. "What is happening?" I cried in desperation. Sean was sitting in the cockpit deep in conversation on his satellite phone to Steve Penikett in Calgary. Eventually he waved at me and yelled from the window that they were not going to take the fuel. Standing in the cold and wind, I watched the aircraft taxi out leaving the fuel like three sentinels standing on the tarmac alone. There was a sinking feeling in my stomach and tears welled up. I was numb.

"I made a mistake, I should have just let the fuel go down there and talked about it afterwards," I moaned to myself. I had been afraid that if they suddenly found three extra fuel drums turn up there they might have refused me permission to land.

I argued again to myself, "My way of doing things is to be up front and honest – that was why I went through all the correct channels." I had taken advice from the Jordan Eleven whose integrity I completely trusted. But I'd been thwarted. Alejo came up. "You WILL do it, Polly, there is ALWAYS a way," he firmly said.

What comforting words, but I was sorely wounded and they no longer rang true. The ongoing ripples would have a profound effect on the whole project. I made myself eat some lunch. Having had no breakfast I knew that I must keep my strength up. I went for a walk to try to come to terms with my emotions. It was windy and it started to rain. Fighting depression I tried to reason with my anger, frustration and desire for revenge. An evil voice inside whispered, "You can just tell the newspapers – give them a press release – BRITISH ANTARCTIC SURVEY STOPS BRITISH ROUND-THE-WORLD CHARITY PILOT." But what was the point? It would only be me and the charity that would be damaged.

I was reading a book about Alaskan bush pilots and as I fell into bed I read *"George left us with a record of quiet courage and faith in ourselves. When things were strange he would say 'don't be afraid of it'. When the problem seemed impossible he would say 'stick with it boy. You will win.'* I gained courage and fell into an exhausted sleep.

The following morning I rang Steve Penikett. "What are you doing down there? – you have started a bloody war," were his opening words. I told him that I was ringing to apologise if I had inadvertently got him into a tricky situation to which he responded, "It wasn't that – this thing started a couple of weeks ago. The National Science Foundation saw that you had put on your website that we were carrying fuel for you and were mad."

In fact the only mention on the website was 'Kenn Borek – logistical support' which could mean anything from giving me hangarage in the Arctic to checking my spark plugs after my Polar crossing. He told me that Raytheon, who were the main contractors for the Americans, were ringing him every half hour to tell him that NSF was upset. When Steve offered to ring NSF Raytheon said "no – don't ring – they are not in the mood for that." "They are just a bunch of schoolboys and just bloody bureaucrats," he continued. "They are threatening to put me on some sort of blacklist if I carry your fuel." It was hard to know who to believe or which way to turn. Everything seemed black and depressing.

Sir Ranulph Fiennes (Ran) and Mike Stroud arrived the same day. They were about to run seven marathons in seven days on seven continents. Ran had had a heart bypass operation just six months previously and he was well into his sixties. One marathon is usually enough to finish most people, but here was someone planning to take it to the furthest limits and to travel around the world to do it. Unbelievable! Ran and Mike were staying in my hotel. As usual Alejo was helping, organising the first marathon to be run on King George Island in Antarctica.

It was a joy to meet them. Ran is one of those rare people who is both captivating and a good listener. He makes you feel that you are the only person in the world. He and Mike too were having their problems. The weather was poor in Antarctica and their flight was cancelled. It was put off the next day too and we all pored over maps trying to find a way out for them. In the end they had to resort to running the first marathon on the Falklands.

At last the weather was good enough for my flight back to Ushuaia. I had done some calculations and with careful fuel management and some luck I could still fly across the Antarctic continent. There was now no point in prolonging my stay in Punta Arenas.

The southern end of the Andes had to be crossed. The weather was closing in as another front approached. The forecaster in Punta Arenas told me to hurry as the front was approaching fast. With a minimum safe altitude of 14,000 ft I did not want to run into cloud and pick up ice. It was hair-

I met Sir Rannulph Fiennes and Mike Stroud in Punta Arenas when they were waiting to run the first of their seven marathons in seven days on seven continents.

raising as I climbed up over the icy Magellan Strait and set course towards the mountains and Ushuaia. On reaching 14,000 ft the outside air temperature was -26° C. I levelled off and tried to pull back the propeller into a coarser pitch but it was stuck in fine pitch.

"It must be the temperature," I reasoned, and on giving the propeller lever a hefty yank, it moved. What a relief! "If this happens here what will happen in Antarctica?" I pondered. Was everything stacking against me? What else was there to go wrong? I made a note to exercise the propeller frequently during the climb.

Huge cumulus clouds built up. It was impossible to avoid going into them. It was like flying into a big black wall which suddenly hits you. All is grey around you and you feel as if you are surrounded by cotton wool. At -26°C it should be too cold to pick up any ice, but a little stuck to the wings adding to my concerns. I shivered at the thought of an engine failure over the sharp Patagonian peaks. There would be nowhere to land safely. My mind was working overtime trying to monitor everything and make sure that nothing *did* go wrong. The views between the clouds of huge fiords, glaciers and snow-covered mountain peaks were spectacular, but I was too busy to care and the forty-five minute flight seemed endless. Finally, I caught a glimpse of the Beagle Channel through the clouds and decided to spiral down directly to the airport. This was a calculated risk. The clouds could have closed up and obliterated the airport from view, but on the other hand I could have run into fatal icing conditions whilst flying the long published approach. It was exhilarating shooting down between huge mountains and vast clouds with the blue sea of the channel stretching in front. It was a risk which worked and after what seemed like an interminable amount of spirals, I was able to join downwind to land.

The warmth of the Aeroclub Ushuaia beckoned as members stood outside to await my arrival. The hangar doors were open – Golf November and I were made welcome. The relief and joy at seeing so many friends was overwhelming.

CHAPTER 15

Patience Tested

Taxis are the main form of transport in Ushuaia. There are 250 of them but none without a multitude of cracks across the windscreen. Many of the roads are still dirt tracks and the stones chip the windscreen. There is no such thing as 'health and safety' or an MOT down this far south. Most people walk down the hill into the town to do their shopping and then take a taxi back. No ride costs more than 50p.

Ushuaia sits on the slopes of the Southern Andes, overlooking the Beagle Channel. The tiny dwellings are all higgledy piggledy, and many are so small they resemble dolls' houses. Each house has at least one dog outside and the incessant barking both day and night echoes around the mountains. Icicles hang on the branches of the pine trees growing on the mountain side and there is a gentle dripping as the snow melts. Huge cumulus clouds move across the sky and a watery sun peeps out whenever there is a gap. It is known as the town at the end of the world and it certainly feels like that. I felt a huge sense of freedom. On the other side of the Beagle Channel are the mountains of Chile and Cape Horn. The only inhabitants live in a village called Puerto Williams and the occasional military outpost. It is desolate.

Yachts come and go in the Beagle Channel and congregate at the quay in Ushuaia. The camaraderie amongst the 'yachties' is overwhelming. Generally they lead solitary lives battling against the elements in their tiny floating homes at the mercy of the winds and waves. They help each other repair their boats and exchange stories of their adventures at sea. Jonathan, Roxanna and Gabriela are at the heart of the yachting community and took me under their wings once again.

"You must meet our friends Keri and Greg," Roxanna enthused. "You will love them," and I did. Keri is a fiery fair-haired energetic Canadian. Greg is a contrasting tall, bearded silent 'kiwi'. They are serious 'yachties'. They live on their boat *Northanger*, and one year wintered over near Ellesmere Island in northern Canada, stuck fast in the sea ice. I tried to imagine what it would have been like knowing that there was no way out from the ice for at least six months. Each day they had to dig the ice away from the edge of the yacht to prevent it being crushed.

We loaded a taxi with my things and went up the hill to the cabañas that Lito Fank, an Aeroclub member had built in the woods. I settled myself in and tried to keep positive in spite of all that had happened in the last week. Every day I walked out of the woods from my cabaña and I looked down the mountain to the Beagle Channel and across towards Cape Horn, wondering what it was like over there.

I hired a little beaten-up Daewoo car and took Jonathan, Roxanna and Gabriela for the eighty-two-mile drive to Harberton as I wanted to say 'thank you' for all that they had done to help me. I had met Tommy Goodall, Harberton's owner, when I first arrived and he had kindly acted as translator. Harberton was of particular interest to me as it was named after a village in Devon near where I lived as a child. It is a huge Estancia (estate) on the edge of the Beagle Channel and is like a small village with a dirt road running between the buildings. It initially belonged to Tom Bridges, so named because he was abandoned as a baby on a bridge in Bristol. He was wearing a shirt with a 'T' embroidered on the front, so the nurses at the orphanage named him Tom. As he was found on a bridge they gave him the surname of Bridges. Tom Bridges was soon adopted by a missionary. He and his wife took Tom to Patagonia where they encountered the Yamana people (pronounced Shamana). As at first the Yamana were hostile, the family retreated to the Falklands but took three Yamana people with them. Tom grew up to speak the Yamana language and compiled the first Yamana/English dictionary.

Near Harberton on the Beagle Channel; the trees are moulded into shape by the prevailing winds.

The drive took us up into the Andes and then onto a dirt road which wove through wooded hills and along the edge of spectacular lakes. Trees that had been blown by the prevailing wind into funny shapes looked like ballerinas leaning effortlessly from the waist at right angles. We just had to stop the car so that we could get out and take some photos. Beavers had been busy felling trees and destroying large swathes of woodland and I learned that the species was introduced by the British and had been wreaking havoc for years. They have no predators, apart from man, in Patagonia where beaver features large on all the menus.

The drive over rough terrain took us three hours but it was worth it. Tom gave us a warm welcome and gave us a tour of the Estancia. We ate a picnic at the water's edge and sipped coffee listening to Tom's fund of stories. They have no telephone in this remote spot and their only contact with the outside world is by HF radio.

Back at the Aeroclub I decided to check over the aircraft with Pilu, one of the instructors there. The oil was still leaking but Pilu reckoned he could fix it. Out came his spanners and he tightened the gaskets even more. I smiled weakly but by this time I didn't believe that anyone would be able to repair the leak. I was still reeling from the shock of my fuel being left behind in Punta Arenas and I felt vulnerable.

We pulled Golf November out of the hangar and did a twenty-minute engine run. After we switched off and put her back in the hangar we took off the cowling and there was a mass of oil leaking all over the engine compartment. "I daren't go to Antarctica with this oil leak," I thought. "It is not exactly like flying up to Manchester, I shall be over the most dangerous stretch of water in the world and once in Antarctica who can repair my engine there?" I called Peter in Australia. "I'm coming over," he said, and I felt a surge of relief.

The cabañā in the woods, belonging to Lito, was like something from fairyland.

It took Peter forty-eight hours to reach Ushuaia from Sydney. He routed via Los Angeles, Miami, Buenos Aires and finally to Ushuaia. I sat at the airport watching every passenger as they walked out, scanning, scrutinising, searching. Then, there he was! It was like the first time I had set eyes on him thirty-eight years earlier. I was a student then, and I never could believe that he would fall in love with me. This handsome man reassuringly appeared when I most needed him just as I had been wondering whether I would *ever* see him again. The joy of seeing him was unbelievable. We had so much to catch up on as we took the taxi up the hill to our cabaña.

Suddenly, the woods became alive and our little cabaña sparkled with warmth and light. It resembled paradise as I began to relax, knowing that I had someone with whom to share my problems and who made me feel secure. The stove burned furiously in the centre, heating the living room and kitchenette and the pretty bedroom on the balcony above. This was spring, but snow still lay thickly on the

Andes behind and the trees dripped and hung with icicles. It was like fairyland with the bright red bunches of *Cytaria Darwinii* on the trees. They resembled coloured oak apples and are known as *Pan de Indio* (Indian's bread), so called because Indians used to eat them. We felt snug in our little nest and I was happy once more.

The following morning we went to the Aeroclub. The hangar with the huge penguin painted on the side loomed in front and the yachts rose and fell gently clanking on their moorings. Little houses nestled against the hillside overlooking the lagoon formed by the causeway. Pilu was there to greet us and I introduced Peter to this bubbly man and the others at the Aeroclub which was fast becoming my second home.

Peter had come well equipped with spanners and overalls. He took one look at the gaskets and immediately pinpointed the problem. He replaced the gaskets which had been distorted by over-tightening, nipping them up just enough but not too much. Within a couple of hours we were able to roll Golf November out of the hangar and perform another engine run. We waited with baited breath. Not a sign of any oil. It was so simple, yet the problem had seemed insurmountable just a few days ago. I felt guilty at having made him travel so far, but I knew I could never have set off across that treacherous stretch of water with an oil leak.

Peter said he would stay until I left for Antarctica. I never wanted to force him to stay, but when he offered I wasn't the one to dissuade him. We settled down into a semblance of routine. I had daily Spanish lessons with Roxanna. She was a wonderful teacher, so patient. I really enjoyed the challenge, but my mind was not fully on the job. I was forever slightly twitchy, waiting for the green light to go, so every day we made our way down to the internet café. There were rows of telephone booths where one could make a call quite cheaply and pay afterwards. It was by far the easiest way. And every day I called Jeppesen meteorology department. This had gone on for three weeks and I was getting used to the negative responses to my call. But one day things changed.

"There's a small window of opportunity tomorrow," said Bill, forever the optimist, "Yes, between 0600Z and 1800Z." However, this created another problem. Z stands for Zulu or Greenwich Mean Time. 0600Z equates to 0300 hours on Argentine time. I couldn't imagine setting off on this the most difficult flight of my life in the dark. My heart sank, yet it also rejoiced. The longer the waiting had gone on, the more difficult it had become to stay motivated to go. Ushuaia was too comfortable. The window did not materialise and it was to be just the first of many false alarms.

A few days later, it was a nice sunny morning again. "Could this be the day?" I wondered. We rushed down to the telefonica. I spoke to Brad this time.

"Yes – you could go today or tomorrow," he said. I wondered whether this would be yet another false alarm, all the same we spent the day preparing. All the clothes needed washing and drying. We took a huge box of chocolates to the Aeroclub as a thank you and rang Jeppesen again in the evening. This time it was Bob. "Oh dear, I don't think the weather looks so good for tomorrow after all. There is a lot of low cloud and icing conditions." I felt completely deflated. Would I ever get that evasive good weather window?

There are three weather systems which would influence this leg of my flight. One over Patagonia (southern Argentina and Chile), one over the Drake Passage and one over the Antarctic peninsula. It was imperative that all three weather systems coincided and there were clear skies all the way. Because of the treacherous weather conditions in this part of the world, and because it was crucial to get as much weather information as possible, the Argentine Air Force were also monitoring the weather for me. Roxanna acted as interpreter and they confirmed the most recent Jeppesen weather report on the phone to her.

I was sure that it would be that day, but I was out of luck again and so I tried to forget about the weather and Antarctica, of the necessity of packing and of waiting on tenterhooks thinking 'maybe tomorrow'. We set off for Harberton as I really wanted to share the beauty of this lovely place with Peter. It was an enthralling drive as over the few weeks since my last trip there everything had

These bright bunches of *Cytaria Darwinii* or 'Indian's bread' added contrast to the snow and ice.

changed. There was less snow and the leaves were coming out on the trees. When we reached the trees blown into funny shapes and stopped the car, Peter said, "Where's the camera Polly?" "On the back seat under my coat," I replied. Peter said in a very strange voice, "Polly that's not my camera - that's my electric razor."

We both looked at each other and burst into fits of laughter. I laughed so much that tears ran down my eyes. I just couldn't stop laughing. The idea of picking up the razor instead of the camera was bizarre. All the tensions of the past few weeks seemed to slip away and I giggled to myself all the way to Harberton.

We had a wonderful day and even took a boat trip to an island in the middle of the Beagle Channel to see the Magellan penguins. There were a couple of scientists tagging them. We looked for the more elusive Gentoo penguins, but were not so lucky. It is amazing to think that there are sixteen different species of penguin and only four types actually live on the Antarctic continent.

On returning to Ushuaia we made another call to Jeppesen. "You took the right decision," Mike assured me. "How are you holding out psychologically?" That nearly cracked me up, they had all become such special friends. Any hint of sympathy was the most difficult to deal with. I gritted my teeth and told him that I was fine and it was great to have Peter with me.

"This is not a suicide mission," I explained, "I will just wait for as long as it takes," sounding much more positive than I really felt. A few days later I heard those magic words, "We think you can go tomorrow – the weather is looking just right – well apart from Rothera." It was Steve at Jeppesen.

I was beginning to wonder whether I would ever get that clear weather window to cross Drake Passage. To get all three weather systems coinciding is a rare event. Here was the old familiar story – it was alright for two out of the three. Would the third fall into line? I rang Rothera and asked if they minded if Jeppesen liaised with them so that I could get the best weather reporting possible. It was agreed that Steve from Jeppesen could speak to Judith, the forecaster in Rothera.

In the meantime Alejo rang. "You must ring Rachel Shepherd in Punta Arenas," he said. "I have organized the fuel for you – Paul will fly it into Sky Blu – also you must ring Morag Howell in Canada." His Chilean accent reverberated down the phone. It was a comfort to know that he was trying so hard to help. I rang Rachel from Antarctic Logistics and Expeditions, the company which had taken over from Adventure Network International. I had a curt response.

"Alejo is always trying to help everyone," she said. I couldn't resist saying, "I hope that is what you are about too," which perhaps was hardly the best way to handle her. I had already had an e-mail from the new director of ALE saying that he would not help me without incorporating his full service which cost $300,000.

"I am not a fuel bowser," were the very words in his e-mail. I understood where he was coming from, but I was sure that I had done nothing to upset him. I rang Morag Howell in Canada. She was both pleasant and kind. She understood the predicament that I was in. She said that all her pilots and engineers would do everything they could to help me. However she told me that her aircraft were contracted to ALE and she could not say they would carry fuel for me without it being sanctioned by them. Antarctica was like a closed shop.

I then had another shock. It had seemed a good idea for Jeppesen to liaise with the forecaster in Rothera in order to gain the very best forecast possible for crossing the Drake Passage. I had a phone call from Steve at Jeppesen. He had contacted Rothera who gave him their forecast but then told him that as they were a government organization they did not want Jeppesen ringing them again. They would speak to Polly but to no-one else. This would mean that to get a forecast I would have to first ring Rothera and then relay it to Jeppesen. All this despite the fact that Jeppesen contract with the British Antarctic Survey to design and publish the landing charts for Rothera, and for all the other countries' bases in Antarctica!

The Argentine Air Force meantime had been supporting me when and wherever they could. Comodoro Jorge Reta ('call me George') was behind it all. Regular weather briefings were provided by them. I asked Jorge about going in to Marambio, the Argentine base on the north east coast of the peninsula.

"That would be wonderful. We really *would* like you to come in anyway," he said. "We are hoping that you can spend Christmas in Marambio, they will make you really welcome." Their hospitality was overwhelming. Jorge went on to say that he had organized for the air force to follow my flights and to provide search and rescue facilities. This was marvellous as the Kenn Borek pilots had already left for Antarctica and I could not afford the services of ALE.

So many people were trying to help find a way to transport fuel into Patriot Hills for me, which was the obvious place to go. Now that I had been held up for so long, there would be people there to help with the re-fuelling. It was just a question of finding someone to take it in. It was sad that I was not allowed to buy a couple of barrels from ALE even though they had a cache of fuel there. I could understand them not wanting to deplete their stocks but two barrels was not excessive. For me to be able to make the extra stop would ensure a safe flight across the continent, but it was not to be.

CHAPTER 16

Solo into Antarctica

I had been stuck in Ushuaia for nearly five weeks when it seemed as if something favourable might be happening with the weather at last. Yet now that it looked as though I would be flying tomorrow or the day after, rather than some indefinable time in the future, I was reluctant to leave.

Peter and I had settled into this small close knit community and had made many friends. We had become familiar with the little streets as we walked down the mountain to the centre of the town to do our shopping and make our phone calls. We never walked down the main street without bumping into someone we knew and we became accustomed to the quaint little shops and the church which towered above the other buildings and was a focal point for this still very Catholic community. Our cabaña had become our simple home and the Aeroclub and Yacht Club were places we gravitated towards. Always there was a welcome and a cup of mate on hand.

Suddenly flying over Cape Horn to Antarctica was no longer an idea but a route on a map that would, in the space of hours or days, become sea and rock, ice and snow beneath my wings. It was mid November and I rang Rothera. With a great deal of persuasion I managed to get an approximate forecast. "We are busy with a Dash 7 coming in – ring later," she said. I rang later.

"Do you have a forecast for tomorrow?" I enquired. "Sorry I can't give you a forecast until the day," she replied. "Can you give me some idea," I persisted. "It looks OK in the morning but there is a moist westerly flow coming in," she grudgingly admitted. "Can I ring you in the morning?" "We are busy until 0850," she replied.

"But I need to leave way before that, please can I speak to you earlier," I requested. It hardly seemed unreasonable considering that I was going to fly over one of the most dangerous stretches of water in the world. I needed as much weather information as I could get. "No, I am busy with briefings until 0850. You don't seem to realise that I get up every day at 0530." If they were up at that time, what was the problem with me ringing earlier? These were my people from my own country! I gave up.

I rang Jeppesen. There was Mike's cheery voice on the end of the phone. "Talk of the Devil," he said with a laugh. "I felt my ears burning!" I replied jokingly. "Oh no – it was nice I assure you," Mike went on. "The weather looks good for tomorrow. You will be best to fly at 5,000 ft as the winds are better lower down. You will only have a 15 kts headwind whereas at 10,000 ft it may go up to 20 kts or more. It should be improving in Ushuaia and if we can get a good forecast from Rothera – oh well it looks good there too – do they realise they are dealing with a British citizen?" he half joked, but I felt embarrassed.

It was time to go. Imagine taking off from Ushuaia. The runway runs along an isthmus and the water from the Beagle Channel laps at the sides. The Aeroclub is sandwiched between two hangars alongside the edge of the taxiway looking out onto the Beagle Channel. The runway leads straight into a hill dominated by the control tower. It is from there that traffic is directed either to the main airport or the old one on which the Aeroclub and Golf November now stood.

"Suppose Golf November is too heavy to take off before she hits the hill." I was worrying again. The aircraft was fully loaded with as much fuel as it could carry. As a result of my barrels being left in Punta Arenas I only had one chance to fly from Rothera to McMurdo. The fuel had to be gauged carefully. It was essential to arrive at Rothera with as much unused fuel as possible, having only two barrels (400 litres) there to top up the tanks before crossing the Antarctic continent. The most dangerous moment of a long distance flight is take-off when the aircraft is fully laden. If the runway is slightly short or there is a strong cross wind, it heightens the risk.

The stiff zips of my immersion suit were fully secured. There would have been no time to put the suit on in the event of an engine failure. Wearing layers of warm clothes under my immersion suit and life-jacket, it was difficult to walk without a definite sideways gait. I gave Peter a last clinging hug and clambered into Golf November with a heavy heart and butterflies rampaging in my stomach. The waters of the Drake Passage are freezing and I would need as much insulation as possible should I have to ditch. I attached my life-raft to my suit. If anything were to happen I was going to give myself every chance to survive. Peter had checked every detail on the aircraft. She was in excellent condition and now that the oil leak had been cured I was happy.

It was the most difficult thing to say good-bye to Peter. He was and is my 'rock' and going to Antarctica was a risky business no matter how well one prepares. I wanted to cling onto him and not let him go, but I had resolutely turned and almost callously dragged myself away.

Would this be the last time I ever saw him? It was like going to the gallows. I glanced at the windsock which was blowing straight across the runway. This would mean a cross wind take-off, the very worst scenario for a fully laden aircraft. Without help from the wind, Golf November roared along the runway. Suddenly her nose reared up and we were airborne and passing the hill with the control tower just underneath my wings. As I felt a surge of relief I was trembling.

Climbing above the airport at Ushuaia I circled to gain enough height to cross the mountains. Peter had walked to the end of the runway because he wanted to see how much distance I used taking off with maximum fuel on board and a crosswind. He wanted to be able to tell me precisely the length I had taken as this was the worst scenario that could occur in the Antarctic. I looked down and I could see a lone figure on the end of the runway as Golf November climbed further and further away. He huddled in his anorak as it was cold and windy, but I also detected another reason for his huddle and it tore my heart apart. A sinking feeling overwhelmed me as the reality of what I was doing began to dawn on me.

What was I doing to this wonderful marriage of mine? Was I throwing away all that had been most dear to me? How would Peter and the boys manage without me? Would I miss Julian and Amanda's wedding? How would they feel on their wedding day if something had happened to me? It was hard not to turn back, but this wasn't an option open to me as it would be suicide to land back overweight with so much fuel on board. The best cure was to keep busy and flying over treacherous seas with only one engine certainly concentrated the mind. I turned south and waggled my wings in farewell to Peter. It was like cutting the umbilical chord.

Alone in the cockpit I tend to shout instructions out loud. "Concentrate on what you are doing," I kept telling myself forcefully. Any mistake could be fatal. This is what kept my desperate thoughts at bay, and thanks to my fifth 'giant', Jonathan Selby, Peter was able to spend the day on his yacht *Anahera* and speak to me on the HF radio every hour. It was a comfort to hear his voice. He always sounded so calm, so in control.

It was an ideal day. The few clouds sitting over the Beagle Channel soon dispersed to expose the mountains and islands forming Cape Horn. It was desolate, but the sunshine added a benign feeling to what is usually a hostile stretch of water. After Cape Horn, it was clear for miles, there was just pale blue sky and slightly darker sea stretching out over the horizon. There were no signs of human existence, and despite the contact with Peter I felt very alone.

I settled down to a long distance hourly routine which included giving a position report, checking temperatures and pressures, doing exercises to prevent deep vein thrombosis, logging details for the two PhD students, nibbling a muesli bar and sipping water. I tried to banish the 'what ifs'. Levelling off at 5,000 ft, the winds were exactly as forecast. There was still the possibility of fog engulfing Rothera, so I was keen to get there as soon as I could. At 65% power to conserve fuel, with a 15 kts wind on the nose, the best I could manage was 99 kts of groundspeed. It seemed painfully slow. Every drop of fuel was critical so I kept recalculating like crazy, trying to work out the best power setting to gain the fastest speed using the least amount of fuel.

A massive tabular iceberg came in sight. It was blue grey in colour with sides like giant cliffs. What utter beauty! It floated by like a huge iced cake sitting on a blue tablecloth. Every hour I spoke to the Argentine base at Marambio on the Antarctic Peninsula, giving them my exact position. The Argentines monitored the whole flight, along with Jonathan and Peter. After a few hours I could see the peninsula in the distance on the port side. It looked spectacular. Tall snow-covered mountains rose steeply out of the blue sea. Antarctica, that focus of so much planning, so many dreams was before me and whatever lay ahead, for the present it was a moment of sheer elation.

My first sight of an iceberg in the Drake Passage en route to Antarctica.

After eight hours Adelaide Island came into sight with what looked like a lot of pack ice surrounding it. As I flew nearer I realized that it was the island itself which was very flat on the western side, but on the eastern side the mountains rose steeply. The crystal clear blue of the sea contrasted with the brilliance of the pristine white snow sparkling in the sunshine. Large icebergs floated nonchalantly around. There was no evidence of anything human. I felt so very small.

Golf November and I flew around the mountain hugging its slopes and wondering at the sheer beauty and majesty. There, at last was Rothera's grey runway stretching in the distance. Once more I had the sensation of skiing down the mountainside as I made a quick descent towards the strip. I could see patches of blue sea with the remains of pack ice and hundreds of icebergs. The whole scene looked like whipped up icing on a cake, the bergs being all different shapes and sizes.

Golf November settled gently on the gravel. A crowd of people were standing outside the buildings watching. The base commander and a couple of pilots and engineers were ready to help me park and tie her down. Even though the weather was clear and calm, the wind could suddenly pick up into a gale and I hoped they would fit Golf November in a corner of the hangar, as the winds here could be so strong that the aircraft might be flipped over like a feather no matter how firmly she was tied down.

Sue, the only woman pilot, showed me to my room. She had kindly made my bed before I arrived. The room had four bunks, but I had it to myself. I made contact with Bob from Jeppesen on my satellite phone. The next flight would be the big one with a distance of 1859 nm to cover to McMurdo. "There is no way that you can fly tomorrow with *your* headwind limitations." Bob was emphatic.

I was glad as I was tired after the day's flight. It had been a wonderful experience and there had been some fantastic sights. The anxiety about the fuel and leaving Peter had taken its toll. I settled down to sleep. It was broad daylight outside. The silence was deafening. There were no traffic sounds, no people sounds and the wildlife was quiet. I had to pinch myself to be sure I really was there.

Rod, the base manager called me into his office the next day. "Please don't feel any pressure to move on from here," he emphasized whilst giving me a general introduction to the base. I felt relieved. I really had no intention of moving on until there was assurance of favourable weather, but it was generous of him to say that and it made me feel welcome. I went up to speak to Andy and Heath in the tower. They had monitored my flight across the Drake Passage. They said my arrival was a great occasion. "We have never had such a small aircraft here before. It was difficult to spot you coming round the mountain." I realised then that all those people standing outside really were there to await my arrival. I felt pleased and began to feel at home.

During the ensuing days I found my way around the base and acclimatised myself to life in the Antarctic. Jane, the doctor, took me for a walk around the point. We sat on a rock overlooking the ice with seals dotted aimlessly on the surface, looking like boulders or logs – motionless. In the silence, she told me how sixteen people had wintered over at the base. We sipped hot tea from her flask. They had had a terrible time. One of the female scientists, Kirsty, was taken by a leopard seal whilst diving as part of her research. Her death cast a dreadful shadow over them all. I could imagine that lithe creature creeping up behind and with a momentary flick pulling her down under the water. "It took a while to beat off the seal with paddles from the boat," Jane continued. "We brought her into the surgery and for an hour we tried to resuscitate her. As the minutes ticked by I knew it was hopeless, but we had to try."

The Antarctic is not to be trifled with. It is harsh and unforgiving, although immensely beautiful. Ice and yet more ice, this is Antarctica. The ice shimmers and shines in the brilliant sun. The deep blue of the open water and the pale blue of the sky contrasts with the white of the snow-covered mountains and floating icebergs. It all seemed so innocuous and it was hard to imagine that death waits around every corner especially for the careless or incautious.

I cast my mind back to when I was flying in on final approach. The icebergs surrounded the

Appearing round the mountain approaching Rothera in Antarctica for the first time...

A little closer to Rothera...

runway which ran out into the sea. They look benign, but they have claimed lives. A couple of years earlier an aircraft had taken off when an iceberg had drifted across the end of the runway. It could not gain enough height and crashed straight into the berg, killing all on board. Since then there is always a rescue boat in the water during any aircraft movement. It was a salutary thought.

On the hill above the base was a seat overlooking the sea. By the seat were a few crosses in memory of those who had died, one for the aircraft crew and one for the three men who had floated away on an ice floe, never to be seen again. I trembled at the thought. Soon the memory of Kirsty too would be immortalised there.

I developed a really bad headache due to dehydration. Little had I realized that Antarctica is so dry. Your skin feels dry and your hair is full of electricity, your urine turns a nasty colour. You are supposed to drink a lot but this is far more difficult than in hot countries because the cold suppresses the inclination to drink. I found the central heating oppressive but if I opened the window I had to turn off the heat in my room and it became freezing cold in moments.

I settled down for what could be another long wait for the right flying weather. Household manager, Rod (yes, another Rod) asked me to take part in GASH duty which entails clearing the meal tables, washing up, cleaning the loos and the living accommodation. Everyone takes their turn from scientists to base manager. It was good to be able to do something useful. On other days I helped Cyril, the French chef, and Izzy in the kitchen. It was amazing the sumptuous meals they were able to produce from tins and frozen food. In between, I occupied myself by reading, working my tapestry and writing my diary. Jonathan Selby had created a special satellite/computer e-mail link. Standing the satellite phone on the windowsill I could send e-mails. It was a slow and laborious process, waiting for a strong satellite signal, then hoping to transmit an email or two before the satellite passed below the horizon. Although I managed to send e-mails by satellite phone from my room, the signal was much improved outside, so each day I stood in the snow to call Jeppesen for weather and speak to Peter.

Soon faces became familiar. The engineers, Paul and Dougie, were very friendly. Some of the scientists explained their research. Cyril and Izzy, the cooks, were always ready to chat. One day on GASH duty, I suddenly heard my name called over the tannoy. I climbed the stairs to the tower and was told that the wind was getting up. Andy in the tower suggested I walk over to the hangar where Golf November would be put inside. I was overjoyed. I had worried about her standing outside, open

Even closer to Rothera…   Touching down at Rothera.

Rothera at last.

With Jane, the doctor and Golf November in the hangar at Rothera. Golf November has an engine cover to protect her from the cold.

to wind and weather. Wrapping up warmly I walked across the runway to the hangar. Sue and Ant, the Dash 7 pilots, stopped me with some welcome tips on flying in Antarctica. They told me not to be in a hurry to be away.

I was relieved to see my two barrels of fuel with a large notice: 'MITTS OFF FIDS! FUEL FOR POLLY VACHER'. (FIDS stands for Falkland Islands Dependency Survey, the name before it became British Antarctic Survey. Employees of BAS are known as Fids.)

Two Canadian mechanics were at the base just to look after the Dash 7. Their names were Eric and Ernie. Of course, they were teased mercilessly. Being Canadian they hadn't heard of the Morecambe and Wise show until they arrived. Coincidentally they worked for Field Aviation in Calgary. The Dash 7 was leased from the company for the season. Field Aviation was one of my sponsors, so Eric and Ernie asked for a photo to send back to Canada.

I went for my customary daily walk. This took me along the shore where seals basked in the bright sunshine, up over the steep hill of the point and over to the seat by the crosses. It was a circular walk which took about an hour or so to complete. Unbelievably, overnight all the sea ice in the bay had melted. Only the day before Weddell seals had been lying on the ice basking in the watery sun. Now it was all gone. The scene looked completely different. The grey shoreline seemed more familiar and resembled the Devonshire coast where I grew up. A part of me is always there, but now it was so far away, it was hard to imagine ever being there again.

Whilst at Rothera I managed to talk to some people about Flying Scholarships for the Disabled. This after all, was the purpose of the flight. Steve, the operations manager, asked for some information about the charity. A lot of people were showing an interest and had said they would like to contribute. I had very little printed information with me because of weight and space limitations, so I asked Susie to e-mail the publicity leaflet. I was pleased that so much interest was being shown.

I settled into the Antarctic way of life. Names became familiar. I really felt I had arrived when my photo appeared on the board with 'Polly Vacher – visiting pilot'. The waiting was not easy although everyone was friendly and most were happy to show me the work that they were doing. Adam spent time explaining the meteorological observations that he took daily, which he then sent back to Exeter for computer modelling.

One evening, I was sitting at supper when Judith the forecaster came over. "I think you will be able to go tomorrow," she said grinning. I could hardly believe my ears. I was just settling down to a regular routine. All hell was let loose. I had to make several phone calls, and make sure everything was packed. Suddenly those butterflies returned with a vengeance.

Was I really going to be able to go so soon? I spoke to Mike at Jeppesen. He told me that I would encounter headwinds south of Rothera. That was not what Judith had on her charts. She had tailwinds levelling out to crosswinds most of the way. Over the Ross Sea there were no winds. Such conflicting forecasts could only add to my apprehension about the coming flight. What would the next day bring?

CHAPTER 17 Point of No Return

7th December 2003 is a date forever indelibly imprinted on my mind. This was to be the big day if the forecasters could stand by their predictions. I rang Jeppesen. "Yep! Today should be good and we have just run a flight plan. The overall winds should be plus 3 kts." This meant I would have an average overall tailwind of 3 kts. It was not brilliant, but it was certainly enough to do the 1,859 nms comfortably. When flying very long distances it is desirable to have the wind coming from behind you so that it pushes you along and you cover the ground faster. If you have a wind blowing against you obviously it slows you down, therefore having a dramatic effect on your fuel endurance.

I rang through to the American base at McMurdo. My satellite phone kept cutting off because there are fewer satellites available so far south, which made conversations disjointed and stressful enough without the addition of unnecessary bureaucracy. I rang the weather forecaster at McMurdo, my destination on the other side of the Antarctic continent. Before they could give me the weather they said they had to take down a number of details first. Surely Erick Chiang had told them about my flight? Why didn't they seem to know anything about it? Surely they were aware that I was due there.

Erick Chiang from NSF had been so adamant that all the weather forecasting would be at my disposal so that I could 'execute my flight as safely as possible'. Now I was having all this hassle. I stuck to my guns. They told me that the weather was clear and looked set to stay good for the duration of my flight. "We will have to log this briefing," was their farewell statement. I didn't care what they did.

Rod organised my bags to be taken to the aircraft. I loaded Golf November and did the final walk around the aircraft. I checked the oil and fuel and all the moving surfaces. We managed to squeeze a few more litres into her already full tanks. With extra warm gear on once more I looked like the Michelin man as I climbed laboriously aboard.

Uncharacteristically Golf November just would not start. Perhaps she was telling me something, but I couldn't think like that. Paul, Dougie and Rod wheeled out the Hermann Nelson, a huge engine heater. This blew hot air into the engine cowling. Within five minutes the engine fired and I gave a huge sigh of relief.

It was a clear sunny day. I taxied down the runway and turned at the end without stopping to avoid chipping my propeller. By keeping rolling potential stone chips fly up clear of the propeller but if the aircraft stops with the propeller running, stones fly up and chip the blades. I started the ground roll. The runway was only 900 metres with the sea beckoning at the end. Loaded down with fuel I had wondered if I would be able to take off in that distance but I need not have worried. Half way down the runway I was airborne and waggling my wings in farewell.

For the first hour I had a tailwind and was making good progress. Relaxed and excited, I was having the greatest of times. Gone were all the anxieties of the past few weeks. The sky was clear with not a cloud in sight and the sun was shining. Undaunted, I was on my way for the flight of a life time. Savouring every moment, I glanced down at the bergs floating in the dark sea. The white mountain tops majestically eyed me up and down as if to say "we are looking after you." It was thrilling.

After an hour I reached the Hampton Glacier. This vast ice stream divides two sets of mountains, the Douglas Range and the Rouen Mountains. I flew up the glacier and over the top. The ice sparkled and shone reflecting a myriad of colours which made me gasp in awe. The tailwind was turning into a headwind which made a considerable difference to my groundspeed. I was unperturbed, thinking that the change of wind direction had been due to the katabatic winds sweeping down off the mountains into the glacier. This local effect would surely vanish once I reached the glacier head.

At the top of the glacier the headwind did not abate, however. It increased in speed and the first pinprick of doubt appeared in my mind. If I continued losing knots in this way I may run out of fuel before reaching my destination. I had planned on having a tailwind to enable me to reach McMurdo in sixteen hours. This allowed a minimum average ground speed of 117 kts. Now everything was changing by the minute. I started to become concerned. I plunged into a series of calculations. At one point the GPS said nineteen hours to McMurdo. I felt sure that the groundspeed would pick up. Optimism reigned supreme. Nonetheless I was now calculating like crazy. I was covering the ground at only 95-98 kts.

Passing over the Beethoven Peninsula, I could see the clearly defined Haydn and Schubert inlets. The Mussorgsky Peaks, Franck Nunataks and Mount Borodin were not so clearly defined, but I was sure I picked them out correctly. It seemed a good omen that I was flying over such a 'musical' area. The sheer size of the continent was overpowering, yet there was a deep sense of freedom. I thought of the Eroica and hummed some of the Ninth Symphony. The contrast between this vast expanse of white and the busy streets of Vienna with which Haydn and Schubert were so familiar was incongruous. The jovial final movement of the Beethoven third piano concerto flitted through my mind. Music filled my very being.

With the Beethoven Peninsula behind me and three hours into the flight, all that lay ahead was white and more white. The wind was building up on my nose and I began scribbling furiously. How far could I get with this headwind and fuel endurance? The clear blue sky radiated a sense of security and the sun shone brightly on the white below. A metaphorical black cloud began to loom on the horizon. Another hour passed and my mind became focussed on one calculation, the Point of No Return. Using wind, groundspeed and fuel capacity I had to make the final decision as to whether I went on or turned back. Once decided, we would be committed. I had another 'fail-safe' system on long flights. I divided the distance into thirds and the fuel endurance into thirds. On reaching a third of the distance the fuel used must be close to a third otherwise alarm bells start to ring way before the Point of No Return.

A huge plateau called Ellsworth Land lay ahead. All around there was nothing but endless white. It was difficult to judge how close the aircraft was to the surface. The ground appeared from the air to be just flat, flat ice. Occasionally sastrugi, lines of wind blown ridges and areas of crevasses, were discernible but generally it was just a bleached sea of white with the contrasting clear blue sky overhead.

Five hours into the flight, a sombre mood was beginning to envelope me. The groundspeed was dropping to 88 kts. If this continued it would take a further fifteen impossible hours to McMurdo. I climbed a bit to see if there was less headwind higher up. It was a calculated risk because Golf November uses 72 litres an hour in the climb as opposed to 39 litres an hour in the cruise. Depressingly the headwind was the same but by descending ever so slowly I could pick up some forward speed. I was excited when I managed to reach 100 kts or even 103 kts. Every knot was beginning to count. Things were becoming desperate. Thank goodness for the satellite phone. Peter was monitoring the flight so I asked him to enquire whether I could go into Patriot Hills. Mike Sharp and Mike McDowell, who ran ALE at Patriot Hills had consistently refused to help. Peter rang me back. "Mike says they will accept you into Patriot Hills," but he did not say whether he would sell me fuel.

I was anxious that if I got there and we started wrangling over fuel, bad winds may pick up and Golf November would be at risk. Mike gave Peter the weather at Patriot Hills: 'Overcast at 800 ft with some snow – winds of 10-12 kts'. These were light winds for Patriot Hills, one of the windiest places on earth. I was not happy about a cloud base of 800 ft, though. Patriot Hills is in the lee of the Ellsworth Mountains. 800 ft would be marginal in the UK where I am familiar with landmarks on the ground, but to go into an unfamiliar landing site near mountains with such a low cloud base could be suicidal.

I was feeling quite calm despite working like crazy. Now that it came down to a vital decision I found my mind was very clear and I seemed detached from any emotional input. Calculating, calculating, every drop of fuel mattered. McMurdo seemed to be slipping into the distance as Golf November and I struggled to gain some speed. I leaned off the fuel perilously close to the limit, burning a smaller percentage of fuel to air than usual. The adverse effect from doing this for any length of time is it will burn out the valves, and if you lean too much the engine splutters and stops. Leaning the fuel meant a sacrifice of a knot or two and it was a compromise.

Vinson Massif, the tallest mountain on the Antarctic continent 16,143 ft (4892 metres), was somewhere in the distance amongst the Ellsworth Mountains. The peaks of the Ellsworth range grew ever closer. It was one of the most beautiful sights of the entire flight and also one of the most frightening. I needed to climb to fly over the mountain tops but I would use twice as much fuel in the climb. After six hours in the air the GPS was still saying fifteen hours to run to McMurdo. The knee pad was covered with calculations. A third of the fuel endurance of eighteen hours had gone. We should have covered 622 miles but I had barely flown 500.

I imagined reaching the massive Ross Ice Shelf and having to land on that, short of McMurdo. The shelf is relatively flat, but its surface is covered by uneven ridges or sastrugi, and a snow layer which can form into uneven piles, blown by the wind. I would be extremely lucky to land without flipping Golf November over. She would be damaged and I would be killed or injured. It was not a responsible option. Running out of fuel is an absolute 'no-no' for pilots.

The situation was desperate. Going back to Rothera was not a good option either. There was no spare fuel at Rothera. There was the prospect of massive bills to have some brought in. Patriot Hills was out of the question because of low cloud.

Would the wind change in my favour? Decision time was approaching. Peter rang Jeppesen. "Stronger headwinds between 78 South and 82 South," they said. I had not even reached 78 south yet and there were already huge headwinds. "Would it improve after 82 South?" No-one seemed to know. "Would it be too late even if it did improve?" Thoughts were swirling and rushing around my head.

I spoke to Rothera. It was a poor reception but they could hear me. "I am considering turning around," I said. "Roger, roger" came Andy's professional voice. Calculating, calculating. Could I do it? – what would happen if I went on? What was the risk?

It took time to sink in, but eventually it dawned on me that there really was no other option but to turn back while I still could. There was a lump in my throat. Exhausted I was resigned. I had been flying for six and a half hours. I had been calculating, calculating, leaning the mixture, climbing, descending, trying to find help from the beastly wind. It was like a demon, taunting, taunting – testing, testing. In all my flying experience, I had never had to make such a cruel decision. The world seemed to evaporate in front of me. Then came Peter's voice over the satellite phone.

"What is your average speed?" he was saying. "Standby," I shouted, but the engine noise drowned me out. "Give me time to calculate," I yelled down the phone, so he rang off. I worked out that I could average 95 kts for the remaining distance. "It's not enough," Peter said when I called him back. Deep down I knew that he was right.

To hell with my sponsors – to hell with records – I won't do anyone a favour if I have a forced landing. I may kill or injure myself – I may kill or injure someone who tries to rescue me. I might ruin Golf November for ever. So there it was. In the end there was no choice. I took a long last look at the spectacular Ellsworth Mountains. It was no time to appreciate the beauty and I had no mind to appreciate it either.

Self pity took over. Tears trickled down my face. My glasses steamed up. Then, miraculously I thought of the disabled scholars and wondered how much more devastated they must feel after an accident, ending up in a wheelchair or without a leg. The flight was to help the disabled but in the end they were helping me! I sat back and enjoyed the privilege of flying over such amazing scenery. I even found time to scribble something for the diary:

> I could not really write anything on the way out. I was trying desperately to find a way to increase my groundspeed. It was dropping down to 88 kts and it was really worrying me – I couldn't film – I couldn't take all the data for the Mirce boys – I was full of anguish – was I going to be able to do this with the fuel I had? – I didn't want to have to land on the sea ice – it was scary.
>
> Antarctica is a beautiful place to fly in but I could do without the hassle.
>
> Now I have to work out two things:
> 1) How to get fuel into Rothera
> 2) How to best get to NZ so that I don't let too many people down.
>
> I guess I'll have to have a good sleep and then work it all out.
>
> The Ellsworth Mountains were beautiful and I got to the foothills of those – that was an achievement in itself – maybe it has all worked out for the best – nothing is irredeemable – I am sure I shall probably suffer a reaction, but I hope I can get over it quickly – I just wonder if I can get to NZ in time for Xmas??
>
> The problem is going to be getting fuel into Rothera and then a good enough weather window.
>
> I should be feeling bitter with all those wallies who wrecked this for me – but – funnily enough – I have got over that and I don't feel a bit like that.
>
> The vastness of this place is amazing – Good tailwind – Now doing 133 kts!! Lots of crevasses below – wouldn't like to have to land there.
>
> Well I guess that not being able to achieve this is nothing compared to say losing your legs or becoming disabled – and at least I haven't injured myself or my aeroplane – and to feel like they must feel must be at least 20 times worse. I have had the pleasure and anxiety of flying on the Antarctic continent and there are many ways to skin a cat.
>
> Art just called on my Iridium – isn't that great – I feel so loved and supported – that has made my face pucker up and tears come to my eyes – how silly!! – I guess I will feel low for a bit – but I am determined not to.
>
> Just passing over Mussorgsky Peaks, Schubert and Haydn inlets. I can see Rothera from 141 miles away!

I sat back and basked in the breathtaking scenery, the snow sparkling in the sunshine, the nunataks, mountain peaks popping their tips up through the layers of ice and snow. Antarctica was impassive to the mammoth decision I had just taken and knew nothing of the turbulence of my mind. I had plenty of fuel and a tailwind so in a way the pressure was off.

So I started thinking, "Can I get more fuel down somehow? If not, do I have enough fuel to get

Numerous nunataks or tops of mountains, poked through the snow as I flew over Antarctica.

me to Ushuaia? Can I go up to California and island hop across the Pacific to pick up my route in New Zealand?" I tried to keep these thoughts at bay. I told myself that I would have plenty of time to sort that out once I was back in Rothera.

"How fast could I get to New Zealand?" The questions kept invading my peace. "I will have to order new maps and approach plates. That will take time." (I had thrown out my maps and charts or posted them home to save extra weight.) "Where will I be for Christmas? What will I do?" Again I tried to push the thoughts behind me and concentrate on the amazing views. "Where will Peter be – poor Peter – he has given so much?" Thoughts, my head was awash with them. "Is this failure, or is it just another challenge the Antarctic has thrown at me? How could I cope with failure? I am sure that I will cope somehow."

I could see Rothera in the distance. I joined downwind and managed to get some photos from the air. As I turned onto final, the sun was shining right in my eyes. The time was 2230 hrs. I couldn't see a thing. The sun was so bright. It was low in the sky and shining straight at me. It was reflecting off the water and the ice – panic – it was blinding me. How could I manage to land?

I kept going. Looking down I could see the crew in the boat below. I rounded out trying to see the grey gravel in front of me somewhere, but I was blinded. I held Golf November in the right position for landing and to my amazement she creamed in and did the softest landing imaginable. She helped me out yet again, as if thanking me for saving her.

There were several people waiting and Ant, the pilot came up and gave me a big hug. "That was absolutely the right decision to take and what is more it was a very courageous one," he said. What a wonderfully warm character. It was lucky I was wearing sunglasses as the tears started streaming down my face again. His words meant so much to me and it was just what I needed after twelve hours in the cockpit.

Cyril and Izzy, the cooks, were there too. They both put their arms around me. "I have left you a curry in the kitchen," Izzy said in her motherly north country way. Rod came up. "You can have your room back and everything will be just as before – don't worry Polly."

It was wonderful to have such a welcome. All those people had stayed up to await my arrival. It was very moving. The lump in my throat was working overtime! Several people came to see me while I was devouring the welcome meal. Jane, the doctor, said, "If you need to bash it out tomorrow, just come and find me." There was no end to their kindness. I felt cocooned and loved. On the notice board I could see 'Polly due back at 2330' in large letters. I arrived back an hour earlier than that. I was glad I didn't keep everyone up even later.

I rang Peter, but it was too soon to make any decisions. I was tired, not thinking straight. I rang Art. He had been so keen for me to get to the Pole. I felt I had let him down after all he had done. I still felt confident that I had made the right decision but it wasn't easy to handle and I had to fight off my emotions. I needed to sleep.

CHAPTER 18

The 'Move Away Clouds Dance'

I am not sure how I got through the next few days. Trying to carry on as normal, I went to the daily pilots' briefing as always. Every morning the pilots gathered with the base manager and operations manager to listen to the meteorologist give a thorough weather report. They then discussed the flights for the day and decided whether the weather was safe to fly.

Sue, the pilot, said, "nice landing last night, Polly." This was praise indeed from another pilot. "At least you are here and alive – a good decision." I found her words deeply comforting because I felt as if I was standing on the brink of an abyss. I felt physically exhausted and washed out emotionally. I really needed all the help I could get. I chatted to Rob, the household manager, over breakfast later. "I so enjoyed GASH – that I felt I just had to come back – couldn't manage without it," I joked, but I was gutted underneath.

A major highlight of the year at Rothera was the arrival of the supply ship *James Clark Ross*. Sitting on a rock overlooking the dock I could see the ship on the horizon and the wharf was cleared. Only the guys unloading the boat were allowed on the jetty as there would be huge cranes lifting the containers off the ship. Everyone else climbed up the hill by the crosses. I noticed a pair of Adelie penguins strutting onto the dock. They looked like two city gents, all they needed was rolled umbrellas under their flippers. They waddled to one corner of the wharf just as if they were checking everything was alright for the ship to berth, then they waddled over to the other corner. The scene reminded me of pompous bureaucratic inspectors! It was bizarre.

We watched the bright red ship make its way through the icebergs. A huge iceberg that was blocking the dock a few hours before had drifted slowly away and the ice crunched and crashed as it gave way to the ship. It was an exciting moment as the *James Clark Ross* berthed gracefully alongside. The snow-covered mountains towered behind us and the sun shone down. Life seemed somehow normal and abnormal at the same time.

Once the ship was safely birthed the containers were craned onto the dock. Everyone formed a human chain to help with the unloading. Boxes of food for the freezers were passed along the line. There was great camaraderie as we all stood laughing and chatting waiting for the next box to arrive. Rolls and rolls of toilet paper were amongst the packages.

This reminded me of a strange notice in the ladies' loo. It said "IN THE EVENT OF A SHORTAGE OF TOILET PAPER – BAS EMPLOYEES TAKE PRECEDENCE OVER MORRISON WORKERS." Morrison was the company building the new Bonner Laboratory. Every time I went to the loo, I pictured the Morrison workers going around with dirty bums!

Whilst I was settling back into the daily routine of the base Peter, Alejo and Art were all attempting to get more fuel to Rothera. I spent hours standing in the snow with the Iridium phone pressed to my ear. It was a marvellous system but most frustrating because I was so often cut off mid

The annual supply ship, the *James Clark Ross* docks at Rothera.

conversation. Yet it was amazing that one minute I could talk to Susie, my volunteer PR manager in the UK and the next to Peter in Australia.

Peter rang. He had spoken to Mike Sharp from Antarctica Logistics and Expeditions (ALE). He said there was no way they could help me with fuel. I was flabbergasted. I knew that they had that cache of avgas at Patriot Hills and I really thought they would help me after what had happened. I was prepared to pay but there was no way. The only thing to do was to just take it on the chin and go on as normal, hoping somebody else could pull some strings.

Steve, the operations manager, called me to see if I had made any progress with fuel. He said that he would do all that he could to help me. Somehow sympathy is more difficult to cope with and as I listened to Steve I burst into tears. The more I tried to stop the more the tears kept coming.

Peter beavered away. He was so calm which is more than I could say of myself. I cast my mind back to the fears I had had whilst in Ushuaia with Peter. The fear of the unknown and fear of flying over such hostile sea and land had all vanished. I had experienced such wonderful flights to and in Antarctica. What was gnawing away at me now was the feeling of letting everyone down. I worried about Peter, my sponsors, my team and the charity I was supporting. The horrors of 'failure' seemed to tower over me like great monsters, their tentacles waiting to entangle me. I fought these feelings with passion. I knew that I had done my best.

I had something very real and practical to worry about too. How was I now going to get out of Antarctica without more fuel? Alejo investigated the possibility of sending an aircraft down to Rothera with fuel for me so that I could have another attempt at flying over the Pole. The cost was astronomical (around £30,000), but I thought that my sponsors might help out if it gave me the chance to cross the continent.

I had too much time to think and ponder on how I had ended up in this situation. I had thought that with meticulous planning I had covered every eventuality but I had not reckoned on Kenn Borek letting me down with the crucial fuel at the last minute. I had organised fuel at McMurdo and was let down then by Antarctica New Zealand but Quark Expeditions had helped resolve that dilemma. There was fuel in Rothera as reserve in case I needed to turn around en route to Sky Blu or Patriot Hills. Then the fuel Kenn Borek was bringing from Punta Arenas was stopped and my only option then had been to use the reserve fuel already positioned in Rothera for my attempt at the Pole. My options had become narrower and narrower until they were like a tightrope and there was no room left to be flexible. Using the reserve at Rothera was always a risk but when Kenn Borek prevented my promised fuel from arriving I dug my toes in and was determined to do it anyway.

One morning I went to the briefing as usual. "There is an idiot who has flown down from Invercargill in New Zealand and across the Pole – he was trying to get to Ushuaia but didn't have enough fuel," said Rod. "He was flying an RV6, so how he thought he would be able to carry enough fuel to fly all that way is beyond my imagination. He kept us up all night and now he has landed in McMurdo."

I later discovered it was Jon Johansen, now well and truly stuck with no fuel. Mine was the only avgas in McMurdo and I was still trying to get fuel brought in somehow to have another attempt at flying across to McMurdo. I thought that if Jon was given my fuel to get him out of Antarctica, I would myself be stranded and unable to fly on to New Zealand. I immediately rang Julian Tangaere at Scott Base. "Don't whatever you do let Jon have my fuel," I shouted down the phone. I felt mean, but there was no point in helping someone and then being stuck myself.

As time moved on, it became obvious that I just could not get more fuel to make a second attempt to cross Antarctica to McMurdo. David Roots from ALE had put the phone down on Peter. Peter must have pestered them too much and they just got fed up. I never did find out the reason for their unwillingness to support me in any way. It would have given their new company excellent publicity. I rang Steve Penikett in Calgary in a last ditch attempt to persuade him to transport some fuel to Rothera. Sean Louttit was back in Calgary so Steve said he would chat to him about it. "Why don't you just go in to Patriot Hills and steal some fuel!" Only Steve could make such a comment. I told him quite firmly that I wasn't like that.

In retrospect it had been just one struggle after another once my fuel had been left behind in Punta Arenas. Perhaps I should have waited until I had a forecast of 20 kts of tailwind, but I might have waited for weeks or missed Antarctica's summer completely. I was not sleeping and began to feel physically lethargic. This was no good at all. Finally, I took a command decision. "It is no good looking longingly at closed doors. Get on with it, Polly. Go back to Ushuaia and make the best of a bad job – go for it."

I spoke to Comodoro Jorge Reta at the Argentine Air Force and our conversation was in complete contrast to all the depressing negatives that I had had to face since my return to Rothera. "We shall be delighted to fly fuel for you from our mainland airfield Rio Gallegos to our base at Marambio on the Antarctic Peninsula," he said. "Can you get drums sent to Rio Gallegos?" Julie Wright at Shell took over and the barrels arrived in Rio Gallegos a few days later. Suddenly things were beginning to look up or at least they were until British bureaucracy came up with an extraordinary edict.

I bumped into the base manager. "Oh Rod – just the guy I want to speak to," I said. "If the weather is good enough I am planning to fly to Marambio tomorrow." "Polly, I am afraid I have something to tell you," Rod said looking sheepish. "I have just had a directive from Cambridge that we are not allowed to give you weather forecasts." "What on earth do you mean? That is positively dangerous," I retorted, swelling with anger. "Well, we can help you unofficially," he said in a weak voice. I shrugged my shoulders and walked away, disgusted.

At the briefing next morning, in front of fifteen people, Rod said, "Well Polly, you know that we are officially not allowed to give you weather, but unofficially we will try to get hold of a forecast from Marambio for you." It was hardly necessary to announce it to everyone. I rather hoped that someone would have the courage to speak up on my behalf but nothing was said, although they all clearly recognised the danger.

I took the bit between the teeth. "Thank you Rod. If I am not able to be sure of the weather at Marambio and en route too, I am just not going. It is not safe to do so and I hope you wouldn't want me ending up on the snow." I was beginning to hate the place.

At dinner that night I sat opposite a guy called Tony. I had not met him before. "How are you getting on?" he said with a kindly smile. Tears welled up and I told him about the weather problem. This great big guy, who I hardly knew, put his hand out onto mine and gave it a squeeze. That gentle act of kindness was just too much. "I am sorry, I will just have to go out," I said to him, wondering which was my quickest escape route so that no one would see. I rushed into the library. Asty, a close friend of Art's was sitting there. I poured it all out while he sat quietly listening. Most of the people at the base were wonderfully supportive and Asty offered help when I most needed it. I was defiant. "To hell with everyone – none of them have done what I have so they can piss off."

I knew there was no excuse for even thinking such words but I was at the end of my tether and raging with anger. Suddenly everyone started talking to me. Perhaps they were impressed with my defiant mood. The forecast at Marambio was for a cloud base of 1,500 ft, a temperature of -6°C and a dewpoint of -6. When the temperature and dewpoint are close or the same it indicates that there will be precipitation and icing. The forecast was not good enough.

Alejo rang. He had never given up on the venture and was still trying to arrange fuel. He told me that DAP could take fuel into Sky Blu. This should have been great news but David, one of the pilots at Rothera had told me that the runway was not long enough that year. Sky Blu has an ice runway but they had only cleared 600 metres. I told Alejo that it wouldn't work. All doors now seemed firmly shut.

Whilst speaking to Peter he told me that Jon Johansen was causing an international incident. "The Americans won't have anything to do with him. He is having to camp under the wing of his aeroplane in McMurdo," Peter said. "They won't give him any fuel. They will take his aeroplane to pieces and send it home on a ship at the end of the season."

Perhaps I could help Jon? "If I give him my fuel, it should be enough for him to fly over the South Pole and on to Ushuaia," I thought. "If I can't do it, the next best thing is to help someone else who possibly can." I rang Peter with my idea. "You know you have kept 'squeaky clean' so far and done everything by the book. I am not sure it will go down well if you are supporting someone who has just gone and done it with no permissions at all." I thought he may have a point and asked Peter to speak to Joe Beeman. Joe has a great legal mind and would know the best way to go.

Peter rang back. "I have spoken to Joe. He thinks you shouldn't give Jon your fuel because it would be seen as supporting a wild adventurer who hadn't done it correctly." I did not altogether agree with him by then and it seemed appropriate to talk to Julian Tangaere at Scott Base. Joe meanwhile was also one of the band of faithfuls who tried to get fuel into Antarctica and was desperately exploring all avenues to enable me to have another go at flying across.

My mind went back to Jon Johansen. By then the Americans had given him space in a hut so he was no longer camping on the ice. He had certainly hit the headlines. Indeed there was a serious diplomatic row going on between the Australian government on the one hand, and New Zealand and the United States on the other. The *Sydney Morning Herald* reported that 'New Zealand Foreign Affairs Minister Phil Goff and his Australian counterpart Alexander Downer met in the Marlborough Sounds, Blenheim at the weekend to discuss a wide range of issues, including Mr Johansen's situation'.

I was happy to give Jon my fuel, but this had to be cleared with Quark Expeditions who had brought my fuel down for me as sponsorship, and Shell who had provided the fuel. It also had to be approved by Antarctica New Zealand and the US's National Science Foundation to make sure that this was what they would want.

Finally the fuel was released to Jon on the understanding that he gave a donation to Flying Scholarships for the Disabled in the UK, and that he supported and promoted Wheelies with Wings, the Australian version of FSD which was established in 2001 by Mike and Liz Apps, David Clegg and Rebecca Sexton during my first round-the-world flight.

The following report appeared in the London *Times* of 13th December:

BRITISH PILOT OFFERS ANTARCTIC AID
From Roger Maynard in Perth

A British aviator whose attempt to fly around the world over both poles was thwarted by bad weather has come to the aid of an Australian pilot stranded in the Antarctic after he ran out of fuel.

Polly Vacher, a 59-year-old grandmother [actually not a grandmother!], has offered 400 litres of fuel to Jon Johanson so that he can fly his homemade aeroplane back to his starting point in New Zealand. Mr Johanson landed at McMurdo Sound in the Antarctic this week when bad weather left him without enough fuel to reach Argentina.

Despite lobbying from the Australian Government, New Zealand and American Antarctic authorities refused to sell the adventurer any fuel.

"The US actually don't run a gas station in Antarctica... and nor does New Zealand" Lou Sanson, chief of Antarctica New Zealand, a government-funded research body, said.

The offer from the British pilot has, at a stroke, saved Mr Johanson, 47, and soothed a potential spat between Australia and its two closest allies.

Alexander Downer, the Australian Foreign Minister, was relieved to announce yesterday. "He will actually be able now to access proper Avgas that'll be suitable for this plane."

The marooned adventurer's partner, Sue Ball, said that she was overjoyed at the offer, describing it as a wonderful gesture from one adventurer to another. "It's just incredibly generous to know that now we can have Jon fly the aeroplane home instead of putting it on a ship – it's just wonderful."

New Zealand had offered to fly Mr Johanson home on a commercial flight and send his RV4 aircraft back on the next available ship. The Government explained to Mr Downer that it did not want to encourage tourists who were not self sufficient when they arrived in Antarctica. Authorities there said that they did not even have the correct type of fuel for Mr Johanson's aeroplane.

Mr Sanson contrasted the meticulously planned British expedition with that of Mr Johanson. He said, "Polly's trip was well organised and properly planned. Her staff spent two years preparing for her flight, with significant advice from the national Antarctic programmes. It is ironic that she is now assisting a stranded pilot who embarked upon an ill-prepared and secret flight over the South Pole."

Mr Johanson denied such claims. He was, however, delighted to be able to fly his aeroplane to Invercargill in New Zealand's South Island from where he began his flight on Sunday.

He was making the first solo flight over the South Pole in a home-built single-engine aeroplane when strong head winds reduced the amount of fuel he had to reach Argentina.

Jon was on his way home and I was still stuck. I continued to attend the pilot briefings in spite of the directive. I also tackled the forecaster daily. I gave her a hard stare as if to say, "don't you dare not give me a forecast." I had to establish that regardless of any instruction from the British Antarctic Survey in Cambridge I was not going to jeopardise my safety as it was essential to have as much weather information as possible. The weather in the Antarctic is fickle and often changes suddenly. Storms can blow up with little warning and forecasting is difficult as there are few people based in the Antarctic to record and report weather on a regular basis. It was essential that I got as much weather information as possible from all available sources to keep me safe.

I spoke to Jeppesen every day, but whereas their forecasting was precise for the rest of the world,

The article which appeared in the *Independent* when I gave my fuel to Jon Johansen stuck at McMurdo in Antarctica.

they too were struggling with Antarctica. I had already encountered headwinds when tailwinds had been forecast for my crossing of the Antarctic and this made me double my efforts to find detailed weather information. I went to the tower and asked Andy to radio Marambio to find out their conditions. Rothera is on the west side of the Antarctic peninsula and Marambio, the Argentine base where I was to stop to re-fuel is on the east side. If one side is experiencing clear skies and calm winds the other could be typically engulfed in freezing fog.

Jonathan Selby played a significant role in my Antarctic flight. His system, Sky Eye, which he and his company Xaxero developed, provided another source of weather information. Sky Eye is typically used to provide sophisticated weather forecasting for ships. Jonathan pioneered a method of tracking weather systems which is then transferred to data for computer modelling to obtain an accurate forecast.

After two weeks, the weather looked good at last. There was another phone call from Peter. "John Apps from Quark Expeditions is a personal friend of Mike McDowell of Antarctic Logistics and Expeditions. They will provide fuel at Patriot Hills if you have a written letter from National Science Foundation to say that they are happy with your search and rescue arrangements."

This gave me another glimmer of hope. Here was a chance to try once more but time was against me. The endless wrangles I had already been through were a salutary reminder that I didn't have time to run down another tunnel only to find yet another dead end. Was this an offer that could materialise or was it another red herring? The Antarctic summer is short, and the sea ice runway at McMurdo is only useable until the end of December. It was already mid December and once the sea ice begins to melt, the remaining ice becomes too thin to support even the weight of my tiny plane. There is a blue ice runway some miles from McMurdo so it was a possibility to use that. It would take time to obtain another letter from NSF and with my previous experiences of lengthy weather delays the prospect of the summer ending and being stuck in Antarctica during the long desolate winters was not an attractive option. I already had letters from Kenn Borek and the Argentine Air Force covering my search and rescue. I had written consent to land at McMurdo from NSF. I had full insurance if anyone else had to come and fetch me, but to get yet another letter out of NSF when I was in Antarctica appeared hopeless.

Nevertheless, I was buoyed up by a series of e-mails. Those who wrote little knew how much they meant to me. There was a wonderful e-mail from Derrick Ings. He was an ardent supporter and sponsor. He said he felt so helpless with me stuck in Antarctica. "I would love to find a way to help," he said. He told me that he had sent a donation to Flying Scholarships for the Disabled as that was the best way he felt he could contribute. I was over the moon. It was truly wonderful to be supported by so many people.

Art Mortvedt had written, "Think of it like this Polly, at least you are not camping under an upturned boat with nothing to eat as Shackleton's party were."

One needed people to put things in the right perspective. I found some of my usual ebullience returning. An e-mail arrived from one of the officers at Marambio. Apparently they were not allowed to fly fuel in drums with personnel on board, and were therefore sending a C130 Hercules from the mainland, solely to carry my avgas. This was fantastic news, I could hardly believe their generosity and willingness to help. Rosemary Taylor told me that donations for the charity were just rolling in. What an outcome! How could I feel miserable when so many were trying to help?

It was another Sunday, 14th December and there were no facilities for any church services at Rothera which surprised me a little. So every Sunday I walked to the crosses on the hill to spend some quiet time. Here I was able to sit in peace – all that could be heard was the odd swish and bang from icebergs as they cracked, melted or bumped into each other. I found comfort from the grandeur of the icy mountains and the contrasting blue sea and skies. I reflected on the different religions I had encountered and I felt an overwhelming sense of unity through the wonderfully spiritual people I had been privileged to meet. David, one of the pilots, invited me to see his video of Sky Blu. It looked a pretty desolate place, so perhaps 'Someone' was looking after me. It was comforting to think so.

The weather was frustrating: either it was brilliant sunshine in Marambio and bad weather in Rothera or the other way around. This was sorely trying my patience. I imagined wintering over and wondered what it would be like. One day the fog was so thick you could not see a thing, everything disappeared under a layer of white and the runway was completely obliterated. It amazed me how quickly things could change. The weather rules in Antarctica.

I thought of my team, Susie, Sue, Valerie and Ro back in England. They all worked so hard to keep the show on the road. They never complained, giving hours of their time and never asking for a reward. Apart from putting all their efforts into raising money for the charity through my flight they were, of course, getting ready for Christmas. It was hard not to dwell on thoughts of home. The shops would be crammed full of tinsel and Christmas trees and everyone would be in a frenzy, wrapping presents, queuing, queuing. I thought of my home with its rickety beams and the smell of wood burning on the open fire filling the air. It was all so far away.

On 16th December I had an e-mail from Marcelo in Marambio:

Dear Polly

The pilots of this Base are planning the SAR (search and rescue) support of your flight to Marambio Base and we need to know how many fuel you have in storage and/or how many hours of flight it represents flying your plane in order to calculate your no-turn back point.
Another question about your plane:

1. Could you please send us the real performance of your plane?
2. Is there any special modification or revision in order to increase the cruise speed?
3. Is there a special restriction that we need to know?

If we have any other question we will write you very soon and do not worry about your flight to Marambio, we are glad to help you.
About your request of laying on some good weather along Rothera-Marambio route, I tell you that we are dancing the 'move away clouds dance' around the runway, but I am afraid the weather is becaming (sic) worst.
At this moment is snowing and there is no probability of getting better until Friday. You must be patient Polly, everything will be alright.
A great kiss for you.
See you soon and best regards
Marcelo

I pictured Marcelo's 'move away clouds dance' with lots of Argentine pilots in uniform dancing around the runway. It made me grin every time I thought of it.

Nick, an eye surgeon, had arrived on the supply ship to study the effect of the sun on people's eyes. "You know, Polly, it is much better for your cause that you didn't reach the Pole – people will equate with that," he said. "It is only fools who go on regardless when all the signs show that you should turn around." This dose of positive attitude was just what I needed. "It is like sailing," he went on. "You go where the wind best takes you and in the end you get to your destination, but maybe not by the route you originally planned."

I felt ashamed of all my negative emotions but it had been hard dealing with bureaucrats and politicians. I had spent too much time worrying about them rather than soaking myself in all the good things that exist.

Alan, the chief pilot, called me in to his office. "All the politics and hassles you have had are dreadful," he said in a whispered voice. "It's time they all grew up." I said, "I am not into politics or reprisals. I understand a lot of it. What I don't understand is the weather directive from Cambridge." But I was flabbergasted no-one felt they could speak up on my behalf.

Suddenly on 18th December I had a phone call from Roxanna. "Jonathan says the weather is good. Can you fly to Marambio today?" It was already lunch time. "At least there are twenty-four hours of daylight," I said to myself with a sigh of relief. I rang Jeppesen and they told me to call back in fifteen minutes. I ran upstairs to find Judith, the forecaster. "Yes it seems to have cleared," Judith said. I rang Jeppesen again. "Surprisingly, it really does look good."

I rushed around like crazy. I spoke to Steve who organized the hangar boys to get Golf November out then I shoved all my things in my bags and took them out onto the deck. It was fortuitous that Tony came in the truck to pick me up. As we drove over to the hangar I told Tony what his gesture had meant to me. "I was so unhappy when I got that weather directive. You just touched my arm. It made all the difference," I told him. Looking at him I could see his eyes were red with tears. "I think they treated you like the pits – I couldn't believe what they did to you," he said.

I felt such a close bond to this huge strong guy who had been so sympathetic to me when I was upset at dinner. I took care not to comment any more but I was grateful for his small acts of kindness. I had no time to say good-bye to anyone. I quickly checked Golf November and told the hangar boys to say farewell for me.

I took off without another thought, climbing as quickly as I could to 9,000 ft. The mountains of Graham Land rise to 7,600 ft. They are spectacular. Brilliant sunshine smiled on me as I climbed over the mountains and glaciers to the Larsen Ice Shelf. The shelf was not how I had imagined it. It was not flat but had nunataks, mountain peaks poking up amongst the icy wastes. The mountain chain of the peninsula rose on my port side and I thought about my departure. It was sad to leave Rothera in such a hurry but at least I had no time to worry about the flight. I had just drifted as quickly out of their lives as I had landed suddenly in. There had been so much kindness, but there had been too many hassles to feel really settled. Nevertheless, I had done my best to help where I could and mix and join in. Steve later sent me a huge framed satellite photograph of Rothera signed by many of those who were there, which moved me greatly and I felt glad that I had made so many friends.

Jonathan and Roxanna followed my flight on their HF radio from their yacht *Anahera*. Memories of Peter and Jonathan monitoring my flight to Antarctica flooded in. Peter's strong, calm voice reverberated in my mind. There was a tremendous tail wind and the groundspeed reached 144 kts. It was exhilarating. Everything was so clear. I couldn't help wondering if the Ross Ice Shelf was anything like the Larsen Ice Shelf; perhaps it was although I now doubted I would ever see it.

Approaching Marambio there were clouds ahead. Cloud cover is measured in octas. For example eight octas is complete cloud cover and four octas is half cloud cover. First there were five octas of stratus in a layer below. The five octas soon increased to seven octas. I began to get worried. Seven octas was too much as I could barely see the ground. It was amazing how quickly the weather could change. I descended to 4,000 ft above a solid layer of cloud. The temperature was -6°C. Ice would definitely form going through the cloud. I would be blinded by an ice-covered windscreen. I looked frantically for a break in the clouds, but there wasn't one. I tried not to panic.

I started to fly the published VOR approach with the printed instructions clipped to my control column. It required flying eight miles out over the sea. I could see a different colour further out and after about six miles there was a small hole. I dived down through the hole while I had the chance. This was not a normal procedure but this was not a normal place. At 2,500 ft I was under the cloud. I could see the island of Marambio standing out of the water like a giant turd. On the top there were bright red objects. As I got closer I realized that they were the buildings of the base. At last I could see flashing lights leading to the runway.

The island rose steeply out of the water to 760 ft and was spectacular in a desolate sort of way, but the landing area ahead was difficult to discern. Without the flashing lights one would not know it was a runway at all. There was a strong cross wind, but I managed to put Golf November down in a dignified fashion. The surface was mud and snow with ruts made by the C130s. As I taxied in a voice from the tower said, "Welcome to Marambio."

A sea of smiling faces was awaiting my arrival. They wore woolly hats, gloves and thick boots. I climbed out into the bitterly cold wind. There was huge excitement. The hangar had a big red door with the name of the base painted in enormous letters. Everyone helped push Golf November up the steep ramp into the hangar. The bags were unloaded. Then a voice from the crowd said, "I am sorry Polly, but every person who visits this base for the first time has to have the snow treatment." There was no time to object. Six guys picked me up and I was dumped in a heap of snow. They pelted me with snowballs. Everyone was laughing as I lay helpless in the snow. All were having a good time. They told me that I had passed the test as I was still laughing at the end. What a welcome!

Inside the buildings, I was shown to my room. It was my room, but in fact it was a dormitory with a row of six sets of bunk beds all very close to each other. There was one loo and two washbasins and a shower. I couldn't help imagining what it would have been like with twelve people sharing. The base was a series of metal container buildings, all painted red, joined by covered corridors.

The warmth of the reception was phenomenal. The base commander invited me to dine with him. He had organized all the English speaking pilots and scientists to sit on our table including Marcelo of the 'clouds dance'. The chatting was incessant and enormous fun. The commander gave me a conducted tour. There was a delightful chapel near my room. We went to the commander's office and rang Jorge Reta in Buenos Aires. He was thrilled that I had arrived safely. "Let me know when you are coming to Buenos Aires and I will arrange for you to come into Aeroparque again."

The welcome I received at the Argentine base was as warm as the weather was cold. Marambio is on a tiny island standing 700 ft above sea level. The biting wind whistles across the top of the island and induces freezing temperatures.

The commander and the pilots took me to the weather department. The forecaster was most helpful and spent about an hour going through the charts. He anticipated that it should be excellent for crossing Drake Passage the next day. The only problem might be with Ushuaia. We arranged to meet early in the morning to get the latest update and take a decision.

The next morning, speaking to Peter on the satellite phone, I heard that Jennifer Murray and Colin Bodill had crashed on the Ronne Ice Shelf between Patriot Hills and Rothera. (Interestingly, I had met Jackie Ronne in Washington, after whom the ice shelf had been named.) They had previously reached the South Pole in their Bell 407 helicopter on 17th December, the actual centenary date of the Wright

In Washington I met Jackie Ronne after whom her husband named the Ronne Ice Shelf.

Brothers' first flight. It was such an achievement, but what had happened to them now? Their emergency locator beacon signal had been picked up in Scotland. I was overcome with a cold sweat. It made me feel more vulnerable. I went into breakfast and met up with Coco and Charlie, two of the pilots. I told them about Jennifer and Colin. They immediately rushed out to find out if they could help in any way. Their quick reactions were impressive. These brave men were prepared to go out and risk life and limb without a thought for their own personal safety.

Meanwhile, the forecaster told me that today was the only chance to fly to Ushuaia before Christmas. I was keen to get back. I had spoken to Jeppesen who advised me not to go and to Jonathan who had confirmed that the forecast for Ushuaia was not so good, but not impossible. What a dilemma, made worse by knowing what had happened to Jennifer and Colin.

With the help of Coco and Charlie I took the decision to go. We went out to the hangar to re-fuel. We checked the fuel drums for impurities and re-fuelled with the hand pump and filter. Everyone was helping and taking photos. The oil was still reading the maximum twelve litres in spite of the three-and-a-half hour flight the previous day. "Golf November is a star," I said to myself.

There were ten people helping. Two enormous heaters were wheeled out. Three of the guys pulled me into the clothing, the Multifabs survival suit and life jacket. I checked the EPIRB (the emergency beacon). All was well. A digger was driven out to clear the snow.

There was a hug and kiss from everyone. Such warmth, it was overwhelming. Coco told me that Jennifer and Colin had been rescued and were currently in Patriot Hills waiting to be flown to Punta Arenas. "Both are alive," he said. "Jennifer has broken her leg." It was a great relief, but sadly they did not get away that lightly. Colin had some serious back injuries which took several operations and months to recover. In spite of his back injuries, he had managed to erect a tent to protect them both. ALE had executed an impeccable rescue operation in the most difficult whiteout conditions, and literally saved their lives.

There were more hugs and kisses. It was sad to leave such hospitality so soon. Climbing up over the island, I waggled my wings in farewell. They all stood watching until they were just dots in the distance. The sky was a clear blue above. "Perhaps it will be alright," I prayed. But I could not get Jennifer and Colin out of my mind.

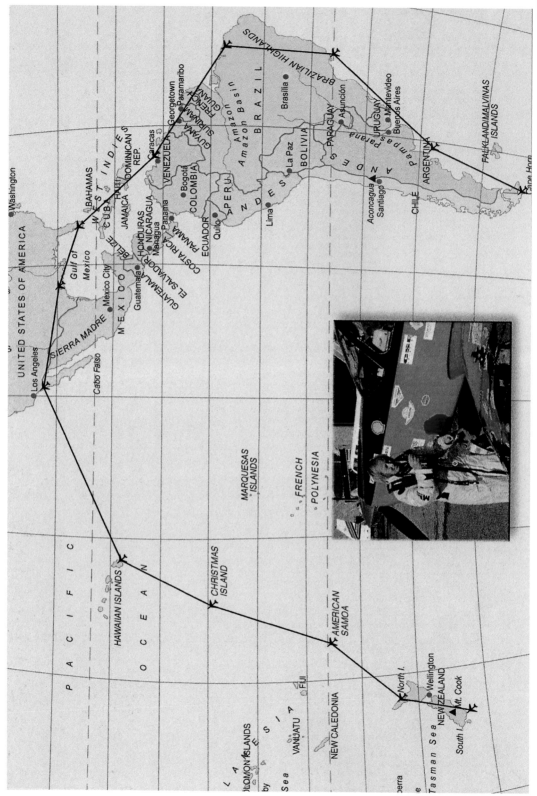

Map of the detour.

The Longest Detour

U shuaia. What a welcome sight! Ice had cracked my side window and the wind was howling through. The noise was deafening and I could hardly hear the controller. Gabriela was jumping up and down as I taxied in. "Polly, Polly," she yelled excitedly. Roxanna said, "You are staying in our house Polly – we will sleep on the boat." What generosity. With just five days left until Christmas I settled into the little house in Teshne.

"You could give up and fly home in time for Christmas," a little voice inside urged, but in my heart I knew this was not an option. I had too many commitments en route from New Zealand back home, so I settled down to planning my long detour.

Jonathan Selby repaired my side window which had been cracked by the build-up of ice on my flight back from Antarctica to Ushuaia.

I would fly back through South America, across to Florida then along the southern United States until I reached the coast. I would then fly island hopping across the Pacific, the largest ocean in the world. The route would take me from Santa Barbara to Hilo in Hawaii – an approximate time of sixteen hours – a further ten hours to Christmas Island, another ten hours to American Samoa and finally fourteen hours to Auckland. A further five hours would get me to Dunedin in the south of New Zealand where I could pick up my original route. It was a daunting prospect, but I just had to get on with it.

I no longer had my maps and charts which I had sent home to lighten the aircraft so I rang Peter Cowley at Jeppesen UK. Peter was one step ahead of me, "The charts for your detour have been despatched from California."

I contacted DHL in Ushuaia and they promised to phone me when the parcels arrived. There was nothing more to be done as it was Christmas. I flew the short distance to Puerto Williams on the other side of the Beagle Channel, as by tradition all the serious yachties meet there for Christmas. There were sixteen yachts of varying sizes, all of which were peoples' homes and each one was so individual. I slept on Roxanna and Jonathan's yacht, *Anahera*, (Maori for Angel). It was like being in the arms of an angel with this wonderful family. Jonathan and some friends even spent Christmas Eve repairing my cracked window.

Christmas Day was a simple affair. Gabriela hoped for just one present from Father Christmas. When she received eight her eyes were wide with wonder and disbelief. Everyone prepared food aboard their own yachts and then came together for a communal feast. It was cold and sunny as we stood sharing our Christmas meals on the deck of the old grey naval ship which had now become the yacht club. All was calm and peace as the children played together on the banks. On Boxing Day, after a long walk amongst the hills and flower-covered meadows, I flew back to Ushuaia.

I wrote my diary on Jonathan and Roxanna's yacht *Anahera* on Christmas Day 2003 at Puerto Williams.

A couple of days later one of the two boxes of maps arrived at the DHL office. Amazingly they were the charts for as far as Trinidad so I was able to pass the time plotting the first part of my return route. But the second box failed to arrive and I was getting impatient. New Year was looming and I knew the office would be closed for three days. How much longer would I have to wait? I decided to stage a sit-in at the DHL office. Jean Paul, the manager was there.

"I wait here until it arrives," I managed to convey, in spite of my poor Spanish and his poor English. He looked perturbed and rang Buenos Aires. The lady who had promised it would arrive was not there and I was put onto someone else. "I am afraid it is not possible," she said. "Everything is possible," I retorted, knowing that at least two flights a day come to Ushuaia. "I will ring you back," she promised.

I buried my head in my book. Jean Paul wanted to go, but I sat resolutely pretending not to notice. The lady rang back, "I am sorry," she said "but it is not possible today." I retorted, "It is possible. You have had it for over two weeks instead of six days. I am sitting here for however long it takes to resolve this." Looking around the stuffy little office I wondered how I would manage camping there for three days – was there a loo? Jean Paul ate a yoghurt. She asked me to hold on while she spoke to her supervisor, "I am sorry, but there is nothing I can do about this," she came back to me.

I resolutely replied, "there is always something you can do about something and I am sitting here until that parcel arrives." I got my book out again. Jean Paul was restless. He put another tape in the machine and ate another yoghurt. Time ticked on. No-one, but no-one in Ushuaia thinks of getting angry or cross.

"The package is in Rio Gallegos and the customs are not working until Friday." The supervisor rang back this time. That was two whole days away. "Don't tell me that the customs are not working for the people wanting to fly to Ushuaia today," I said. "Can't you get someone to take the package through customs?" They have this peculiar rule that even though Ushuaia is in Argentina, anything or anybody going to Patagonia has to pass through customs.

Ten minutes later Sebastian, the supervisor rang back. "I have good news and bad news," he said. "I cannot get the package to Ushuaia, but if you like, I can get it back to Buenos Aires and have it delivered by 1000 on Friday morning in Buenos Aires." I asked him how I could be sure that would happen. After all they said the package would arrive yesterday and it had not and then they said it would arrive today and again it failed to materialise. He gave me his direct telephone number and told me that he would make sure the parcel arrived himself personally.

He then said, "Before you go Polly I want to say I am so very sorry this has happened." How could I be cross? It was disarming, but nonetheless I was desperate. In fact the Argentines are not used to people insisting. They look drained and go pale and you feel bad. I never heard a cross word in all the eight weeks I spent in Ushuaia. I had always tried so hard to be an ambassador for my country. I knew I should be patient, but my patience had run out. I needed to move on.

New Year's Day and the weather was reasonable. Golf November was packed and ready. With grim determination I left Ushuaia once again but with a nostalgic backward glance to the town at the end of the world. I wondered how soon I could get back to that beautiful place where I had experienced such wonderful friendship even though I had gone through some agonising moments. Now I had serious business in front of me. I had to make up lost time. The pressure was on.

I flew up the coast of Argentina to Buenos Aires. There, as promised, was my parcel of maps. As I left Argentine air space two pilots spoke on the radio. "Good Luck – Good Luck!" said one whilst the other said "Beautiful!"

I rose early each morning and pushed on, but now I was flying to make up time. Every day it was a slog, and every day I kept at it. As I flew northwards through Uruguay to Brazil I couldn't stop myself from wondering what I was doing. I had been away from home for eight months and the flight of my life over Antarctica had come to an abrupt end. Now I was retracing my steps trying to recover

Gerard and Margy Moss at home in Rio de Janeiro. Gerard has flown a Ximango motor glider around the world.

what I felt I had lost. Every evening I was exhausted yet not having planned for this detour every night I had to work out the route and flight plan for the next day's flight. Still tired in the morning I had to keep going and it was a challenge to keep up the momentum but I had many moments of sheer elation as I marvelled at the desert and rain forests I was flying over. I often glanced at all the names on the wings and wondered what they were all doing. I still considered it a comfort to see them there and I felt a real sense of everyone willing me on.

Golf November just kept going, she didn't seem to care whether it was extremely hot or very cold. The early aviators had less reliable aircraft and very basic navigation aids. Those heroic days will never return but modern aviators face different challenges, the most significant of them being, from my experience, bureaucracy.

In Rio de Janeiro Margi and Gerard Moss were once again my generous hosts. Gerard is a very experienced long distance pilot and his wife Margi is a navigator, writer, organiser and founder of Earthrounders, the website recording all solo world flights. In spite of them being in the midst of a major project measuring the water pollution in the lakes and waterways of Brazil, they found time for me to stay and hosted an enjoyable and relaxing dinner party in my honour.

Golf November was due for a fifty-hour inspection and Gerard recommended an engineer at another airport, Jacarapantua, ten minutes flight down the coast. He duly dropped me at Santos Dumont airport so that I could fly on to Jacarapantua. Horror of horrors, I had forgotten to bring my pilot's licence. They refused to let me through to my aircraft. I even had the number of my licence but that was no good. There was nothing for it but I had to get a taxi back to Gerard's house to pick it up. In vain I had been trying to travel light by leaving my flight bag behind and just taking the essentials for a ten-minute flight.

At Jacarapantua I taxied up to Jato, the company who would do my maintenance check. Apolo, the manager, asked for my overflight documents. Despair! I didn't have those with me either. "No problem," said Apolo. "We will ring Gerard and get him to fax them through to us." I was anxious not to keep worrying Gerard but I knew that without those documents, I would not be allowed to return to Santos Dumont, the airport in the middle of the bay where I had first landed.

Golf November was gleaming and rearing to go. Then the fun began. I had to go to one office to show my flying licence and file a flight plan. We then went to another office. Here they scrutinized my overflight clearance which Gerard had faxed. They shook their heads, "We need to see the original."

This was ridiculous as I was only going ten minutes down the coast, all in the same city. They copied the details onto a computer from the faxed copies. I was then ushered to see the head of the airport. I felt as if I was some sort of criminal.

The airport director was most perturbed because I could not produce the originals. He asked to see all the aircraft documents and my flying licence again. He started taking all the pages out of my flying licence one by one. He then asked if I had my medical to see if I was fit to fly! "You will have to produce all the documents at Santos Dumont," he said as he finally released me after two hours. I was exasperated, and felt like hitting him, but smiled sweetly instead.

I flew back to Santos Dumont not feeling at all happy and fighting to keep my cool. I was met by Edouardo the handler who had an important looking official with him. I wanted to scream, but held my hand out to the official with a broad smile. "Where are your original documents?" he launched in without a smile. I don't know where he thought I was going to spirit them from. Edouardo was translating. "He says that you must go and get them NOW."

I had had enough and was determined not to take a taxi back to Gerard's just to get the document. I was hot, tired and cross. The refueller turned up so I started the refuelling process whilst the official was standing by. Edouardo came up. "He wants to see your aircraft documents."

I handed him the documents and continued helping the refueller. He then asked for my licence. I handed that to him. He scrutinised it carefully. He spoke no English so I am not sure what he deduced from my licence. He said again that I would have to go and get the original documents. This would entail a half-hour taxi journey in each direction. I was most certainly not going to do that. Edouardo said, "He insists you go and get the original documents." I replied, "He has the copies. I am NOT going back to the flat and coming back again tonight. I'll bring them in the morning." The official replied, "You can't do that as I won't be on duty." To which I retorted, "You can leave a note for someone else," feeling extremely angry with his uncompromising attitude.

He stomped off saying, "You'll be punished for this!" I wondered what exactly he thought he would do to punish me. I was amused and thought it would be funny if he caused a diplomatic incident because I had shown him a copy instead of the original and all for a ten-minute flight! My imagination ran riot thinking of policemen and prison cells. The next morning I presented all my documents to the officials on duty. The problem had stemmed from the fact that the officials in Porto Allegro where I had first entered the country had given me a copy instead of the original. The official made a phone call and all was resolved in just a few minutes. I was free to go.

My troubles were not entirely over, however. I suffered the most dreadful stomach upset en route to Salvador. Sickness overcame me and I went into a cold sweat. Trying to fly the aircraft and cope with sharp griping pains became a battle. At one point I doubted that I could land the aircraft as I was doubled up with pain and nausea. I had to keep saying to myself, "whatever you feel like you *must* put the aeroplane down safely – concentrate." Summoning up all the effort I could find, I managed to land Golf November in spite of the agony I was in. After that it was impossible to continue and I spent a day in bed in an attempt to recover.

In spite of ever present nausea I pushed on. As I approached the north coast of Brazil, I entered the Inter Tropical Convergence Zone (ITCZ), and now I faced build-ups of cloud and monsoon. Huge clouds towered above and all around me. It was hard work dodging the largest clouds but exciting flying in between them. Really early morning departures were the order of the day, to avoid the huge build-ups from the steaming midday heat.

After an eight-hour flight it took four hours to clear customs in Trinidad. And I thought I had left bureaucracy behind... Ro rang. Anthony Mollison had just sent £24,000 to Flying Scholarships for the Disabled. This was tremendously good news. When Ro opened the cheque she thought it was for £24 – she did not have her glasses on. She tried to ring Anthony to thank him and tell him that she would put his name on the wing. She was going to add a pound to make it up to £25, the minimum donation required. Luckily she didn't get through. When she put her glasses on she realized her mistake and had to sit down with a gin and tonic!

I stayed with Eve John in Antigua. Eve had lost her husband, Hugh, about six months before. She was devastated. I mentioned to her that I had just heard we had had a large donation for the charity from a chap who owned a flying school in Bournemouth. "Was it Anthony Mollison?" Eve enquired out of the blue. "Yes," I replied with surprise. "Do you know him?"

"Rather," she said. "It was Hugh's flying school and he passed it on to Anthony when we came to live out here." She went on, "He is the great nephew of Amy Mollison, the famous aviatrix Amy Johnson who married Jim Mollison. Eve perked up when she heard this news. "I have been waiting for a sign from Hugh," she said. "This is it." Her whole countenance changed.

The flight across the Bahamas to Fort Lauderdale in Florida had a certain poignancy. It was my sixtieth birthday. I wanted to forget it. I told everyone firmly that I was "twenty-one and some months" and I kept telling myself, "you are only as old as you feel."

The flat islands, lagoons and reefs of the Bahamas looked like pancakes sitting on a shallow lake. There was a huge sandbank in the middle of the ocean. It reminded me of the sandbank in the middle of the Solent where the 'Island Yacht Club' play 'The Royal Southern Yacht Club' at cricket once a year. Peter and I were once invited for the day on a friend's boat to see the 'J' class yachts racing in the Solent. In the evening we landed on the sandbank as the tide receded. Everyone was dressed in white. Wickets were set up and the game proceeded. After twenty minutes the tide began to rise and everyone rushed for their boats. Where, other than England would you see such a crazy event?

On arriving in Florida the man in Immigration looked at my passport. "Happy Birthday," he said. "In fact it's a big one." I put my finger to my mouth and said "shsh" whilst thinking that it was sharp of him to pick that up.

"I hear it's your birthday," the lady in the Fixed Base Operator (FBO) said, and produced a box with a birthday cake in it, which was a wonderful surprise. I had been flying for eight hours across the flat islands and lagoons of the Bahamas, but I had another hour's flight up to Vero Beach. There I was meeting Clive our middle son who would spend a couple of days with me. Piper Aircraft replaced the window that had cracked in the ice. It was a real tribute to the ingenuity of Jonathan and the yachties that the repaired window had lasted that long.

The pressure was on. This detour had been different from the rest of the flight. There was no publicity, no television, journalists or presentations but there was no let up. I had to make ground as fast as was safely possible. The international language for air traffic control is English. I really doubt I would have learnt to fly aged fifty if I had had to learn another language. However, the English spoken is not always easy to understand. Flying into Houston air space in Texas I contacted air traffic control. Houston is a busy airport with a lot of jet traffic. It is class A airspace, meaning that you *must* do what the controller tells you. The controller said "G-FRGN – fly direct Chony."

I wrote C-H-O-N-Y on my kneepad. I looked everywhere on my chart for a radio aid called Chony. Not a trace anywhere. It was imperative that I did what the controller said. I put my finger on the button and said, "Say again." He said, "Fly direct Chony," even faster than before.

I combed my map for Chony. I just could *not* find it anywhere. I was getting desperate. Again I put my finger on the button and called, "Sir – please could you spell it as I don't understand your accent." He responded in a slow drawl, "Ma'am – I don't *have* an accent!" He did, however spell it for me, "Tango, Romeo, India, November, India, Tango, Yankee." – TRINITY! John and Susanne York met me at Houston. Susanne learnt to fly after she discovered she had Multiple Sclerosis (MS). She now has her instrument rating as well. She had a keen interest in the charity. Sadly, no-one with even mild MS is allowed to fly solo in the UK.

The maintenance check at Santa Barbara before my sixteen-hour crossing of the Pacific, with the singing mechanic Jose Corral and assistant Joan Steinberger at Stratman Aviation.

As so often during this big dash to make up time, I had to leave before first light. Checking the aircraft in the dark was not easy. It was vital to look for water or other contamination in the fuel but torchlight created all sorts of shadows and it was difficult to see. Checking the oil was a problem too. Being short I could not reach the top of the cowling. I had to stand on tiptoe, pull the dipstick right out and then hold it in front of me to read. Doing this in the dark with a torch was precarious. Dropping the dipstick on the ground would pick up debris which could land up in the engine, not to mention the fact that oil might splatter all over my clothes.

The amazing thing about flying in the States is there are no landing fees. Facilities at Fixed Base Operators are free. They generally have comfortable areas to sit, with coffee and biscuits on tap. If you are out in a rural area they will often lend you a car. Access to a full weather brief and filing a flight plan over the phone is free too. You just dial 1-800-WX BRIEF and you are through to a briefer who does everything for you. You are given full weather details for your route and updated on all the NOTAMS (Notices to Airmen) which alert you to any changes in equipment at airports and temporary restricted air space. They file your flight plan for you. The whole system is remarkably 'user friendly'.

At Santa Barbara Golf November had a thorough check to prepare her for the long Pacific crossing. The first leg from Santa Barbara to Hilo, Hawaii is 2,068 nms. Once more I questioned what I was doing taking a single-engine aircraft over such long distances of water. I had to make myself get out of bed the morning of departure. I was so apprehensive, even though I had made the same crossing in the reverse direction several years earlier.

I knew that some of the flight would inevitably be in the dark because it would take me sixteen hours. Imagine what it was like taking off from Santa Barbara to cross such a huge expanse of water. Leaving the safety of land is the most difficult thing to do. My hourly diary written in the aircraft says it all.

1st Hour

I have had conflicting forecasts and it is very marginal. I may have to turn around. Feeling most anxious and I have some headwind at the moment so feeling decidedly uncomfortable – I really DO want to get there but I DO have to have enough fuel and unless I gather a lot more speed, I am not going to make it. Established contact on HF radio with San Francisco who will watch me all the way – just not loud and clear. Filled in Mirce forms – done fuel calculation – have 18 hours at 65% power – Jepps forecast N. winds to begin with and changing to East for most of the flight which would work OK – but it has to be there within 3-4 hours.

2nd Hour

It's just about OK – I've picked up some speed – now doing 125 kts (speed over the ground 'groundspeed') – I'm sitting on top of cloud and feeling slightly more relaxed (not much) – just doing 126 kts and feeling excited, but hardly dare 'hold my breath' – had half a muesli bar and some sips of water – have done lots of exercises to keep the circulation going – now GPS says 14 hours 35 minutes to go – I've just done 2 hours so hope to get some improvement on that or I'll have to turn around. The first couple of hours are the worst and then you settle down a bit. The sun is shining – I have done some exercises to prevent deep vein thrombosis, also to keep the limbs from getting stiff – now 125 kts – gloom – 2 hours has just whizzed by – I wish I could pick up some more speed. Now 124 kts which is not good enough – sometimes, I hardly dare look – still over 1,825 miles to go – it is a long way and I must be careful – picking up speed again 125 kts – now 126 kts – this is a knife edge.

3rd Hour

Another hour has gone and it's still marginal – what a nightmare and knife edge – can't seem to get more than 123 kts – more nightmare – done some exercises – done Mirce charts – rang Peter – he could hear me quite well – want him to ring Jepps about wind etc. – need to pick up more wind (I am heading slightly south of course as suggested to pick up what wind I can) – another half muesli bar – I must be crazy doing this without a good tailwind.

4th Hour

Some high cirrus clouds here – still only doing 118 kts – surely it must get better soon – this is a nerve jangling affair – now only doing 116 kts – I still may have to turn round. This is like a mini nightmare – beautiful 'on top' with some cirrus clouds obscuring the sun which keeps it cooler.

5th Hour

Now done 5 hours and picking up speed so feeling a lot better – clear skies ahead – even the cloud beneath me disappearing – there is a definite line where it ends and it looks as if I am on target – not holding my breath just yet!! 11 hours 37 minutes to go and if I keep this up I will do it in sixteen and a half hours – but may not be able to keep it up – mustn't get too excited. Did a bit of filming in the last hour – just spoken to American 39 – they had a message from San Francisco with a different HF frequency – this is even beginning to be some fun – but mustn't get too excited – darling Peter is monitoring me and I bet he won't get much sleep tonight – it is 1940Z and thus the same time for him – poor chap – will speak to him soon.

6th Hour

Over a third of the way and feeling better as long as I can get 9 hours out of ferry tank – always a worry – there seems to be one worry after another – now doing 125 kts – wish it would pick up just a tiny bit more – I'd feel safer. Beautiful sunny day – no clouds to speak of – just a few 'puffers' around – time going quickly as so anxious – will have to take final decision Point of No Return (PNR) at about 8 hours. Am doing a TAS (true air speed) of 126 kts and groundspeed of 132 kts!! 9 hours 34 minutes to go – been in air for 6 hours 40 minutes – must be lovely to sail in the Pacific when it is as calm and sunny as this.

7th Hour

Doing much better speed – nearly half way – well that makes me feel better – actually I've got 172 nms to go to half way, but I feel as if I'm getting there – now doing 134 kts so getting quite excited. The beginning was a bit nerve wracking – one watches the GPS like a hawk and if it moves up or down a notch, you get correspondingly excited or despondent. Just over 9 hours to run and have done just 7 – so feeling quite good as long as the fuel lasts out which it should do (calculating all the time – no let up) – almost got to a real safety margin – then can relax! Might be going into some puffy cloud but temp. now +14C so should be "icing no factor" as the Americans would say. Hardly dare feel better yet – but beginning to enjoy – now doing 141 kts – yeehaa (Jepps were absolutely spot on with their forecasting).

I can't understand what has happened. For some reason, I ran the left tank dry – I couldn't possibly have done seven hours on it so would like to know when and how it got changed – now I AM in a muddle as haven't a clue how much is left in the ferry tank. I am now really scared as if the ferry tank runs dry now – I won't have enough fuel left to go either way.

8th Hour

I decided that I must climb over and check the big tank. This entailed setting the auto pilot, undoing my seat belt and with a lot of contortion turn myself around to kneel on my seat – thank God there's at least a third there – can't think when and why I changed onto the left tank – must have been sleep walking – gave me a scare – now just under 7 hours to run – Talk about being in a pickle – I decided to go to the loo while I was in control and not bursting. I knew that even I couldn't manage 16 hours! I got all my gear off – easier than last time – I'm becoming more adept (the guys don't know how lucky they are!) The top of my 'Lady Jane' is cracked so some of it leaked – so now I am sitting in wet pants with wet seeping down my legs – most undignified and uncomfortable. BUT I feel heaps better for having relieved myself – not sure how I am going to clean inside immersion suit – I guess I'll just have to sponge it – AND I've got nearly 7 more hours sitting like this – ugh!

9th Hour

The sun is now in the west and shining in my eyes – if I can keep this speed up I'll just have 6 ¹/₂ hours more – the worry of the fuel and the anxiety of whether to turn round makes these long flights more of a challenge than a pleasure – you sit and listen for that engine 'cough' which signifies an empty tank as you want to use every drop of fuel you can. Speed dropping off now – only 137 kts (the highest I got was 147 kts) – horrors – God – I hope I can make it – what a dreadful thought – I am really 'bricking it' (an expression my children tell me I shouldn't use!). Mad at myself over the tank – I usually use the left tank as a quick change over when I am just about to run the auxiliary tank dry and now I don't have that facility which means I have to be even quicker off the mark changing the tap which lies behind me and under the suitcases – this requires considerable contortions. Just romping along – how long can this last? – not long – it's dropping off again. Magical sight with sun shining in front and a few puffy clouds over calm greyish sea. I've just seen a boat – heavens! – It looks a big one too. I bet the sea is choppier than it looks – it looks like a millpond – 5 hours 42 minutes to go.

10th Hour
Well I'm two-thirds the way through the flight which is a good feeling – still plenty of fuel and it's just a matter of being patient before I push up the power – I want to be 100% sure that I have more than enough – it's a beautiful evening and the time has gone really quickly – 'Someone' is looking after me – as always. Doing lots of exercises and feel quite good. I am not speaking to Peter until 0400Z as poor chap needs some sleep – gosh my transponder is bleeping – I can't believe it if they can pick me up from out here – just over 5 hours to run – It's been magic once the really scary bit was over.

11th Hour
Back up to 140 kts which is exciting – sun right in front of me now – but still quite high in the sky – hopefully there won't be too much flying in the dark. Last time I flew this long leg – in the other direction – 9 hours was in darkness – I didn't really mind it 'tho' as I had that lovely view of the two moons which was a real bonus. The speed has dropped to 130 kts – so glad I didn't put full power on – not yet anyway. Beautiful sun shining on mid size cumulus beneath me – it's magic – maybe the other side of these clouds we will pick up speed again. Sure enough it has picked up a bit the other side of these cumulus clouds which were visibly collapsing in the evening sun.

12th Hour
Have just been through some build-ups with light rain – that slowed me down to 120 kts but now doing 132 kts again – long may that last – I see a big nasty one ahead – but hopefully it's isolated – I could do without these hassles at the end of a long flight – trouble is when it gets dark, I can't see them – gosh – how I would love to be there. 3 hours 41 minutes to go.

13th Hour
I've had to stop looking at the clock because I am becoming impatient – three more long legs over the Pacific, but none as difficult as this one – I shall be glad when it is over. Now doing 130 kts with just 2 hours 39 minutes to go – should be able to speak to Hilo soon. The sun has set so it will be dark soon. It is not quite dark but there is a beautiful new moon and the evening star shining brightly.

14th Hour
It is now virtually dark although there is a red glow in the distance – spoke to Peter at 0400 and he is going to ring Jepps to get the latest weather for me – I'll ring him at 0500.

I had no chance to write more. As soon as darkness fell I could see lightning flash on the horizon. I was plunged into horrendous storm clouds as the stars disappeared. The strobe lights at the ends of the wings reflected off the surrounding clouds and the rain had a weird effect. Everything was jolted around the cockpit as I reduced to 'turbulence penetration' speed. I wished I had a Stormscope. I gathered from the Hilo controller that there was a whole line of storms. I could hear airliners making eighty-mile detours. My fuel limitation did not allow me that luxury. I had nowhere to go except straight on.

'Carby heat – on – lean the mixture – carby heat off – richen the mixture – on and off – on and off' as the rain beat down. The strobes flashed and I had a job keeping altitude. No good using auto-pilot in these conditions so it was hand flying and concentrating like mad, nearly two hours of this hell. Peter rang, but I cut him off. All my focus was on flying the aircraft. The controller gave me ILS for runway 08. The plate for ILS r/w 08 must have been floating around the cockpit somewhere. I tried to get out the Jeppesen book to check but I was tossed around and it crashed to the floor. Everything fell off the tank in the back.

"God – this is ghastly," I thought but it was no use feeling sorry for myself, I had to get through it. There was no time to think of anything else. It was a life and death situation. If I let up just for a few seconds I would have been in the drink. It was interminable. Lightning was flashing not far off. The controller vectored me as best he could. He was great. He gave me ILS r/w 26. It made no difference as there was a crosswind. They had just had a massive thunder storm at Hilo. I had been in the air for sixteen hours. Exhausted, yet relieved I came in on final. The runway lights shone reassuringly at last. It wasn't over yet. I got all the speeds wrong and bounced about four times. Realising that Golf November would not settle, "Full power on – go around" I yelled to myself as I left the runway wondering how on earth I would ever manage to land.

"Golf November is going around," I told the controller sounding much calmer than I felt. "God – will I get it down this time?" I wondered, feeling worn out and scared all at once. On the second attempt I executed what we call 'an arrival' which just means I managed somehow to put the aircraft safely on the deck. I had not bounced so many times since I first learnt to fly.

Tim from the handlers had been worried as he had been told I was due to arrive at 1630 local but I did not land until 2030 – I don't know who told him that. I filed for sixteen hours and actually did it in sixteen hours and five minutes, a pretty good estimate over such a long distance. I struggled out of my immersion suit. My legs felt stiff and seemed to have a mind of their own.

Tim took me to the hotel but there was no chance of a meal as the restaurant had closed at 2100 (about when they open in Argentina!). I could have done with something light like soup, but the best I could do was a bottle of fizzy drink out of the machine. I soaked in a bath or at least I tried to soak, but the plug was useless and I had to keep the tap running to keep the bath full. I lay wide awake, my mind churning over the events of the last day and my adrenalin still flowing. I had sat in the cockpit for sixteen hours, flown through thunderstorms and come through unscathed. I rang Peter and relived it again. He had sat up all night monitoring my flight. It amazed me that someone could love me so much.

It was definitely time to rest and recover. Wanting to see the volcanoes I hired a car and went to the local supermarket for some food to make a picnic. I love avocado sandwiches and there was a great big pile of avocados. However, fingering them, I found they were all rock hard. There was a tall young guy also feeling the avocados and he managed to find a ripe one and then one which wasn't quite so ripe. "You have the soft one and I'll take this one," he said. It was little kindnesses like this that really gave me energy.

Finally, I gave into exhaustion. After a while the adrenalin wore off. I slept for fifteen hours. The following day I packed my back pack with avocado sandwiches and the camera and drove out of the hotel onto Banyon Drive which is flanked by huge banyon trees. These massive multi-trunked trees formed a tunnel. Each one had a plaque at its base, planted by someone famous. There was Ellsworth, after whom the mountains in Antarctica are named, Amelia Earhart, the aviatrix lost somewhere in the Pacific between Lae, Papua New Guinea and Howland Island, and Richard Nixon.

Feeling very relaxed after my long sleep, I ambled along in the car soaking in the green grass, tall trees and ferns along the Hawaii Beltway, the road which circles the island. It was Sunday and I had not been to church for ages. I wished I could find a nice church, but it was already past eleven in the morning. By now I was about ten miles out of Hilo, driving along at a leisurely pace, enjoying the scenery and ruminating quietly to myself. Suddenly, as if by magic, a little wooden church appeared. It was standing on top of a small raised mound and looked quite delightful in its cream and brown paint and little wooden spire. As I drove past I noticed the door was open and there was a crowd inside.

The strangest thing then happened. I tried to continue my drive but a voice inside was urging me to turn around and go back to the church. The voice nagged and nagged and in the end I just had to go back. I parked the car and crept into the rear seats. The church was full. All the women were wearing white, a lot of them with exotic white flowers in their dark hair. The choir was singing. The air was filled with the most wonderful harmony and rhythm. The warm breeze wafted the rich scent of tropical flowers. It reminded me of the Inuit Church in Resolute Bay. So much had happened since then, yet here, so far away from that remote icy corner where the warmth of the people was so overwhelming, I was once again uplifted by a spiritual experience beyond my control.

It was not until the last hymn that I discovered a hymn book beside me. I opened it at the appropriate page. Everything was in the native language so I did not understand a word, but I can read music so I joined in the singing lustily. It was more than a coincidence that I was wearing my white shirt that day. At the end of the service everyone came up and shook hands and gave me a kiss. They invited me to stay for a Hawaiian lunch and I decided to 'go with the flow'. The avocado sandwiches would make a good supper. In the church hall at the back a magnificent feast was spread out on trestle tables.

Everyone came up and spoke. On enquiring why they wore white, they told me that four times a year the two Hawaiian churches on the island gather together for a service and feast. These churches like to keep the Hawaiian traditions alive. I sat next to a remarkable lady who was ninety-five. She did not look a day older than sixty-five and was sharp as a razor. Before I left I was given a quotation to take with me from Psalm 139. Driving away, I saw my new friend waving energetically from the roadside. She was blowing kisses.

Driving back to Hilo the heavens opened and the rain beat against the windscreen. By the time I reached the airport the rain was torrential. There was no way I could refuel Golf November in such a downpour. If water got into the fuel it could be fatal. It was just not worth the risk and besides

Lunch at the little church in Hawaii where all the women wore white.

Cassidy International Airport, Christmas Island comprises a runway and a hut.

which the storm had put out the runway lights. I was forced to spend another day at Hilo. This was frustrating, but in retrospect I was still mentally tired from my long flight that another day of enforced rest was in fact just what I needed.

I rose earlier the following morning. Even at 0500 Tim was waiting at the airport to help me file my flight plan. "The runway lights are still not working," he said "but you can use the short runway." The aircraft was fully laden so I was not keen on using the 'short' runway, especially in the heat, but at least we were at sea level. The air is denser at sea level so aircraft need a shorter take-off run, however if it is hot the air becomes less dense cancelling out the sea level effect and a longer take-off run is needed. Anyway I told myself that the shorter runway would be fine.

I was taking off for Christmas Island where I had had a bad experience on my last flight. I had been obliged to land at Aeon, the runway the British had built for nuclear tests in the 1950s. No-one had been there when I landed and I had no means of contacting anyone. The main and only other airport, Cassidy International, was only open on a Monday! Millions of crabs had crawled across the roads and the driver had tried to weave his way between them to avoid their claws puncturing the tyres. This time, after a ten-hour flight, the island stood out peacefully in the sun with its beautiful lagoon dominating the whole aspect. I stayed in the Captain Cook Hotel, the only one on the island. There was no evidence of crabs and I was able to sit on the coral beach for an hour before sunset.

The pressure was still on and I took off early the next day for another long flight to Pago Pago (pronounced Pango Pango) in American Samoa. En route I had a call from Martino at Jeppesen UK. "Pago Pago are saying the airport is closed." Panic, where could I go? "From 0630Z," Martino went on.

Why didn't he say that at the beginning? That was much later than my estimated arrival time. I was shaking at the thought of having nowhere to go. In fact Western Samoa is close by, but I knew they had no avgas, so I would be stuck if I landed there.

Nine hours later I arrived at Pago Pago. Last time there had been an arch of sea water forced up through blow holes at the edge of the runway which is built out into the sea on the coral. It made a spectacular sight. This time the sea was calm and the tide was low so the runway was clear of spray. The airport manager and Janet, whom I had met before, were standing on the apron.

"We are closing the airfield for repairs. What time do you want to leave tomorrow?" they asked. "I would like to leave at 0600." "OK – I will tell the runway workers that they can't start until you have left." The manager replied. That was something of a relief. Janet was not sure if there was any avgas available. Could I wait until the morning to refuel?

"Definitely not," I replied, knowing how long these things take. It was +30°C. I could have done without hassle. I still had all my survival gear on. Janet took me to her trailer which had been trashed recently in a hurricane. I sat around feeling impatient. "When will the fuel be ready?" I ventured to ask every so often. "Soon, soon," Janet replied.

I continued to wait. Apparently they had to decant the fuel from drums into a cart. I had had a nine-hour flight from Christmas Island. There was nothing I could do. Eventually they turned up and re-fuelling began. I always do the internal fuelling myself, using my hand filter. The whole operation took an hour. Thank heavens I had insisted on refuelling that evening. They never would have done it in time in the morning.

The following day I was at the airport at 0500. The head of the tourist office was already there. They held a little ceremony and I was presented with a 'Chief's Talking Staff', a beautifully carved wooden pole about the same height as myself. The Chief always holds the staff when addressing his audience. On showing it to Peter later he said, "Polly, you talk enough anyway without that!"

As dawn broke the stunning view of the runway running out into the coral lay before me. At cruise altitude I had a big headwind once more and was only doing 95 kts groundspeed. At this speed I would be cutting it fine to reach Auckland with enough reserve. I started to scour the maps for alternate landing sites. Nadi in Fiji was out because I knew that they had no Avgas. Gradually I picked up speed to 110 kts. I called Jeppesen on the satellite phone. "You will have neutral winds at 25 South and a tailwind for the last quarter." Steve was confident.

I sat back and began to enjoy being alone in the skies. I had a glimpse of Tonga on my starboard side. This brought back memories of Queen Elizabeth II's coronation in 1953. The Queen of Tonga insisted on driving in an open carriage in spite of the fact that she was over eighty and it was raining. I was eight at the time and very well remember sitting on the floor all day in front of a small 14" black and white television screen.

Approaching Auckland the sun shone through layers of cloud onto the grey blue water. A line of puffy cumulus clouds reminded me of a row of grey-haired ladies sitting at the hairdresser. It was comic and beautiful all at once. In front of me was the blue purple outline of New Zealand. I became really excited. Peter would be in Dunedin. I had one night planned in Auckland before flying to Dunedin, but the excitement was already getting to me.

I contacted Auckland Control. "Would you like vectors for a visual approach. That way you can have a sight seeing tour over the city?" he said. "Affirm," I replied, and felt warmly welcomed by the controller who was happy to spend time vectoring me when the easiest thing would have been to give me an instrument approach.

I taxied up to the handling agent, Air Center One. The first thing that happened was they passed an aerosol spray can through my little window to me. I had to spray the cockpit in case of unwanted 'bugs'. It was horrid stuff and made me feel nauseous. I had to sit there for five minutes before opening the door. I filled in all the logs whilst waiting and pretended not to notice the foul odour from the spray. I was approached by a man from 'Agriculture'.

"Have you any fruit or meat on board?" he enquired. Luckily I had eaten my last apple en route. "What is that?" he said pointing at my Chief's Talking Stick. "Where did it come from? Let me see it."

He took the staff and inspected it all over. To my astonishment he hung onto it. I did not want him confiscating that, I really loved it. He started to walk off with it. I was standing on my wing. I shouted after him. "Are you really going to take that away with you?" He turned round rather sheepishly and said, "Oh no! – it's fine, I just forgot I was holding it." "Lucky I spoke up," I thought as I smiled at the man.

'The longest detour on earth' was coming to an end. I was finally flying to Dunedin. The last I heard from Peter was that he had been seriously delayed at Heathrow. Unknown to me he had managed to get re-routed via Sydney and was well on his way. There was no response from his mobile phone. My flight to Dunedin was just four and a half hours. It was one of my shortest but seemed to be one of the longest. It was so near the end of the detour and Peter would be there. I could hardly contain myself. When I was overhead Christchurch I finally had a response from Peter. "Where are you?" "I am in Christchurch," he replied. What a coincidence that he was immediately below me.

I continued on what seemed like an endless flight. I was on top of cloud so I had to fly rather a complicated instrument approach. At last there was the airport in front of me. "Yeehaa! I've done it – I wasn't beaten after all." I felt triumphant. "Welcome to Dunedin," said the controller as I landed.

As I parked Golf November on the grass Peter Glaister rushed up with a picnic bag. He pulled out a mug and there at last was the long awaited cup of coffee! How I had longed for that coffee all the way through South America. How I hated drinking watery tea. It was manna from heaven. I grabbed my camera and asked someone to take a photo of the momentous occasion. What a welcome. It was 31st January 2004. I had left Ushuaia on 1st January so it had taken me exactly a month to do an extra 14,000 nautical miles and 133 flying hours to be able to rejoin my original route.

Coffee at last! – Peter Glaister in Dunedin.

I was greeted by a host of people all wanting to hear the story. There were schoolchildren, journalists, Rotarians and more. One lady, Zali Brookes, had flown in with her flying instructor. She was most interested to hear about Flying Scholarships for the Disabled as she was planning to start something similar in New Zealand. Suddenly I saw an aircraft land and within minutes of my arrival, there was Peter. I had not even drunk my coffee. He had just managed to catch the flight. It was all overwhelming and so exciting.

Peter and Sonia Glaister drove us back to their lovely home. We soaked in the huge spa bath and my Peter told me his story. The doors had just closed on the Cathay Pacific 747. A man had a call on his mobile from his mother who was ill. He had to get off. But was his story true? They were concerned there might have been a bomb on board. The aircraft was evacuated. All the passengers were corralled so that no-one could escape. The plane was thoroughly searched. This delayed the flight by four hours. Peter consequently missed his connection in Hong Kong. Cathay re-routed him through Sydney. He flew direct to Christchurch and then to Dunedin. He arrived exactly ten minutes after me.

CHAPTER 20 Back on Track

A heavy schedule awaited us in New Zealand. We were to be there for two weeks and every day would be spent in a different place. I was due to fly to each destination whilst Peter would follow in a rental car. Our route was planned to take us through the South Island up to the North Island right to Whangarei in the tip. We would finish in Auckland where Peter would fly to Sydney on scheduled airlines whilst I faced the long thirteen-hour over-water flight in Golf November.

Dense cloud hid the mountains as we drove up to Wanaka. Because of the weather we had to leave my aircraft in Dunedin. It was eerie and quiet driving up the mountains as if some ghostly figure would emerge to scoop us up into the unknown. We were to be the guests of Sir Tim and Pru Wallis. Tim has a magnificent aircraft collection and hosts the 'Warbirds over Wanaka Airshow' every second year. He pioneered deer farming in New Zealand, initially dragging deer off the mountains in helicopters. He has suffered many helicopter and aircraft accidents, miraculously surviving them all.

Lisa and Max Wenden who had helped so much with my Antarctic preparations, met us in Wanaka and over dinner I related the whole story. It was the least I could do after all they had done for me. Lisa had been at McMurdo when my fuel barrels arrived. She told me how the helicopter had 'underslung' them over to Scott Base from the ship and how everyone had helped roll the barrels up to the base.

The Dunedin school children welcomed me with a Haka, the Maori ceremonial war dance and chant. Links with the schools worldwide had added an exciting dimension to my whole trip. Manley Hot Springs in Alaska had been the northernmost school and here I was at the most southerly one.

Rosa and Graham Peacock own Orari Gorge Station near Timaru in New Zealand. Here was a peaceful haven where I could relax for a few hours amongst rhododendrons and azaleas. The station was a sheep farm with a long history. One of the most famous visitors was Ernest Shackleton. He had stayed at Orari Gorge for two weeks when he was invalided back to New Zealand from Scott's expedition in 1903. It was very exciting to sign my name in the visitors' book which dated back to 1870 and included such an illustrious name.

A short flight took me to Christchurch, the Mecca for Antarctic operations. I felt a shiver of excitement and expectation as I approached this place so inextricably linked with Antarctica. The American Antarctic Division base is situated on the edge of the airport at Christchurch from where the Americans run the majority of their Antarctic operations. The massive hangars house C130s and C17s which fly personnel and equipment to McMurdo and on to the South Pole. Next door is Antarctica New Zealand whose director, Lou Sanson, had been so helpful. A tall smiling man with a moustache approached me. "Polly!" he exclaimed grabbing my hand. "I am so pleased to meet you at last – let's go and have lunch." This was a warm welcome indeed and I felt sad that after all the effort

Lou Sanson, director of Antarctica New Zealand, who was so supportive of my flight.

from ANZ storing my fuel and offering to have me to stay at Scott Base that I had been unable to get there.

Lou introduced me to Neil Gilbert. I did a quick 'double take'. I had last seen Neil at the Foreign and Commonwealth Office in London. "What was Neil doing there?" I wondered. Neil greeted me like a long lost friend. He had indeed been most instrumental in helping me obtain my Antarctic permit. He had emigrated to New Zealand. He told me he loved living in New Zealand and did not miss the FCO one bit.

The conversation soon moved to Jon Johansen. As this was a courtesy visit I had decided not to broach any controversial subjects myself. "Jon said on television that he taught you everything you knew about Antarctica," Lou said. I bit my tongue and said nothing for this was so far from the truth to be ridiculous.

I did, however, take the opportunity to suggest to Lou that as long as Antarctica was there, solo pilots would take up the challenge. I advocated that the preparation of any pilot wishing to land in Antarctica should be scrutinised by an independent body at the pilot's expense. If a pilot passed established criteria it would be sensible to grant a permit. If it was made possible to obtain permission then pilots would stop going down there without approval. This would create a safer environment for all. Lou agreed with me. I also put this viewpoint to John Pye at the British Antarctic Survey. He too was in agreement but to date I have not heard whether any scrutinising body or guidelines have been established.

Before leaving ANZ Lou said, "Would you like to speak to Julian Tangaere at Scott Base?" He picked up the phone and the next thing I knew I was speaking to Julian in Antarctica, who said how sorry they all were that I did not make it across to them. Lou gave me a ticket to enter the Antarctic Museum next to the ANZ building and I spent a wonderful two hours there including a go in the blizzard simulator. Clothed in warm jackets and overshoes, a howling wind blew while one watched a huge thermometer drop to -25°C. It was all very realistic.

It was not possible to see Jon Johansen whilst in Australia, but I did have a very pleasant lunch later with Dick and Pip Smith. Dick is one of Australia's great entrepreneurs. He has flown five times around the world and in a Twin Otter to the South Pole with Giles Kershaw. When Jon was stuck in McMurdo, Dick was very vocal with his support. His attitude was to encourage people to just openly go down there and flaunt the rules. I explained why I disagreed with this attitude. "Surely, a more softly, softly approach would be better for us all. We must try to work with the governments. We must explain that adventurers will keep coming to Antarctica," I argued.

Dick promised to keep an ear out for Wheelies with Wings, the Australian version of Flying Scholarships for the Disabled, as they were very moved on hearing some of the success stories about the British scholars.

We spent a night on Rangitata Island. Russell and Linda Brodie and their family own an airstrip which leads up to a cottage which they kindly lent us. The cottage is called Moth Manor Cottage and their home Moth Manor, so it came as no surprise to discover that he was rebuilding a Tiger Moth. Russell was particularly interested in our charity. In spite of the fact that he only has one eye, Russell is an instructor, but he had had a huge battle with the CAA to keep his licence.

From Rangitata I planned to fly to Taraunga. It was a long way to go but it was an important stop as it was the Sport Aircraft Association's annual rally. Mike Paauwe had contacted me and asked me to attend the meeting. "We would like to start Flying Scholarships for the Disabled in New Zealand," he told me. "Please come to the rally. I think they may support the enterprise." His voice was confident.

I roared down the little grass strip and waggled my wings in farewell to Peter and our newly made friends at Moth Manor. Mountains drop steeply to the coast along the east of New Zealand's South Island. I flew over the sea as much as possible because of the danger of rotors, wind flowing strongly down the mountain sides in swirling circular bands. Even with full power and the climb attitude it was impossible to maintain altitude at times. The danger was that Golf November might stall which means that the aircraft wing enters such an angle that it will no longer fly. This is usually caused by a steep nose up attitude and slow air speed. The concern was the possibility of descending below the minimum safe altitude which could be a lethal situation in the vicinity of mountains. I was over the sea so it was not that alarming, but it was an interesting experience and I made a mental note to be more vigilant in the vicinity of mountains. I had magnificent views flying across Cook Strait to the North Island. The route went over Wellington and Palmerston North. Turning north east, I flew over more mountain ranges to Rotorua and Taraunga. It was a long four-hour flight.

Taxiing to the display area I was immediately surrounded by a host of people. Mike Paauwe introduced me to a lady who had built her own aeroplane. I was full of admiration as I could not imagine even starting to build one. Trish and Ike Stephens were my hosts and they took me to their lovely home in the hills. I was able to give a short speech at the annual dinner to an audience of 200 and before leaving the next day I addressed Young Eagles, a charity initially established in the United States but now spread worldwide. Its purpose is to give young people the chance to experience the freedom of flight, often aimed at children with disabilities and from disadvantaged homes. In the UK it is known as the 'Greenhawk Trust'. It was a magic hour talking to the kids.

Heading south west again I flew to Paraparumu near Wellington. The weather forecast wasn't good and many of the pilots at the rally were deferring their flights until the next day but I was keen to be back with Peter. I was also anxious not to be taking unnecessary risks. I filed an IFR flight plan and climbed above the clouds. Peter had followed me gallantly around New Zealand in the car. My short journeys by air took him several hours on the ground. He did however see more of New

Zealand than me. It is known as 'The land of the long white cloud' and it certainly did not let us down. Most of my flights were in or above cloud. I only had the chance to see land as I approached my destinations.

John and Jane Wallart live in the mountains outside Paraparumu. John, a keen pilot, had made contact through my website. Jane showed us to our room where we were greeted by a huge poster reading *WELCOME PETER AND POLLY*. On the dresser in the kitchen was a clay model. It was of a ring of people all holding hands. Jane had a plant standing in the middle. This immediately reminded me of the Inuit experience when I visited the church in Resolute Bay. All the Inuit congregation had stood encircling me and laid their hands on me to pray for my safe flight. This clay ring was in fact a Maori artifact. Because of the weight limit in my aircraft I had not been able to purchase anything during my flight, but this circle of figures seemed an irresistible symbol of my journey.

The Maori ring which reminded me of the Inuit people in Resolute Bay.

"Where can I get one of those?" I asked Jane telling her the story about the Inuit at the other end of the world. "It is yours," Jane said. "I couldn't possibly do that, I would just like to know where I could purchase one." "No, no it is *definitely* yours," she insisted.

As Peter did not want to carry it home with him – he was afraid something might happen to it – we found an appropriate shop and bought a box and some polystyrene packaging and then wedged the box on the back parcel shelf of Golf November. Here it travelled all the way back from New Zealand and it still adorns our dining room table. Whenever we have guests I place three lighted candles inside. The faces glow in the candlelight and I am once more transported to the icy north with the warm friendly Inuit, to be reminded of the harsh conditions of their lives and the contrasting warmth of their personalities.

Peter and I were able to snatch a couple of days together at Rotorua in a quiet hotel on the lake and away from the smell of sulphur which the hot springs produce in the centre of town. There had been endless media interviews and speaking engagements. We were both very tired but the reception everywhere in New Zealand had been overwhelming. Now I was becoming anxious about the long sea crossing to Australia.

To begin with it was a scary flight. The weather was shitty and I was struggling with rain, clouds and turbulence. This is never easy with two pilots, but with one it was full on all the time. There was no let up. The auto-pilot cannot be used because it puts too much strain on the servo motors in the wings but hand flying in cloud and turbulence is hard work and very challenging.

"Keep your eyes on the artificial horizon – scan, scan – artificial horizon, altitude, airspeed, temperatures and pressures, artificial horizon." A moment's loss of concentration and the aircraft can enter a spiral dive within seconds. I noticed that the exhaust gas temperature (EGT) gauge was reading way above normal. I checked my magnetos. Sure enough I had knocked off one of the magnetos with my knee. I switched it back on. The EGT gauge went down to normal. This had been a problem at Baton Rouge in Louisiana where I had made an unscheduled landing and waited overnight for the engineer to change the probe, all quite unnecessary but I was not to know at the time.

I relayed position reports via the airliners flying many thousands of feet above me, NZ70, NZ75, Kiwi 218 and Qantas 45. The Qantas guy said, "You're a long way from home" and there were numerous short comments from the others. The 'air to air' VHF frequency 123.45 was a psychological lifeline and the frequency 121.50 could have been a real lifeline. This frequency is monitored by all aircraft in case of emergency. That way a 'mayday' call can be picked up and relayed immediately.

At last I flew into Sydney's Kingsford Smith airport. The runways are built out into the ocean and the sea laps up against the edge of the platform they are built on. The bright blue of the sea and sky contrasts with the sparkling white of the concrete and the effect is similar to that of the Opera House which dominates the bay. Here I did my first instrument training in 1995 and it brought back many memories. Airports with runways built out into the water like Pago Pago and Sydney provide some of the most magic flying moments.

Having checked through customs, I flew the short hop to Bankstown, the busiest airport in the Southern Hemisphere. There are three parallel runways and it is not unusual to have three aircraft on finals all at once. It can be scary, but it seems to work. The controller said, "Welcome to Bankstown – Ray Clamback has got out the tea and cucumber sandwiches for you!"

I would have died for this but the controller was being funny and there was no sign of the tea and cucumber sandwiches. Ray Clamback is an experienced ferry pilot. He runs a charter company and flying school with Aminta Hennessy. It was with Aminta that I did my Australian instrument rating so I had known them both for several years. Ray has done about 150 ferry crossings from the States to Australia in light aircraft. He has had to ditch twice in the Pacific and both times he survived.

It was 29°C and very humid. Peter and our friends Ross and Lyndal were there to meet me and there were hugs all round before we off loaded Golf November of all her baggage. She was going to have her big annual check with Hawker Pacific while Peter and I spent a happy week in Canberra with friends and in Narooma with Patsy and Brian Gorman. We timed it perfectly for their daughter Sarah and Michael's wedding, and it was wonderful to be with old friends again.

Soon it was time to say goodbye to Peter. Each parting became more difficult, although none was as heart wrenching as the farewell at Ushuaia. I now had to face the long haul back home. Mentally exhausted, and with so many miles in front of me, I braced myself for the final journey.

CHAPTER 21

Bhutan Lost in Cloud

Bright red ridges resembling sastrugi shone in the merciless sunshine. The Simpson Desert in Australia reflected as many different hues from orange to maroon as the sea displays a multitude of taunting blues. There was colour everywhere but all variations on a theme. Fear of the unknown had disappeared for this was a familiar route. All the same, the desert needed to be treated with respect. Caution dictated that there were gallons of water on board because, in the event of a forced landing, I would quickly succumb to dehydration and die.

The Simpson Desert is one of the world's most spectacular deserts, comprising miles of red dunes, and in the couple of hours it would take me to cross I had time to reflect and look back at the journey that had brought me to this place. I was going home, but what did that mean? My life had changed from mother and music teacher to pilot and adventurer in the space of ten years. The metamorphosis from skydiver to world aviatrix must seem meteoric to an outsider but I could see that it was the culmination of a lifetime of growth and change.

Flying from Bundaberg to Alice Springs over the red Simpson Desert.

"I have had an amazing adventure," I thought. "Now I will have to settle down to a quiet life at home – but will I really be able to after a year of constant excitement?" Life in the limelight appears glamorous and for a while it is. However, gradually the somewhat superficial existence of always smiling, always meeting different people becomes more like hard work. The lack of privacy, the absence of quality time for oneself creates an unending strain.

The McDonald ranges and Uluru passed beneath Golf November's wings like a kaleidoscope as I crossed one of the hottest continents in the world, having so recently been challenged by the coldest. As always my musings were interspersed with a series of obligatory checks and came to a definite halt as I came in on final to land. I had no intention of staying any longer than overnight in Port Hedland for I was eager to be on my way. The Inter Tropical Convergence Zone was looming large again and that meant a really early start in the morning.

At 0200, I walked the short distance to the airport through the long grass shining my torch to look for snakes. Glancing at the row of trucks parked outside the motel, I couldn't help looking behind in case someone was following me. The stillness of the night made the airport an eerie and ghostly place but I was not alone after all. Every mosquito in the vicinity was circling around trying to take their share from this feast which appeared out of the dark. Checking Golf November by torchlight, I was pricked and stung on every part.

I slunk away from my beloved Australia, not wanting to face a farewell to a land that had become my second home. Out over the ocean Golf November and I flew and as the sun rose in the dawn sky, so did the thoughts of this flight of my life come scrambling back. "My flight was to promote Flying Scholarships for the Disabled. Fame is transitory." I was trying to sort things out in my mind. "Quit long distance flying while you are at the top," my inner voice advised. "After all, you have had a good run, give it up before something happens — you don't want to reach the stage when you hear 'God, not that woman again'."

The sun rose in the east and cast an orange glow over the inky sea below. Once more I was trussed up like a chicken in my immersion suit and life-jacket with life-raft beside me ready to push out of the door in the event of ditching. Glancing at the menacing ocean, I tried to ignore the irritating mosquito bites. Jittery Jakarta awaiting elections lay steaming in the foothills of the island mountains. I had dinner with Didit, who was a prime mover on my first round-the-world flight. She introduced me to Hermen Herry, an MP and one of the presidential candidates. I rather unwisely went with them to a nightclub in a bullet-proof Range Rover along with an armed bodyguard. What on earth was I thinking of? The following day, I thankfully climbed out of that volatile city.

I headed north west over Sumatra where the jungle vegetation fought for the light and the orang-utans fought for existence. The black paint on the aircraft certainly absorbed heat, designed as it was to minimise the extreme cold in the cockpit in the polar climes. In Kuala Lumpur the inside temperature gauge read + 67°C before it broke! In Singapore, Kuala Lumpur and Bangkok it was time to repay the sponsorship from Oris Watches. It was a frenetic round of one promotion followed by another. Oris had produced a limited edition pilots' watch. The 'Wings Around the World' logo featured on the front of each piece and the back sported my signature. Watch collecting is big business in the Far and Middle East. Potential purchasers know what they are looking for. It was exhausting. I was beautifully looked after, but I will never know how I got through those few days of endless receptions, presentations, interviews and press conferences.

Bill Heinecke and his wife Cathy looked after me at the Riverside Marriott Hotel in Bangkok which was extreme luxury. Bill was the first person to drive from Singapore to Bangkok before there was a proper road. He is also a pilot flying a Piper Malibu with a PT6 engine conversion to a turboprop. This aircraft, about twice the size of mine, is fully pressurised and capable of climbing to 27,000 ft. They hosted a dinner with Sunder and Chanda, our Indian friends who coincidentally happened to be in Bangkok. We had acted as guardians to their son Viku whilst he was at school in

Claude Hertz (left) and Jurgen Gross (right) based their doctoral thesis on my flight at The Mirce Akademy of System Operational Science in Exeter. Dr Knezevic is holding a certificate of appreciation for his support.

England. We always refer to Viku as our fourth son.

Bangkok International Airport boasts two parallel runways like Heathrow in London. Unlike Heathrow there is a golf course in the middle! I couldn't resist a giggle and wondered how many golf balls had hit a jumbo jet. I set off for Calcutta, but my Global Positioning System (GPS) steadfastly refused to receive a signal from the satellites. The GPS was not essential to this part of the journey as there were sufficient ground radio aids, but I was acutely aware that my next leg was from Calcutta to Bhutan. I would certainly not wish to venture among the Himalayas without a fully on-song GPS. I also doubted whether it could be fixed in Calcutta. So after two hours I turned back to Bangkok. Bill Heinecke's engineer Khun Direg took a look and fortunately had the idea of switching on a GPS in another aircraft. It too was receiving no signal. It turned out that the whole system in that part of the world had gone down, a salutary lesson never to wholly rely on the GPS. I spent another night in Bangkok.

The spectacular jungles and mountains of Myanmar provided a wondrous panorama beneath Golf November's wing. Years ago they had provided cover for many refugees fleeing to India during WWII as the Japanese invasion encroached further and further into Burma. It was hard to imagine the hardship they had endured and many perished on the way.

"Check temperatures and pressures – give a position report to Rangoon control." I jerked myself back into the present. It was time to document the hourly reports for the 'Mirce boys'. I enjoyed collecting data for the two PhD students, Jurgen and Claude from the postgraduate college, Mirce Akademy of Systems Operational Science in Exeter. Their research had been invaluable during the year prior to departure. The flight data would make a fascinating record. Hopefully they would come to some useful conclusions about how the aircraft responded in extreme climates.

Flying over Bangladesh, brown muddy water stretched for miles. Little wooden houses appeared to be afloat like boats on a huge brown 'lake'. What hard lives these people must live. My mind lingered on the Antarctic and I was unwilling to let it go. I thought of the comparisons. How did Scott and Shackleton manage in such harsh conditions – how did they live on tiny quantities of food?

How did Scott, Bowers and Wilson feel when they lay down in their tent to die, just eleven miles from their next depot.

In hot, humid and polluted Calcutta the air was filled with noise, honking horns, screeching brakes, shouting, rattling, tingly sounds. Pungent and varied smells mixed equally with exotic perfumes of jasmine and josticks, burning in every little store and bazaar. Behind high walls lay the tranquil green lawns of Minnie and Kochon Bhattacharjee's garden. Their home provided a perfect antidote to the rush and bustle of the street outside.

With a now fully performing GPS, Golf November took off for Bhutan. I was honoured to be asked to visit this mountainous kingdom nestling in the Himalayas and to meet one of the King of Bhutan's four wives, who was in charge of care for the disabled. Mine would be the first single-engine aircraft to fly into Paro, Bhutan's only airport and I knew that a great deal had been laid on for my visit. I was faced with a monumental decision which, like every decision I had made as pilot in command of my small craft, was non-negotiable.

Just thirty-six miles from Paro, the Himalayas rise steeply from the plains. Because of the sudden steep rise of the mountains the minimum safe altitude is 17,500 ft and Golf November just could not climb that high. The advice from Tensing, the national airline Druk Air's chief pilot was to follow the river valley to Paro. The pollution haze hung heavily below 10,000 ft blocking visibility in every direction and from 8,000 ft upwards huge towering cumulus clouds reached seemingly to infinity. I could not see the ground, the mountains or the river below. In aviation speak, high mountains are known as 'granite cumulus'. No pilot wants to go into those. Gutted, my head ruled my heart for the third time and I turned around.

Back in Calcutta I was invited to a school for the disabled. The work that was being done for disabled children in this seething city of some eighteen million people was an inspiration. Meeting the youngsters brought tears to my eyes as I witnessed amazing love and care in extremely simple surroundings. The contrast to the wealth of the western world was overwhelming. Then I was introduced to a remarkable man. Tim Grandage had worked for HSBC where he had a high powered job in Calcutta. One evening he had parked his car outside a five-star hotel where he attended a dinner and reception. When he came out there was a crowd of boys standing around his car.

"Thank you for looking after my car," he said to them. "Where are you from?" They told him they had nowhere to go and were living on the railway station. He piled them all into his car and drove them to his smart apartment where they slept on the floor. That was the start of Future Hope. Now he has a big house where the boys live in dormitories according to age. There are still many in a small space, but the conditions are clean and well kept. He has three other houses and a school. When I visited Future Hope the youngest boys were getting ready for bed. First they had to wash their own dinner plates, then their clothes every night. Even the smallest ones did this. They put up their sleeping mats and mosquito nets. Tim educates them and encourages them to be proud of what they do. They even learn to play rugby. He now has four students at university in England.

I flew 868 nms across northern India to Jodhpur where Viku and his wife Gayatri invited me to join them in their private Hindu temple. The Guru sat cross legged, chanting. There was an aura of peace and as I relaxed, my thoughts turned to my flight which had had far reaching effects in promoting Flying Scholarships for the Disabled. Money had poured in whilst I was stuck in Antarctica. It was a sign of solidarity and a reason to rejoice.

From Jodhpur I flew south 430 nm to Mumbai, the old Raj Gateway to India. Tea on the lawn at the Cricket Club of India in Mumbai with Peter's relations was a reminder of those far off days. Peter's grandfather was a Parsee in Bombay. The Parsees were refugees from Pars in Persia. They settled in Bombay in the eighth century AD. His grandfather studied civil engineering at a university in Germany. He fell in love with the daughter of the family with whom he lodged. They married and shortly after Peter's father and two aunts were born. Peter's mother was English but Peter still has many cousins living in Mumbai.

Once more a huge ocean stretched before me and I taxied out to begin the six-hour flight across the Arabian Sea to Muscat. Endless miles of water lay beneath my wings. It is never easy combating the fear of leaving the coast behind. On this very stretch of water I remember talking to the journalist Carolle Doyle on the radio, relieving my fear as she flew overhead in a Gulf Air jet on my first world flight. In those days it was possible to go to the flight deck and talk to the captain. That enabled her to contact me on an air-to-air frequency, and chatting to her helped immensely.

Muscat was a complete contrast to Mumbai. Clean white houses and shops lined the streets. Khimji Ramdas, an Oris watch distributor, laid on a dinner and press conference and put me up in a luxury hotel. From Muscat I flew the relatively short distance to Dubai which is situated in harsh desert running into the blue sea. Sue Hanisch, one of Flying for Disabled's previous scholars who had lost a foot in an IRA bomb attack in London, was passing through Dubai at the same time. It was exciting to see her so vibrant and full of life. She has since climbed Mount Kilimanjaro to raise funds for charity. Her courage is an inspiration.

Yvonne Trueman, an English lady pilot and friend flew from Bahrain to meet me. She had asked me to fly into Bahrain, but as the first Formula One Grand Prix was being held there, only aircraft involved with the race were allowed into the airport, so Dubai it had to be. Yvonne and I had last met in Prince Rupert just south of Alaska. What a lot had happened since then. She gave me a wonderful foot massage and we talked about what I would do next.

"No more long distance flying for me," I firmly said, although a feeling of bereavement was already creeping in. Yvonne had lost a son in the British Army in Belize. Memories of Belize, on the way south to Antarctica, came flooding back as I thought of my few days with Zoe and Paul Walker who run an outward bound school. There I slept in the jungle and wandered the mangrove swamps in a boat. Yvonne supported an orphanage there, the government-run Belize Child Care Home which I had been to see. I vividly remembered visiting the orphanage en route to Antarctica nearly six months before. It was the most distressing visit of the whole flight. Fifty orphan children were crammed into a tiny building. They all had conjunctivitis and nits in their hair. Dirty nappies lay on the floor and the kids cried and begged you to pick them up. It tore my heart apart. I felt so utterly helpless.

This local who had a fierce looking machete guarded my aircraft for twenty-four hours a day for three days in Sartaneja, Belize. I was glad he was there.

CHAPTER 22
An Unresolved Conundrum

Crossing the massive desert of Saudi Arabia, I glanced down at the odd green irrigated circles which surround small settlements. Suddenly I recalled the engine failure over the Arctic wastes and prayed it would not happen again – here. My mind began to wander over the many issues that I had faced.

Why did the US National Science Foundation (NSF), the British Antarctic Survey (BAS) and Antarctica New Zealand (ANZ) give their approval for me to land at their bases? Or indeed why shouldn't they? There is nothing in the Antarctic Treaty of 1959 to say that they should or should not grant permission. Antarctica belongs to no-one, the treaty clearly states. Yet one would never enter someone's house without their permission, so it seemed courteous and wise not to turn up without prior blessing.

Hour upon hour of dusty, sandy haze passed. My thoughts meandered through the maze that was Antarctica. The Foreign and Commonwealth Office (FCO) maintained it could not grant a permit without written permission from the National Science Foundation, the British Antarctic Survey and Antarctica New Zealand. NSF were not keen to issue their permit without the backing of FCO. The British Antarctic Act 1994 states that any British citizen entering Antarctica without the correct permit may face a period *not exceeding two years in prison or a fine*. Languishing in gaol was not an exciting prospect.

A thick murky haze engulfed Golf November and me. It was like forcing one's way through an endless grey brown curtain. The eight-hour flight to Jordan through all the murk reminded me of battling through a bewildering Scotch mist of bureaucracy.

Why did 'they' try to stop my Antarctic flight? Who was behind it all? It was frustrating not knowing the full story which had culminated in the cancellation of my fuel transportation. My curiosity was more than aroused. Why if 'they' gave me permission in the first place did 'they' then spend all that time trying to stop my flight – I did nothing wrong, but somehow I 'got up someone's nose'. I resolved to try to solve the mystery. Who indeed were my mysterious but effective opponents?

The sandy haze was so thick that it was impossible to see the propeller. I had a headwind but slowly, with a groundspeed of a tantalizing 100 kts the huge Saudi Desert passed beneath me.

Was a company as large and prestigious as Raytheon really involved with something as insignificant as three barrels of fuel? It was hard to believe that this was the case, although there had been pressure on Steve Penikett at the end. It was a mystery fit for the investigative talents of Sherlock Holmes or Poirot.

Check temperatures and pressures. An engine failure over this desert would be a disaster. "How would I be treated, a woman on her own?" I wondered, imagining a forced landing there. It was hard

A rare picture of myself in the cockpit, balancing the camera on the dashboard.

to see anything except immediately below me because of the sandy haze. My thoughts went their own way again.

Why would a company like Raytheon care about a small event like my flight? If they were aiming to stop my fuel, what was their motive? When did the Raytheon or NSF contract begin? If it began when the Twin Otters reached their destination in Antarctica did they really have the right to threaten Kenn Borek for taking my fuel if they were not technically at that stage under contract? My mind was racing, but it was all surmise.

Why had there been such a problem then? I sighed and took a bite from my muesli bar. I always munched muesli bars on my long distance flights because they stoked up my energy level whilst not leaving a smell or mess. They were the perfect food, but I never ever want to see another one.

I tried to get sight of the ground but the sand-filled smog surrounded me. It was like flying in brown cotton wool, it was the essence of nightmares. Nightmares! I had had plenty of those on the icy continent. And so my thoughts returned to the Antarctic.

What had made Antarctic Logistics and Expeditions so unwilling to help? They had avgas at Patriot Hills. They were trying to run a successful business, so why were they so reluctant to sell me fuel? I was not even asking them to give it to me. The cost was $4,000 a barrel and I needed just two." It was true that I could not have afforded the whole $300,000 package, which entailed positioning fuel caches along the route and having aircraft on standby just in case I had an engine failure.

"I am not a fuel bowser," Mike McDowell had said as if I was suggesting he was. It was a funny thought! This was a charity flight. I had more than enough insurance to cover any eventuality in the Antarctic thanks to my sponsors Global Aerospace. By the end of the flight we had raised the equivalent of £350,000; how could I have justified spending that sort of money on one fuel stop in Antarctica when the motivation behind the flight was to promote and raise funds for a charity? I couldn't.

After what seemed like an interminable eight hours I crossed the border into Jordan. The relief from tension was spontaneous, for Jordan is a small haven in the Middle East, although the air traffic controller was impossible to understand. A great friend of Sir Douglas Bader, the late King Hussein had been patron and actively supportive of Flying Scholarships for the Disabled from its inception in 1983. Her Majesty Queen Noor took on the role of patron when the King died. His Royal Highness Prince Feisel, Chief of the Air Staff of The Royal Jordanian Air Force has been actively involved for many years.

Jordan represents an oasis in the desert as it stands geographically in the centre of the Middle East and acts as a buffer between the different countries. It is crammed full of history and delightful people. A visit to the Al Hussein Society for the Physically Challenged enabled me to meet Princess Majda, a charming down-to-earth lady. "Call me Majda," were her first words.

It was exciting to see the education of disabled people taking shape in countries where previously disability brought shame on a family and was something to be hidden away. Majda was keen to establish a flying for the disabled charity in Jordan, but it would take a while. Meanwhile I met a Jordanian fighter pilot, Mohammed, who had had an accident and become a paraplegic. He was back flying a light aircraft, so 'big oak trees out of acorns do grow'.

I had fun too as Captain Muwafaq Al Khalayleh took me for a daring flight in a Seeker. This is a tail-dragger two-seater aircraft which looks like a helicopter but is in fact an aeroplane. Its performance and use is similar to that of a helicopter. They manufacture these in Jordan and he was proud to show me its capabilities. I enjoyed flying it too.

I flew over the Dead Sea and Petra which brought back vivid pictures of previous experiences in Jordan. The Sinai Peninsula, the Suez Canal and the deserts of Egypt all greeted me as a huge map lying beneath my wings. I landed in Alexandria, thus entering the record books as being the first solo round-the-world flight to land on all seven continents. It was exciting and heady stuff, but I paid a price. I was developing the real 'heady stuff' and the cold I had been fighting was beginning to take control.

As I left Alexandria and set Golf November's nose towards Crete, I tried finally to sort out the Antarctic queries in my head.

What about ANZ? They had let me down over fuel transportation too, but apparently that was pressure from a journalist. Why had this man acted as he did? The media in general had been incredibly supportive of me. My thoughts meandered on. ANZ had suggested alternative options, thus supporting me in any way they were able. After all they were really sticking their necks out by offering to store my fuel and have me to stay at Scott Base. I knew that Lou Sanson, director of ANZ was fully supportive of my venture. He was impressed with the level of preparation and continually said so. In the end was his organisation worn down by one journalist?

What is it about Antarctica? The Antarctic Treaty is probably the most successful world agreement ever. It was established between twelve initial countries to protect the last pristine continent in the world. Its main purpose is to ensure that Antarctica is only used for peaceful purposes such as scientific research. No nuclear activity is allowed and no exploitation of minerals. All expeditions entering Antarctica have to account for their environmental impact and ensure that everything that is taken in is removed on completion of the expedition. There are now forty-five member states and most of them keep a presence in Antarctica at least during the summer months.

Then there were the Argentines. They were my ultimate saviours. Argentina was an original signatory to the treaty, yet they saw fit to cover for search and rescue and to carry fuel for me too. They insisted I stayed at Marambio, their base on the Antarctic Peninsula, and gave me the warmest of receptions on my arrival there.

I came to the conclusion that I never would find out the whole truth of what led to the fuel being stopped and finally surrendered to the running nose and sweaty head in Crete. I felt wretched, and exhausted and succumbed to my bed for forty-eight hours. Even the bright warm sunshine seemed to have lost its power and I spent most of the time in oblivion. I had to push on, so after a couple of days rest I set out for mainland Greece. The new airport at Athens, built for the 2004 Olympic

Games, came into view across the water.

Here I was forced to abandon Golf November to the harsh sunshine. As the weather forecast for further north was atrocious, I was forced to catch a commercial flight to Belgrade, which had been incorporated in the route because lectures, receptions and Easter with Dr Knezevic's (from Mirce Akademy) family were planned there. I snuffled my way through those few days. The weather clamped down in direct opposite proportion to the warmth of their welcome.

Reunited with Golf November in Athens I was made acutely aware that Greece is part of the European Community. All flight plans have to be sent to Brussels. However, the computer there seems to have an inbuilt resistance to private flights, and plans are refused on a regular basis. The battle with European bureaucracy became the norm again.

I was to fly to Rome's Ciampino airport. As I flew over the Corinth Canal and across the coast of Greece I was reminded of the four weeks I spent in Greece as a student many years previously. On approaching Brindisi, the clouds built up. Golf November began to pick up ice as I tried to skirt around the clouds. It was impossible to climb above them as they were too high. I tried to fly below them, but they were too low and the mountains beneath buried themselves in their base like a child nestling into its mother's breast. I felt no such primitive emotions. I needed to get through to Rome but that was proving to be impossible. Forced to land in Brindisi, I spent a night there and was infuriated when my camera was stolen. The next day I headed over the mountains to Rome.

"G-FRGN, squawk 7531."This is a number unique to you and comes up on the controller's screen so that he knows which aircraft is yours. "Roger, squawk 7531," I repeated the number as required. "G-GN – please ident," which entailed pushing a button so the number flashes on the controller's screen. "G-GN – negative transponder," which meant he was not picking it up on his screen. I continued onwards. "G-GN," the controller harassed me. "Go ahead.""G-GN negative transponder." "Roger" I could not understand why he was not picking it up. I was sure it was working. Perhaps it was the mountains.

"G-GN you must turn back immediately. Rome won't accept you without a transponder." "Negative," I responded in defiant mood. After all what would I do if I turned back? "G-GN you must turn back immediately."

My welcome back in Birmingham International Airport, 27th April 2004.

"Negative," I said continuing on my track. I was amazed at how assertive I had become.

Meanwhile I called Naples Control and they could see my transponder easily. Obviously they had more up-to-date equipment. I told the Brindisi controller that I was changing to Naples, and all was well after that.

Here was Rome, where General Franco Cataloni and Michelle Bassinet are involved with Baroni Rotti, the organisation for pilots with disabilities. In Italy disabled people can only fly microlights. Franco and Michelle, along with help from Steve Derwin, past chairman of The British Disabled Flying Association, are working to have that changed.

Because of the weather I was stuck in Rome for several days. I stayed in Castel Gandolfo where the Pope's summer residence looks out over a volcanic lake. My hotel overlooked the lake too, but I only once caught a glimpse of the water through the low cloud and fog. The cloud was on the ground, and there was continuous rain.

My thoughts went to my family and my excitement rose. I was getting so near yet so far. My husband, Peter and our sons, Julian, Clive and Brian had all been so incredibly supportive and never once suggested that I should give up or come home. This story started with skydiving and now Brian, our youngest son, was making his career in the sport. It was exciting to see this development. He was a champion in the new discipline of 'swooping', a canopy piloting competition which is measured from ten feet before landing. It requires high levels of skill and precision and makes a wonderful spectator sport. I also thought of Julian and Amanda's wedding drawing closer by the day. I wondered how my mother had fared, now in her ninetieth year. She had been immensely brave watching me fly off into the distance from Birmingham.

In marginal conditions I flew on to Clermont Ferrand in France where student friends had made their home. I too made it my home for nearly a week as the frustrating weather prohibited my flight to Hanover where my major sponsor, Sennheiser, the headset manufacturers, had laid on various promotions and receptions. It was another disappointment. I tried twice to make the flight but ice built up as I flew IFR, and trying to fly VFR beneath the clouds I found the mountains rising and the cloud lowering. There was no way through. The weather ruled yet again.

Finally I had a short weather window to return to the UK even though the huge front which had dominated my European flights from Italy was still in control. As I flew north from Clermont Ferrand to the UK I tracked alongside the distinct dividing line of the front as it moved slowly eastwards. Approaching the coast of France I could see the white cliffs of Dover. Tears of emotion filled my eyes. When I heard the distinct clear voice of the first English controller, I was unable to respond.

A reception for my return had been planned for Tuesday 27th April 2004. I arrived in the UK three days earlier. I had been concerned that the poor weather still persistently hanging over Europe may prevent me arriving on time so I came back early. We hid Golf

Coverage of my return included an interview with Graeme Bowd from Central News.

November under numerous aircraft covers in a corner of a hangar on a little airstrip at Brimpton. I crept back home and had three wonderful days with Peter.

Flying into Birmingham on the morning of 27th April there was a distinct feeling of 'déjà vu'. The months dropped away as I taxied beneath a glorious arch of water formed by two fire engines. What an honour. "Golf November needs a wash," I laughed to myself. Had I really been all that way? Already it seemed like a figment of the imagination. Photos, friends, press, TV, flying scholars, sponsors were all there to greet me, just as they had been there to see me off. It seemed as if it was just yesterday.

More speeches and flowers and hordes of people awaited our arrival back at Oxford. This was Golf November's home and it was as if she knew that she was returning. It was cold and low cloud completely obliterated the sky. No-one seemed to mind. Golf November was pushed into her hangar just as if she had never left. There were more flowers and one admirer thrust a bag of delicious coffee into my hand. I went home to a dinner in our kitchen with giants, family and friends. Once more I could indulge in coffee, wholemeal bread and good old fish fingers!

Re-united with Peter after 345 days away from home.

In the peace of our old Oxfordshire farmhouse my thoughts tied up the loose ends. This had been more than an adventure and challenge, it had been a journey – like gathering a huge bouquet of flowers, each bloom having its own special beauty, some not being immediately so appealing as others, yet being a part of the whole. I sipped from a mug of steaming coffee as I lay in the sun by the stream in our garden. I thought again of the metamorphic growth from mother to aviatrix, but it was more than that. I knew that I could not have faced the challenges without the support of so many people. It mattered not what was their culture, colour or creed. The vast majority were just trying to lead good and useful lives.

The last word must be with Luis in Porto Allegre who had told me, *"There are two seats in your aircraft – one for you and one for God."*

Epilogue

The whole flight took 352 days. The distance flown was 60,000 nautical miles, equivalent to nearly three times around the world at the equator. The detour alone was 14,000 nms. The total flying hours were 550, of which the detour took 133. The longest leg of 2,068 nms between California and Hawaii took 16 hours and 5 minutes. The flight took in thirty-four countries and all seven continents; there were 106 stops. I gave around one hundred talks and presentations en route. Golf November had twelve scheduled maintenance checks. She had one brake failure, one oil leak and a cracked window. She carried sixty spare parts of which only the oil filters were needed.

During the preparation and throughout the flight I was buoyed up by a huge body of people which in my mind resembled a pyramid. At the base were those who had so generously put their names on my wings along with the many supporters around the world. On top of that were my sponsors who stuck with me through thick and thin and gave so generously. The next layer comprised my 'giants' who gave unstintingly of their time and expertise. Then there was my voluntary team who worked behind the scenes for the flight and the fund-raising, and were such a tower of strength as friends when most needed. Next were my close friends and family who always encouraged me and never once suggested I should not go. Finally, there was Peter, my rock. Without him, nothing would have happened.

As a result of all of this effort over £400,000 has been raised for Flying Scholarships for the Disabled. Australia's version Wheelies with Wings has been established for five years. Flying Scholarships for the Disabled/USA is getting under way. Norway, Chile, New Zealand, Oman, Jordan, Italy and Switzerland are all expressing an interest in starting similar programmes to rebuild disabled people's lives using the challenge of learning to fly.

Dr Knezevic of the Mirce Akademy of Systems Operational Science in Exeter commented:

> The Wings Around the World flight has changed the syllabus of the Master of Science programmes in Reliability Engineering and System Operational Effectiveness which have been run at Exeter University (1991-2001) and at the Mirce Akademy (1999-2004). As a direct result of the flight, the studies of Human Performance and Reliability have been included into the curriculum, as well as the studies of the Natural and Environmental Impacts on the System Operational Effectiveness. These changes have significantly increased the accuracy of the reliability engineering predictions, which in return have improved the maintenance and logistics planning, leading towards higher operational reliability and availability, while reducing operational costs.

Three records were established during the flight:

The first woman to fly solo across the North Pole in a single-engine aircraft.

The first woman to fly solo in Antarctica.

The first person to fly solo around the world landing on all seven continents.

The Sponsors and Charities

The Principal Sponsors

Birmingham International Airport: Departure, return and financial support

Jeppesen Europe: Maps, charts, approach plates

Jeppesen UK: Overflight clearances, flight following, handling

Jeppesen USA: Weather forecasting

Oris Swiss Watches: Financial support and official watch sponsor

Sennheiser: Financial support and headsets

Shell Aviation and Shell Aircraft: Fuel provision and aircraft painting

The Major Sponsors

Aon: Insurance

CSE Engineering: Engine rebuild, launch and open days

Global Aerospace: Insurance

Hartzell: Supply and fitting of new propeller

Honeywell Bendix King: Avionics

Lycoming: Engine rebuild

Quark Expeditions: Logistical support

The Supportive Sponsors

Aircraft Owners and Pilots Association: Charity donation

Derrick Ings Aircraft Sales: Financial support

Far North Aviation: Logistical support

Field Aviation: Financial support

Fujifilm: Digital camera and software

Guild of Air Pilots and Air Navigators: Charity donation

HR Smith Group: Personal locator beacon

Imagecare.com: Photography, press pack, and media material. Design/production

Kenn Borek Air: Logistical support

Kingfisher Graphics: Wing names and sponsors' logos

Martyn and Tanya Brigden Gwinett: Wing name marketing

Mirce Science: Study of aircraft performance in extreme operational conditions, seminars and hospitality worldwide

Mountain Hardware: Annapurna tent

Mountain High Oxygen Systems: Personal oxygen system

Multifabs Survival: Survival suit

New Piper Aircraft Corp: Aircraft parts

Packsome Clothing: Tropical flight suit

The Park Club: Financial support and fitness training

Photo-Graphic-Art: Financial support

Planeweighs: Aircraft weighing

Red Tail Associates in conjunction with
Mantau eCommerce Solutions: Website design build and hosting

Ross Consular: Visas worldwide

Rotary International: Hospitality worldwide

Royal Institute of Navigation: Charity donation

RSH Airwear: Financial support and charity donation

Selby Wilderness: Hospitality and survival training

Shell Education: Schools' website

TNT: Logistical support

Virgin Atlantic Airways: Overseas travel

Warner Lewis: Hand fuel pump

Wilmslow Life Rafts: Life-raft support

WL Gore Associates UK: Polar clothing

Xaxero/SkyEye: Technical support

Flying Scholarships for the Disabled charities have now been established in the following countries:

Australia – since 2001
'Wheelies with Wings'
www.wheelieswithwings.com.au
Contact – David Clegg: cleggair@optus.com.au

Norway
En Ny Dag (A New Day) Foundation
Stiftelsen "En Ny Dag"
Vendla 72
1397 Nesoya, Norway
gstoe@online.no

United States of America
Flying Scholarships for the Disabled – USA (FSD/USA)
http://home.earthlink.net/~flying-scholarships/
Contact – Bill Murrell: billmurrell2004@earthlink.net

The following countries have shown interest in starting similar programmes:

Italy:
Contact: mash@centropilota.it

New Zealand:
Contact: ikest@xtra.co.nz and zalibrookes@xtra.co.nz

Sweden:
Contact: jens.sternberg@gmx.de

Switzerland:
Contact: josua.roffler@deep.ch

United Arab Emirates
Contact: rimzie@dca.gov.ae

Chile

Jordan

Index